Illuminating *Torchwood*

CRITICAL EXPLORATIONS IN SCIENCE FICTION AND FANTASY
(a series edited by Donald E. Palumbo and C.W. Sullivan III)

1. *Worlds Apart? Dualism and Transgression in Contemporary Female Dystopias* (Dunja M. Mohr, 2005)

2. *Tolkien and Shakespeare: Essays on Shared Themes and Language* (ed. Janet Brennan Croft, 2007)

3. *Culture, Identities and Technology in the Star Wars Films: Essays on the Two Trilogies* (ed. Carl Silvio and Tony M. Vinci, 2007)

4. *The Influence of Star Trek on Television, Film and Culture* (ed. Lincoln Geraghty, 2008)

5. *Hugo Gernsback and the Century of Science Fiction* (Gary Westfahl, 2007)

6. *One Earth, One People: The Mythopoeic Fantasy Series of Ursula K. Le Guin, Lloyd Alexander, Madeleine L'Engle and Orson Scott Card* (Marek Oziewicz, 2008)

7. *The Evolution of Tolkien's Mythology: A Study of the History of Middle-earth* (Elizabeth A. Whittingham, 2008)

8. *H. Beam Piper: A Biography* (John F. Carr, 2008)

9. *Dreams and Nightmares: Science and Technology in Myth and Fiction* (Mordecai Roshwald, 2008)

10. *Lilith in a New Light: Essays on the George MacDonald Fantasy Novel* (ed. Lucas H. Harriman, 2008)

11. *Feminist Narrative and the Supernatural: The Function of Fantastic Devices in Seven Recent Novels* (Katherine J. Weese, 2008)

12. *The Science of Fiction and the Fiction of Science: Collected Essays on SF Storytelling and the Gnostic Imagination* (Frank McConnell, ed. Gary Westfahl, 2009)

13. *Kim Stanley Robinson Maps the Unimaginable: Critical Essays* (ed. William J. Burling, 2009)

14. *The Inter-Galactic Playground: A Critical Study of Children's and Teens' Science Fiction* (Farah Mendlesohn, 2009)

15. *Science Fiction from Québec: A Postcolonial Study* (Amy J. Ransom, 2009)

16. *Science Fiction and the Two Cultures: Essays on Bridging the Gap Between the Sciences and the Humanities* (ed. Gary Westfahl and George Slusser, 2009)

17. *Stephen R. Donaldson and the Modern Epic Vision: A Critical Study of the "Chronicles of Thomas Covenant" Novels* (Christine Barkley, 2009)

18. *Ursula K. Le Guin's Journey to Post-Feminism* (Amy M. Clarke, 2010)

19. *Portals of Power: Magical Agency and Transformation in Literary Fantasy* (Lori M. Campbell, 2010)

20. *The Animal Fable in Science Fiction and Fantasy* (Bruce Shaw, 2010)

21. *Illuminating Torchwood: Essays on Narrative, Character and Sexuality in the BBC Series* (ed. Andrew Ireland, 2010)

22. *Comics as a Nexus of Cultures: Essays on the Interplay of Media, Disciplines and International Perspectives* (ed. Mark Berninger, Jochen Ecke and Gideon Haberkorn, 2010)

23. *The Anatomy of Utopia: Narration, Estrangement and Ambiguity in More, Wells, Huxley and Clarke* (Károly Pintér, 2010)

Illuminating *Torchwood*

Essays on Narrative, Character and Sexuality in the BBC Series

edited by ANDREW IRELAND

CRITICAL EXPLORATIONS IN
SCIENCE FICTION AND FANTASY, 21
Donald E. Palumbo *and* C.W. Sullivan III, *series editors*

McFarland & Company, Inc., Publishers
Jefferson, North Carolina, and London

LIBRARY OF CONGRESS CATALOGUING-IN-PUBLICATION DATA

Illuminating Torchwood : essays on narrative, character and
  sexuality in the BBC series / edited by Andrew Ireland.
      p.   cm. — (Critical explorations in science fiction
    and fantasy ; 21)
  Includes bibliographical references and index.

  ISBN 978-0-7864-4570-7
  softcover : 50# alkaline paper

  1. Torchwood (Television program)   2. Science fiction
television programs — Great Britain — History and criticism.
I. Ireland, Andrew.
PN1992.77.T67I45   2010
791.45'72 — dc22   2009052865

British Library cataloguing data are available

©2010 Andrew Ireland. All rights reserved

*No part of this book may be reproduced or transmitted in any form
or by any means, electronic or mechanical, including photocopying
or recording, or by any information storage and retrieval system,
without permission in writing from the publisher.*

Cover art ©2009 Kimberly Slayer

Manufactured in the United States of America

McFarland & Company, Inc., Publishers
  Box 611, Jefferson, North Carolina 28640
  www.mcfarlandpub.com

Acknowledgments

Special thanks go to Donald E. Palumbo for being so supportive and helpful along the way. Thanks also to the Science Fiction Area of the PCA / ACA Conference which, in 2008, included a panel session on writing book proposals which led to the genesis of this book. To all the contributors on both sides of the Atlantic, I give my heartfelt gratitude for their enthusiasm and hard work. Finally, thanks to my colleagues at Bournemouth University who supported the project, and also to my family for their endless understanding and love.

Table of Contents

Acknowledgments	vii
Introduction — Reading the Rift (ANDREW IRELAND)	1

PART I:
Narrative and *Torchwood*

One — Playing to the Crowd: *Torchwood* Knows We're Watching (ANDREW IRELAND)	11
Two — Existentialism and Christian Symbolism (R. C. NEIGHBORS)	22
Three — Policing the Rift: The Monstrous and the Uncanny (SUSAN J. WOLFE *and* COURTNEY HUSE WIKA)	30
Four — Touching the Other: Alien Contact and Transgressive Touch (RIA CHEYNE)	43
Five — More Than Just a Hero's Journey: Harry Potter, Frodo Baggins, and Captain Jack Harkness (VALERIE ESTELLE FRANKEL)	53
Six — Screwing Aliens and Screwing with Aliens: *Torchwood* Slashes the Doctor (RICHARD BERGER)	66

PART II:
Character and *Torchwood*

Seven — The Eternal Vigil: Captain Jack as Byronic Hero (G. TODD DAVIS)	79
Eight — Gwen's Evil Stepmother: Concerning Gloves and Magic Slippers (VALERIE ESTELLE FRANKEL)	90
Nine — Transgressive Torch Bearers: Who Carries the Confines of Gothic Aesthetics? (DANIEL J. RAWCLIFFE)	102

Ten — The Alien Woman: Othering and the Oriental (CARRIE DUNN) 113
Eleven — Outside the Heroic Paradigm (TOM POWERS) 121

PART III:
Sexuality and *Torchwood*

Twelve — "Love the coat": Bisexuality, the Female Gaze and the Romance of Sexual Politics (CHRISTOPHER PULLEN) 135

Thirteen — Fashioning Masculinity and Desire (SARAH GILLIGAN) 153

Fourteen — Sexual Relations and Sexual Identity Issues: Brave New Worlds or More of the Old One? (SHERRY GINN) 165

Fifteen — "Loving the Alien": The Erotics of Technology (PAUL WINTERS) 181

Sixteen — Cyberwomen and Sleepers: Rereading the Mulatta Cyborg and the Black Woman's Body (ELSPETH KYDD) 191

Seventeen — No Consent Necessary: A Feminist Perspective on Non-Consensual Penetration (CARRIE DUNN) 203

Eighteen — Out in Space: Masculinity, Sexuality and the Science Fiction Heroics of Captain Jack (LEE BARRON) 213

Episode Guide 227
About the Contributors 231
Index 235

INTRODUCTION

Reading the Rift

ANDREW IRELAND

"Excellent bottom."

The world's first glimpse of Captain Jack Harkness is at the height of the Blitz; the Germans are bombing a war-torn London during World War II in the 2005 *Doctor Who* episode "The Empty Child." In the midst stands Jack (John Barrowman), ogling a "damsel in distress" hanging from a weather balloon. After peering at Rose Tyler's (Billie Piper) derriere through futuristic binoculars at a balcony window, and uttering those defining first words, he then flirts with a male officer before rescuing said damsel with an invisible spaceship. As one does.

The character of Captain Jack is arguably one of the most fleshed-out, unique and multi-dimensional in recent television history. First *Doctor Who* (BBC, 2005-present, UK), then *Torchwood* (BBC, 2006-present, UK), provide the "omnisexual" Jack with an extraordinary journey, through time and space, death and rebirth, betrayal and regret.

Torchwood's first season aired in the UK, in the autumn of 2006, as 13 45-minute episodes on the public digital station BBC3. It was a huge ratings success, with the opening episode attracting 2.4 million viewers and a 12.7 percent share of the audience. This made it at the time the most-watched non-sport digital program ever in the UK. The second episode (which was screened immediately afterwards) achieved 2.3 million viewers, and a 13.8 percent share. The second season continued to be as successful, airing first not on BBC3 but BBC2—a more established, mainstream channel. The opening episode achieved an excellent 4.2 million viewers. The third season moved again, this time to BBC1, the corporation's primary channel, and launched with 5.9 million viewers. When it launched in America, it proved to be the most successful series to air on BBC America with the highest ratings ever for the channel.

Torchwood is a unique television drama series, and the present work examines the qualities and approaches that define it as such. The blend of adult language, tongue-in-cheek dialogue, subversive sense of humor, archetypal characters, and openly homosexual/homoerotic and bisexual storylines provides much material for scholarly analysis. Ultimately this collection of essays seeks to provide an interpretative framework for understanding developing forms and genres of television drama, through the locus provided by the analysis of *Torchwood*. Russell T. Davies has been instrumental here — he has designed a show that is forever challenging the accepted norms of the genre, and has drawn successful audiences on both sides of the Atlantic.

The book is presented in three parts and with three overarching themes — "Narrative," "Character," and "Sexuality." However, it is important to note that the chapters present significant cross-referencing between these relatively general ideals. *Torchwood* is a dense, rich text, ripe for textual analysis, and due to the relatively limited number of episodes to consider, certain "key moments" and text-defining characteristics re-surface in multiple chapters. However, each chapter brings with it different foci, providing recurring elements with new lenses for analysis, and fresh perspectives to consider. What follows, then, is a 360-degree, in-depth analysis of the fresh, innovative and stimulating *Torchwood*.

Narrative and Torchwood

The first part looks at issues relating to narrative in the *Torchwood* text. My essay "Playing to the Crowd: *Torchwood* Knows We're Watching" argues that *Torchwood* marks a transition to a new form of drama where the position of the audience as a "critical, experience-laden" element has an effect on the way stories are told on screen. The storylines and characters portrayed are distorted by the overriding presence of the audience as they no longer *peer inside* the narrative, but are *inside, peering around*. In this chapter I discuss how this post-modern shift to co-presence leads to new approaches to *re-enable* the audience's ability to achieve a satisfaction of engagement with a text. I focus on two specific episodes, "Everything Changes" and "Reset," to investigate how the narrative and direction within them has been influenced by the extra-textual co-presence of the audience. I argue that *Torchwood* takes advantage of such notions to "play to the crowd" and engages with the audience in a sparring power-play.

The second essay looks at existential questions of "life without an afterlife" in the *Torchwood* universe. R. C. Neighbors, in "Existentialism and Christian Symbolism," postulates that without a promised reward after death, moral acts must find new motivation, must be performed for their own sake, and must have intrinsic value, or at least a value that we attribute to them.

In addition, without an afterlife, the question of an existential "point" of being arises. What does Suzy's proclamation that "life is all" mean for the characters and for us as viewers? How does the proclamation relate to *Torchwood*'s fluctuation between the view of "life as beauty" and "life as misery"? Neighbors argues that the implication is that the characters of *Torchwood* must embrace the valuable aspects of life, while learning to deal with those that are not so great because these combined characteristics are the sum total of reality.

Susan J. Wolfe and Courtney Huse Wika's "Policing the Rift: The Monstrous and the Uncanny" discusses the liminal space within which *Torchwood* exists, as much as the monsters and aliens it guards against, as Uncanny. *Torchwood* puts the mundane to good use in creating uncanny situations, for a creature that looks human may turn out to be a creature that devours sex, or both feeds upon and implants memories in order to manipulate humans. Actual human beings may be monstrous themselves, butchering fellow humans for meat or carving steaks from a harmless sentient alien. The authors argue that, like protagonist Gwen Cooper, the viewers are kept continually off-balance by shifts between the ordinary and the eerie, the humorous and the horrible, the human and the monstrous, and discomfited by the sense that little enough separates them.

The notion that *Torchwood* is constructed around the concept of "alien encounter" is discussed in the next essay, by Ria Cheyne, entitled "Touching the Other: Alien Contact and Transgressive Touch." The chapter conceptualizes human-alien contact in terms of touch, arguing that representations of touch are key to determining a character's status as either human or non-human, and that *Torchwood* pushes the boundaries in its depiction of alien touch. Drawing on recent theoretical work on touch, studies on the psychological and physiological significance of touch, and Cyborg theory, the chapter will discuss the role of human touch within the series. It then considers key moments of alien contact and the implications of these.

Valerie Estelle Frankel's essay, "More Than Just a Hero's Journey: Harry Potter, Frodo Baggins, and Captain Jack Harkness," argues that the program offers a unique science-fantasy approach that may appeal just as strongly to Harry Potter fans as it may to science fiction viewers. The chapter focuses on the fantasy elements present, including the quest that Captain Jack travels in his "hero's journey." It also considers the fantasy creatures that surface — from savage faeries to Weevils, the latter being monsters in every sense of the word. She discusses the mysterious happenings that have no readily available or offered scientific explanation, including ghosts, fortune-telling and prophecy, and the arrival of the biblical demon in the episode "End of Days." Notions of hero and anti-hero are developed further in the next part.

"Screwing Aliens and Screwing with Aliens: *Torchwood* Slashes the Doctor" locates the series in the context of developing cross-platform, 360-degree production. Author Richard Berger discusses the dialogic relationship between the revitalized *Doctor Who* series and *Torchwood*. Berger argues that the series has its origins firmly embedded in fan communities and activities (such as original *Who* novels in the 1990s) that had taken place during *Doctor Who*'s hiatus from 1989 to 2005. Berger discusses the dialogics of the series, and makes connections between "slash fiction" as it developed from the 1960s, to the internet, and to the origin and development of the cannonical *Torchwood*.

Character and Torchwood

Part II is book-ended with investigations into the concept of the hero in relation to the series, and in particular, the lead character, as a continuation of the "hero" theme that Valerie Estelle Frankel discussed previously. G. Todd Davis's essay "The Eternal Vigil: Captain Jack as Byronic Hero" leads the way.

Valerie Estelle Frankel, in "Gwen's Evil Stepmother: Concerning Gloves and Magic Slippers," argues that the story of the heroine has been neglected in favor of notions pertaining to the hero's journey. Frankel addresses the balance by exploring the notion of the heroine's journey through an investigation of Gwen Cooper, starting with her first encounter with the Torchwood team in the premier episode. Captain Jack is portrayed as the beast to Gwen's beauty, concealing secrets, and having returned from the dead. Like heroines from fairytales and myths, Gwen's heroic journey takes her into the realm of death itself for an encounter with Abaddon, the "great devourer," in the season one finale. Frankel argues that the "revitalizing" kiss she gives Jack after he dies defeating Abaddon symbolically assures her place as a healing mother, and ascends her to "successor-queen" status as a new head of Torchwood.

Daniel J. Rawcliffe provides an analysis of the Gothic notions that reflect aspects of *Torchwood*, in a continuation of the work presented in Chapter 3. "Transgressive Torch Bearers: Who Carries the Confines of Gothic Aesthetics?" argues that Cardiff, as the setting for the show, features myriad examples of the uncanny and therefore can be deemed a Gothic liminal environment. The chapter offers an analysis of Gwen Cooper, as Gothic heroine, and Jack Harkness, as Gothic hero. Rawcliffe argues that the latter's masculinity as an "omnisexual" being enables him to escape the trappings of the Gothic. Referring to current discussions of the Gothic, the chapter discusses identity politics, with a particular focus on issues of sexuality.

The next chapter, "The Alien Woman: Othering and the Oriental," examines the depiction of female characters in the series, arguing that they are often represented as physically Other, and requires others to free them of their Other status to enable them to return to their previous state. Author Carrie Dunn argues that the only reoccurring female character *not* to undergo a transformation to otherness, Tosh, is treated thusly because she is of Japanese heritage, and therefore is already deemed exotic and Other in nature. The chapter will examine instances of female characters being "Othered" to their disadvantage, and will refer to key theorists of the Other, extending into Orientalism.

To conclude this part and the notions of the hero, Tom Powers, in his chapter "Outside the Heroic Paradigm," offers an exploration of how *Torchwood* develops the concept of the anti-hero. Powers draws from other classic science fiction anti-heroes, and with anti-hero theory, leads us through the evolution of the concept of the reluctant male lead with a particular emphasis on the characters in Torchwood and how they overcome their human foibles to become truly heroic.

Sexuality and Torchwood

Part III shifts the focus to issues pertaining to sexual identity and sexual representation. The first chapter in this part provides a comprehensive examination of the series, a series that offers complex imaginings of sexual identity, and where bisexuality and homosexuality are foregrounded. "'Love the Coat': Bisexuality, the Female Gaze and the Romance of Sexual Politics" discusses the bisexual desire that runs throughout the series. Author Christopher Pullen examines the narrative construction of *Torchwood*, which, Pullen argues, sensitizes mainstream audiences to gay and lesbian lives through the filter of bisexuality. In this way Captain Jack's eternal sexual arousal, largely directed towards potential male (rather than female) bisexual partners, stimulates audiences to engage with same sex narratives previously untold. Pullen uses the term "love the coat" as a subtext for the sexual attraction between Captain Harkness and Ianto Jones, and explains how these two characters and their frequent engagements provide a continual point of reference; where external and sometimes superficial desire is juxtaposed with intensity and depth. Pullen expresses this as in the same way that a coat covers the intimate body, yet traces and compliments that form, *Torchwood* stimulates audiences to engage in deeper surfaces that are not expressly revealed.

Following on from Pullen's work and his "love the coat" concept, Sarah Gilligan provides an analysis of fashion in respect to masculinity, gendered identity and sexuality. "Fashioning Masculinity and Desire" offers a textual analysis of Captain Jack Harkness and Captain John Hart, and argues that the fashioning of their masculine identities creates its own discourse through which costume drama and Post Heritage cinema's escapism flows. Gilligan argues for the central role that the male's costume plays in relation to the representation of masculinity, and the popularity of *Torchwood* and the two captains.

Sherry Ginn's chapter, "Sexual Relations and Sexual Identity Issues: Brave New Worlds or More of the Old One?", continues the theme of sexuality by exploring popular science fiction's mixed messages. Characters in shows such as *Star Trek* may become (usually implicitly) involved in sexual activity; any such activity is usually "safely" contained within monogamous or heterosexual relationships. *Torchwood* has broken the mold by including male characters openly involved with other males, and females are depicted as actively engaged in sexual activity with both males and females. Ginn extends her analysis by reviewing the impact such a "bold" approach has on viewers and in media comment. The chapter then concludes with an analysis of firsthand research conducted with a class of students to see their reactions to the unusual, high-profile sexual activity on display.

Paul Winters' chapter, "'Loving the Alien': The Erotics of Technology," argues that beyond the speculative nature of science fiction television, and a broad desire for technological evolution, there is an "erotics of technology" at play. He argues that the desire for technology can be extrapolated into human sexual desire, something that the storylines, themes and motivation of the characters of *Torchwood* exemplify. His subsequent discussion brings in the notion of "strangeness," a notion related to the work of the show's creator Russell T. Davies, from examining the perceived influences on the show's genesis.

The next chapter, "Cyberwomen and Sleepers: Rereading the Mulatto Cyborg and the Black Woman's Body," examines the racial subtext present in two key episodes of *Torchwood* where black women embody the concept of the mulatto cyborg. Elspeth kydd argues that both the episodes "Ghost Machine" and "Sleeper" provide instances where the series presents the ambiguities of racial identity and envisions black cyborg/alien women as ambiguous embodiments of Otherness.

The penultimate chapter, "No Consent Necessary: A Feminist Perspective on Non-Consensual Penetration," critically analyzes the program's fluid approach to sexuality. Carrie Dunn examines instances where apparently consensual acts of sex are not what they first appear to be when portrayed as such on screen, with consent being manipulated on several occasions. Unusually for a television series, this unacceptable behavior refers not just to "bit part" characters, but also the leads. Dunn then progresses this by discussing non-consensual penetration in a non-sexual context, including the use of the "resurrection glove" and mind-probing. The chapter refers to feminist theories of rape, and examines why non-consensual penetration can be acceptable for contemporary mainstream television audiences, and the issues that acceptance raises.

The final chapter, "Out in Space: Masculinity, Sexuality and the Science Fiction Heroics of Captain Jack," by Lee Barron, examines the representation of sexuality in the show with a specific emphasis on Captain Jack. He argues that the show combines alien menace (from *Doctor Who*) with an added focus upon sexuality, bisexuality, and homosexuality. The chapter examines how these aspects function together, critically discussing the ways in which *Torchwood* "fits in" with both British science fiction traditions and previous representations of homosexuality.

The third and most recent season of *Torchwood* culminated in some of the most unusual, brave, and daring narrative developments in the context of popular television drama. Hero Captain Jack sacrificed his grandson's life, purposefully and with intent, and in so doing lost the love of his daughter too. The world was saved in the process, but at a level of cost that is rarely, if ever, required in television drama. Broadcast in the UK during the latter stages of this book's development, it provided a somber reminder of why this series requires scholarly analysis. It is the unusual fusion of science fiction drama, soap, sex, violence, representation of bisexuality and homosexuality, notions of the gothic and the uncanny, the Other and the hero, that makes it such a "fresh" text to study. Enjoy.

Part I

Narrative and *Torchwood*

ONE

Playing to the Crowd:
Torchwood Knows We're Watching
ANDREW IRELAND

The opening voiceover of the show tells us: "The 21st century is when it all changes. And you've got to be ready." But whose voice is telling us? Certainly the voice sounds like the lead character Captain Jack Harkness. Or is it the actor, John Barrowman? The register of the voice can be interpreted in different ways, depending on who we consider the voice is speaking to. If it is Captain Jack Harkness speaking, then surely it is to the fictional inhabitants of a Cardiff ravaged by a rift in time and space. If it is John Barrowman speaking, then surely it is to the audience of a television show entitled *Torchwood*? The show itself is defined by this duality, a commentary on itself and its progeny text, *Doctor Who* (BBC, 2005-present, UK).

Torchwood, a scripted and performed 21st century text, is a contemporary advancement of Roland Barthes' notion of the death of the author and birth of the reader.[1] Barthes indicates that the meaning of a text is not affirmed by the author, but rather in the interpretation of the text by the reader. The contemporary audience has grown sophisticated and discerning in their reception of media texts, a fact which could be argued has been embedded into the identity and discourse of the *Torchwood* brand. According to Barthes, the author only lives at the moment of writing; the reader then takes over to receive the text. I would argue that here in *Torchwood* we can see the author co-present with the reader, the audience, jostling for space, sparring to see who can outdo the other with their meaning and interpretation of the text. The boundary between author and reader blur and reduce, for the reader knows not just how to interpret meaning from a text, but is now a maker of text themselves. Thus, author and reader combine into a gestalt entity. So, in a sense, the production of *Torchwood* implicates fans of *Doctor Who*.

The presence of the audience as a critical, experience-laden element has an effect on the way stories are told on screen. The storylines, the characters, the tone, the style, the method of presentation, all are distorted by the over-riding presence of the audience that no longer peer inside the text, but are now inside, peering around. The cast and crew have to make room for them, and make them feel at home, lest they feel unwanted and turn away.

In this chapter I will argue how this shift to co-presence has led to new approaches to drama production, evidenced in the television series *Torchwood*, a show I would offer as a marker for change through its use of the audience — explicitly their experience, their knowledge, and their *presence*, to influence how stories are told. I will primarily focus first on the premiere episode, "Everything Changes," and the episode "Reset" from the second season.[2] The latter episode introduced the character of Martha Jones from *Doctor Who* into the show, and I will offer a comparison with Einstein's theory of relativity to demonstrate the effect that her presence has within the text.

Michael Rabiger argues that literary texts and moving image texts invoke different techniques of storytelling.[3] While a literary storyteller is constructing a story based on past events, storytelling for the screen has an added complication of events that appear to unfold in real time — in our present. How can one narrate a story set in the present? Rabiger explains that "the most you can do is to observe, react, and navigate, which is what the camera does unless it serves to reproduce what a character is experiencing."[4] Rabiger goes on to discuss that this passive narrator takes on the role of a "Concerned Observer," and in so doing represents the audience's connection to the text. The Concerned Observer provides a viewpoint into a text. Television drama though requires more than passive observing — it requires a Storyteller, one "through whose active, creative intelligence we perceive the film's events."[5] Controlling what the Concerned Observer witnesses is the work of the Storyteller, who figuratively stands behind, with his hands on either side of the head of the Observer, controlling what they will see, hear, and feel. Behind the Storyteller is the audience that finally receives the relayed experiences of the Observer.

Torchwood represents a shift in the balance of power. Not content with merely observing, the Observer has shrugged off the controlling hands of the Storyteller. John Fiske states that there "is a drive for innovation and change [which] comes from the audience's activity in the cultural economy."[6] Fiske continues:

> The audiences' freedom and ability to make their socially pertinent meanings out of television's text ... is, at one level, exactly what the producers want: they neither know nor care what meanings and pleasures their audiences produce, their concern is solely with the headcount and the demographics.[7]

Torchwood takes this a step further by not only accepting the positioning of the audience as makers of meaning, but is also willing to engage with them in a sparring power-play — beyond the headcount and demographics (although, ultimately, the power-play and headcount are inextricably linked concepts). Only some producers would have the confidence to undertake this very public challenge. Perhaps the death-defying Resurrection Glove that features in the premier episode is in fact the gauntlet that producer / author Russell T. Davies threw down moments before, to take up the challenge? And perhaps the new life that the Glove breathes into the body of a murdered man in the opening scene is indicative of the new life that is breathed into television drama? Not Barthes' "birth of the reader," but rebirth? Stronger and equipped with what would be described in *Doctor Who* as the most powerful weapon of all — knowledge.[8] The author's awareness and utilization of the reader's knowledge is what constitutes the essence of *Torchwood*.

The premiere episode, "Everything Changes," follows Gwen Cooper, a regular beat cop. Walking into a pub in one of the episode's early scenes, Gwen's partner tells her this: "It's all DNA these days. Like that CSI bollocks. CSI Cardiff, I'd like to see that. They'd be measuring the velocity of a kebab." But who is speaking? I'd argue this is Russell T. Davies, sparring with the audience. Until this line is delivered in the narrative, *Torchwood* appeared comparable (for the most part) with slick U.S. shows. The series isn't afraid to name-drop to demonstrate its own contextual awareness of TV.

Another example of this power-play features later in the episode, and is a direct, if relatively subtle poke at the genre-aware audience, who are now fully engaged in a "spot the reference" game which Davies has initiated:

> CAPTAIN JACK: Torchwood 1 was London, destroyed in the battle. Torchwood 2 is an office in Glasgow, very strange man. Torchwood 3, Cardiff. Torchwood 4, kind of gone missing, but we'll find it one day.

Presumably this is a sly reference to *Babylon 5* (Warner Bros. Television, 1993–1998, U.S.), where a similar list of previous stations is discussed in its premier episode; notably Babylon 4 vanished without a trace.[9]

Aside from textual references, the audience's highly developed genre-literacy is used as a way to develop new approaches to telling stories. We all smirk at the notion of *Star Trek* where a man in a red shirt is "beamed down" to a planet. We know that this poor unfortunate, who probably hasn't been afforded a character name, will be vaporized within moments. This foreknowledge affects how audiences read television texts that have relied for too long on the same set of codes and values. In a "whodunit," we are immediately suspicious of a character that emerges from a background of non-speaking extras, to deliver a line of dialogue. Our eyes narrow as we consider the cost afforded to give this newcomer a higher fee than the rest. Why wasn't this line deleted at the scripting stage? Often, the character is played by an actor the audience will recognize. The fore-knowledge may be used to attract audiences to watch the program, but can be to the detriment of the unfolding narrative. This character must be the murderer! At least, they must be highly relevant to the unfolding plot.

This cynicism-inducing fore-knowledge is turned back against the audience in the sparring *Torchwood*. Consider the scene: Gwen Cooper, a cop who has been established as the audience's main reference point in the story as we have been following her from the start. Persuaded into being a "Concerned Observer," we follow her steps. The camera hovers around her face, showing us her doubts, her worry, her determination, to find the mysterious Captain Harkness. She eventually tracks down the Torchwood address by pretending to be delivering pizza. Gwen enters the Torchwood hub for the first time—as do we. We are provided with a long, dramatic sequence of discovery—dark corridors, a huge rolling door, and then a magnificent underground laboratory complex. There are people here, hard at work. They are all going about their business, seemingly unaware of Gwen's presence and of the presence of the audience. The non-diegetic music that has accompanied the scene swells to a crescendo as Gwen moves enters the main staging area—and then suddenly, the music stops and the Torchwood gang collapse into laughter. It seems the characters, the writer, the director, are all in on the joke. And it is at the expense of not just Gwen, but also the audience, duped into being her Concerned Observer! Point scored for Russell T. Davies, and the game continues.

The re-purposing of the audience's television literacy becomes a key tonal quality in storytelling throughout the episode. The first view of an alien in the series is particularly worthy of note. In a hospital, Gwen walks down a lonely, sealed-off corridor after chasing Captain Jack's coat-tails. At the far end, stands a creature: a Weevil. Tall, dressed like a man, only the hands and face betray alien origins. As Gwen gets closer (and so, therefore, do we, as Concerned Observer) more detail becomes apparent. We see the eyes, the teeth, the mottled skin, and the cleverly controlled sneering mouth. What is on display is not an alien—but a production team showing the audience a lifelike, animatronically controlled prosthetic mask. The Storyteller proudly shows us this with some lengthy close-ups. A hospital porter appears at Gwen's side and echoes what the Storyteller wants the Concerned Observer to be thinking: "Bloody hell, that is brilliant! That is *Hellraiser*, that is. Look at that!"[10]

As well as dropping another cultural reference to which *Torchwood* may be compared, the script is drawing attention to what the program designers and prosthetics makers would naturally be trying to hide — any clue that this is a mask, and not reality — and to always maintain the suspension of disbelief.[11] But that is an outmoded concept — the audience has no suspension of disbelief anymore, and would willingly cast it aside in order to become more involved. The increasing use of "special features" on DVD and behind the scenes shows such as *Doctor Who Confidential* and *Torchwood Declassified* expose the methods of production and the mechanics of storytelling like never before. That insider knowledge that audiences now possess can be used by production teams, to invigorate the dramatic text. For the methods of production, the show utilizes its audience's acceptance of behind the scenes tricks revealed. For the mechanics of storytelling, we are presented with, for example, the hospital porter in this scene. A character so brashly ignoring the rules of the grammar of production, defying the nature of the text's construction, is surely doomed to die a violent death. And the audience understands that — and this represents a new direction for drama to take — this sparring with the audience's prior knowledge provides fertile ground to move and excite audiences anew.

Torchwood, in its fragile first days between conception and taking its first faltering steps, could have developed into an oppressed sibling eager to escape the dominance of its older brother, the behemoth super-brand *Doctor Who*. Indeed, it seemed that every article in the popular press that discussed the series included the phrase "*Torchwood*: an anagram of *Doctor Who*."[12] From the very beginning, the production team were keen to distance themselves and allow *Torchwood* to mark its own territory.

Russell T. Davies made the following comment at the first production meeting to set up the series: "Compared to *Doctor Who* especially, this series is real. It's really set in Cardiff."[13] This quote is interesting for two reasons — firstly, it sets out the very conscious mission by the executive producers to separate it from *Doctor Who*. Secondly, that this series is real — really set in Cardiff. This move to a grittier, darker depiction of the city is one of the key methods *Torchwood* has of defining itself as a series in its own right. *Doctor Who* is a program designed as a Saturday night, 7 P.M. series for family viewing. As such, it is bright, fast, colorful, rich, and larger than life. *Torchwood* is designed for a later time-slot, that of 9 P.M. in the UK. As such, it is aimed at an older, more adult demographic, and so can afford to be darker, moodier, more suspenseful. The premiere episode wastes no time in highlighting this different tone — we are given a night setting, with lots of rain. Certainly, this is Cardiff. This is not to say that *Doctor Who* never featured rain — but invariably this was simply due to filming in the UK, with rain often unavoidable. The rain in *Torchwood* is more forceful — full-on, wild, and added at some expense by the production team to create a very different tonal "feel" to the series. This heightened sense of realism creates a contrast to *Doctor Who*. The realism soon extends to feature copious blood, violence, and swearing: "Don't ask me. There's no procedure anymore. It's a fucking disgrace," says a crime scene investigator to Gwen Cooper, standing in the rain, in the dark, at the gruesome murder scene.

The dialogue, featuring taboo language, has been renounced by the producers as a mistake, in hindsight. On repeated viewing, it stands out awkwardly as a line delivered not to Gwen, but to the audience. Watch out, the subtext not so much whispers, but rather, thunders: this is *not Doctor Who*. The production team are very aware of their primary audience—a *Doctor Who* audience—and they over-react to its presence, fearing them peering critically into their precious new text. This paranoia about brand separation juxtaposes with the sparring, friendly quality of the storytelling between the author and the reader. The contrast between opposing behavioral traits may well be the real rift in *Torchwood*.

In order to create a unique identity, the program strives both to remind viewers of its family ties (from which it draws viewing figures), and tries to distance itself from them. As Captain Jack tells Gwen at the end of the episode: "something happened to me a while back. A long story and far away." This pull-towards, push-away "arms length" relationship has defined the very essence of the series.

As *Torchwood* entered its second season, with a now established audience, it delivered a succession of strong, dramatic stories. In particular, a three-episode story arc in the middle of the thirteen episode run is worthy of analysis within the context of this chapter.[14] The episode "Reset" introduced the *Doctor Who* character Martha Jones into the *Torchwood* brand. It is interesting to note that this was broadcast sixth in the run, halfway through the season. The affection afforded to the Martha Jones character brought a fresh surge of media interest to the show that helped to "prop up" ratings at this point. A similar ratings-driven tactic was employed in the revitalized *Doctor Who*, notably in the first season broadcast in 2005. The Daleks were not featured in the first episode, but saved for the sixth, again the mid-point of the run and helped to counter an inevitable fall in ratings once the initial media speculation and hype had began to die down. Daleks are synonymous with *Doctor Who*, and therefore would be expected to appear in the show.[15] *Torchwood* however bears no such relationship with a character such as Martha Jones, and it could be argued which one came first—the idea of introducing Martha into the show, or the consideration of a strategy to increase the ratings? Certainly I would argue that the placing of the episode itself is a tactic to draw on audiences. But how evident is the presence and impact of this augmented *Doctor Who / Torchwood* audience within the episode itself?

In the teaser sequence, we are introduced to the character Martha Jones through the use of a point of view shot (POV). As Rabiger notes, this technique can be employed for a variety of purposes, and to reflect different points of view.[16] I argue that the use of POV here, where the identity of the character is not revealed on screen, provides the audience with a key signifier that separates the character from all others. Character POV is not a tool generally utilized in *Torchwood* (or television drama for that matter), and it serves to build up tension.[17] As it serves to hide the identity of the character from the audience, it provides the opportunity to develop a sequence where this secret can be gradually revealed, in layers, like the careful removal of wrapping paper from a present. First we are presented with a POV that signifies power and significance, and then we have the reaction of Ianto as the POV moves into the hub. We hear dialogue: "The VIP visitor is here," again raising expectation and intrigue. Then we are presented with a tantalizing extract of Martha's signature theme music from *Doctor Who*, intermingled with *Torchwood's* theme. Then we see Martha herself. Interestingly, when we first see her in shot she looks quite small and timid, in contrast to the power afforded her by the POV. This only lasts a moment though as we are then presented with a close-up, where she smiles confidently. As such, her change in visual signifiers from "powerful," to "timid," to "confident" provides the narrative with a developmental framework that the audience can follow and enjoy — pleasure and satisfaction, a reward for watching the episode, and for removing the layers of the wrapping. The sequence concludes with Martha's close-up, and Captain Jack's words "Miss Martha Jones!" providing a clear exclamation, echoing that of a child crying, "A train set!" after unwrapping a present on his birthday. Martha has now been unwrapped and stamped with the *Torchwood* brand, accepted into the fold. The program maker's understanding of the audience's response to a character such as Martha, have dictated the construction of her arrival at the hub.

The mixing of the Martha Jones theme and the *Torchwood* theme indicates the blurring of boundaries between brands. Martha brings her character, with its values and *Doctor Who* family-friendly tone, into *Torchwood*. This is a character who will not engage in swearing and sexual acts: Martha is bound by *Doctor Who*'s audience — and thus, *Doctor Who* functions as the dominant narrative, imposing its rules. When the dialogue turns to sex, the term itself is not mentioned, but coded as "dabble" instead. This dancing around the subject fits uneasily into a *Torchwood* scene, which previously would have shown no such restraint. It demonstrates awareness of Martha's audience in the scene, an extended audience beyond *Torchwood*'s norm, which are being made to feel at home. So, *Torchwood* is an ambivalent text in that it seeks to present itself as autonomous from its progeny text, *Doctor Who*, but at the same time it annexes that text in a way that replicates the audience's reception of *Torchwood*; the audience is seeking for fidelity to its progeny, so *Torchwood* does too.

To further discuss the impact Martha Jones has on the *Torchwood* brand, we can turn to Einstein's theory of relativity, which tells us that space-time is curved by the presence of matter. "Einstein's idea [is] that the gravitational field is represented by curved space-time: particles try to follow the nearest thing to a straight path in a curved space, but because space-time is not flat their paths appear to be bent, as if by a gravitational field."[18] Stephen Hawking describes this as the effect of putting a heavy ball onto a rubber sheet. As objects pass by the ball, they are attracted towards it and curve inwards.[19] I would go as far here as suggesting that the presence of Martha Jones within *Torchwood* leads to a similar effect. All other elements of the text, including narrative and construction techniques become distorted by the presence of the "heavy ball," and curve inwards towards it. Martha is thus center of the text, in all senses.

Characters within the frame are affected (curved) by the presence of Martha. With gravitational force, they orbit her. Examples of this include scenes set within the hub — an early autopsy scene has Martha center stage, with the other characters physically placed on a gantry above her, looking down, in a ring — as spectators themselves. A later scene includes the team experimenting with a device (known as the Singularity Scalpel) that can remove objects from inside other objects. Jack actually *takes* Martha's shoulders and *moves* her into center-frame during the sequence. Is he aware of the audience angling for a better view?

The plot of the episode has been fashioned to serve the motivations of this character. The story orbits around medical issues, hardly surprising as it presents a rationale for Martha's presence there. Again the presence of Martha curves the plot. She goes undercover once Owen has been seen by those they are trying to infiltrate. He would have been the likely choice as the medical officer of the team, but now Martha must play the pivotal role. POV is once again employed at this point to curve all aspects of the story around her perspective — plot developments and focus, the framing of shots, character actions and motivations, the position of the audience — all serve the presence of Martha Jones.

The analogy with the theory of relativity can be developed further through consideration of the POV technique. At a critical mass and size, all matter in a star is compressed into a region of no volume, leading to the density of the matter, and the curvature of the space-time, becoming infinite. This is known as a singularity[20] (and coincidentally forming a connection to the Singularity Scalpel discussed above). As Stephen Hawking describes, at this point the heavy ball would make a bottomless hole in the rubber sheet and matter would fall into it, and not be able to escape.[21] This is how stars collapse into black holes. If we substitute the heavy ball for Martha Jones, we can see why, as the story progresses and Martha's stake in the plot increases (as she goes undercover), we are presented with a POV sequence. The density of the matter (the story), and the curvature of the space-time (the narrative techniques) become infinite, and the author / reader presence falls into the resulting singularity, becoming the central point, at one with the character, and as Proferes' describes the POV technique: "[it] contains the dynamics of the spatial relationship, thereby conveying an awareness in the audience."[22] Through the use of the POV, author, reader and character combine as a singularity, an extension of the gestalt entity discussed earlier.

At the conclusion of the episode, the playful *Torchwood* responds again to the awareness of the Martha-augmented audience. Owen, the medical officer, is shot dead. Previous dialogue in the episode planted a seed in the audience's collective mind. Jack has already told Martha, "If you wanted a job you should have given me a call." Now it looks like there may be an opening, and Martha would fit right in. This *excites* the audience, who put the pieces together and sees a connection. Their awareness of how television drama plots develop is being utilized. But unlike the seeding of the Singularity Scalpel, this seed is not set to germinate. But the tactic wins out — the audience is being lulled into watching the following week — a bid to retain Martha's fans for subsequent episodes. However Owen is subsequently revived and Martha leaves the show after the three episode story arc has concluded.

Torchwood continues to offer ways of playfully engaging the audience to interact with its storytelling. The production team's understanding of how best to utilize the *Doctor Who* audience to maximize ratings was put to use in the season three story "Children of Earth" broadcast over five consecutive nights on BBC1 and BBC HD in the UK. This specially extended story, branded "event television" in the UK, was a ratings success with 5.9 million viewers watching its opening episode, 1.5 million more than the previous record held by season two.[23] It is interesting to note that this season was broadcast on BBC1, the flagship BBC channel home to the natural *Doctor Who* audience. Previously the series had premiered on BBC3 (season one), and BBC2 (season two). Earlier in *Torchwood*'s run, the Doctor character had rarely been mentioned explicitly. Indeed, in "Reset," in recognition of the presence of the *Doctor Who* augmented audience watching Martha, there was a reference to the Doctor, spoken by Martha: "We were both under the same Doctor." Now, in "Children of Earth," references come in thick and fast, taking an opportunity to spar with the BBC1 *Doctor Who* audience. This builds to the final installment with Gwen Cooper's brief video diary of what is happening:

> GWEN COOPER: There's one thing I always wanted to ask Jack. Back in the old days. I wanted to know about that Doctor of his. The man who appears out of nowhere and saves the world, except sometimes he doesn't. All those times in history when there was no sign of him. I wanted to know why not. But I don't need to ask anymore. I know the answer now. Sometimes the Doctor must look at this planet and turn away in shame.

I argue that this is seeding the audience's expectation of how the plot will develop in much the same way as the foregrounding of Owen's death seeded an expectation that Martha would join the *Torchwood* team. Here though, it is seeding, and *feeding*, the *Doctor Who* audience into hoping that the Doctor will arrive on the scene to save the day. This idea infects all aspects of the tone and story development of "Children of Earth." We are shown a bleak, ugly world where there is no hope and no savior. Therefore we crave one. The video diary, used twice in the episode, purely works to underline the Doctor's absence from the story, and reinforces the idea that we miss the Doctor. *Torchwood* is again sparring with its audience, reacting against a *Doctor Who* craving audience, ultimately leaving them feeling empty. I argue it does this as a means to heighten the level of anticipation for *Doctor Who*, always the prime and dominant super-brand, set to return to television in the fall of 2009. But while this chapter has dealt mainly with *Torchwood* being the agent of the sparring, I argue that in this case it is being used as an object to spar with; an audience-curving weapon wielded by the producers of *Doctor Who* as a marketing tool.

As well as dealing with the extra*terrestrial*, *Torchwood* has always embraced, as part of its very DNA, the extra-*textual*. Returning to the question of the voice carrying the opening narration, perhaps it is not simply a question of whether it is Captain Jack, or whether it is John Barrowman, or even Russell T. Davies speaking. For *Torchwood*, the extra-*textual* includes the notion of the audience itself. Perhaps the voice belongs to the audience, the newly empowered, media-savvy, cynical awkwards who know too much about how television is constructed, and are now forcing television to rise to the challenge of surprising them anew, to engage them in a sparring match. The audience is game. Spoken by them, the opening narration carries a powerful message for the medium: "The 21st century is when everything changes, and *television* has got to be ready."

Notes

1. Roland Barthes, "The Death of the Author," in Stephen Heath's translation, *Image, Music, Text* (London: Fontana Press, 1977), 142–148.
2. "Everything Changes" established the tone and *modus operandi* for the show. "Reset" is the sixth episode of the second season and introduces *Doctor Who* companion Martha Jones into *Torchwood* for a three-episode mini-arc.
3. Michael Rabiger, *Directing: Film Techniques and Aesthetics* (Burlington, MA: Focal Press, 2003), 54–55.
4. *Ibid.*, 54.
5. *Ibid.*
6. John Fiske, "Moments of Television," in Ellen Seiter, *Remote Control: Television, Audiences, and Cultural Power* (London: Routledge, 1991), 62.
7. *Ibid.*
8. The Doctor's preferred weapon of choice is knowledge — to think his way out of situations (a different solution to the gun-toting Torchwood crew). See the *Doctor Who* episode "Tooth and Claw" (BBC, 2006) where the Doctor declares, in a library: "the greatest weapon of all: Knowledge."
9. The *Babylon 5* episodes "Babylon Squared" (Warner Bros Television, 1994) and "War Without End" (Warner Bros Television, 1996) tell the story of the Babylon 4 space station which mysteriously vanished during construction only to resurface years later to play a part in the war against the Shadows.
10. See *Hellraiser* (New World Pictures, 1987).
11. The phrase "suspension of disbelief" was coined by Samuel Taylor Coleridge in 1817 and means "the temporary acceptance as believable of events or characters that would ordinarily be seen as incredible. This is usually to allow an audience to appreciate works of literature or drama that are exploring unusual ideas." *http://www.phrases.org.uk/meanings/suspension-of-disbelief.html* (accessed 16 July 2009).
12. It is thought that the anagram "Torchwood" was first utilized during the production of the 2005 series of *Doctor Who*. It was written on the tapes in an effort to prevent advance copies being leaked. Russell T. Davies later adopted it as a title for the spin-off series a year later. *http://www.imdb.com/title/tt0485301/trivia* (accessed 10 June 2009).
13. See Special Features on the *Torchwood: The Complete First Series* (BBC DVD, 2008).
14. The season 2 episodes "Reset," "Dead Man Walking," and "A Day in the Death" tell the story of Owen's death and subsequent revival. Freema Agyeman (Martha Jones) guest stars.
15. Since *Doctor Who* began on British television in the 1960s, there have been Daleks. They were first introduced in the second story in early 1964, and helped secure the longevity of the show thereafter. Since that first encounter, the Daleks have returned time and time again, increasingly to boost ratings.
16. Michael Rabiger, *Directing: Film Techniques and Aesthetics*, 193–203.
17. A similar POV technique was employed in the television series *Babylon 5* to maximize the "final reveal" introduction of the wife of Captain John Sheridan, who had been missing and presumed dead for years. See "Z'ha'dum" (Warner Bros Television, 1996).
18. Stephen Hawking, *A Brief History of Time* (London: Bantam Press, 1992), 135.
19. Susan Andrews review of a Stephen Hawking lecture, *Black Holes: Eternal Prisons No More* (USA, 2009). *http://www.physorg.com/news156450506.html* (accessed 22 June 2009).
20. Stephen Hawking, *A Brief History of Time*, 49.
21. *Black Holes: Eternal Prisons No More*, *http://www.physorg.com/news156450506.html* (accessed 22 June 2009).
22. Nicholas Proferes, *Film Directing Fundamentals* (London: Focal Press, 2005), 41.
23. See *http://news.bbc.co.uk/1/hi/entertainment/8138514.stm* (accessed 15 July 2009).

Two

Existentialism and Christian Symbolism

R. C. Neighbors

In his seminal article "Ideology and Ideological State Apparatuses," theorist Louis Althusser describes ideology as "the imaginary relationship of individuals to their real conditions of existence."[1] In other words, ideology negotiates an imagined relationship between an individual and society. These ideologies, Althusser argues, are produced by what he calls ideological state apparatuses, such as the educational system, the media, etc. In this sense, one of the most prominent producers of ideologies is religion and, in historical Western culture, specifically the Christian church. According to Jean-Luc Comolli and Jean Narboni, these ideologies can be used to categorize entertainment media texts — the ideologies either being reproduced by a text, contested by a text, or unintentionally reproduced in an attempt by a text to contest them.[2] One television show that specifically contests religious ideology — by perpetuating existential thought — is the BBC television program *Torchwood*.

Torchwood is a science fiction spin-off of the long-running program *Doctor Who*, the former centering around a quasi-governmental organization based in Cardiff, Wales, a team sworn to protect the world from aliens and other fantastic creatures and happenings. As a post-watershed show, *Torchwood* deals with many mature themes, and perhaps the most prevalent mature theme in the program is that of existentialism, a search for an understanding of the human condition involving ideas like individual freedom, meaninglessness, and the concrete nature of existence. In *Torchwood*, this theme manifests itself in a number of ways, including dealing with the randomness of existence, meaning, mortality, and the afterlife.

An existential worldview pervades the episodes of *Torchwood*. For instance, when confronted with a possible apocalypse in the episode "End of Days," team member Ianto begins reading a prophetic section from the

Book of Daniel. The team's leader, Jack, who it can be argued is often a mouthpiece for the show runners, comments on humanity's obsession with anything that "denies the randomness of existence," an obvious existential notion. Here Jack takes for granted that existence is random, completely disregarding out of hand religion or any other explanation that would claim otherwise. Perhaps, though, the most prevalent existential concepts in the series are those dealing with mortality and the meaning of life, predominately dealt with through the possibility of an afterlife.

The belief in life after death has been nearly universal among human cultures throughout history, even if not among all individuals in those cultures. Accordingly, most people today, whether religious or not, believe in some form of an afterlife. Many envision a bright light at the end of a tunnel, rewards for behaving properly, or a reunion with loved ones. However, this heavenly spirit world does not exist in the fictional universe of *Torchwood*. In fact, several characters have died and been brought back, only to report the same thing: death is nothingness, darkness. Life is all that there is.

From the beginning of the program, the idea of no afterlife existing is a recurrent theme. In fact, the concept is featured in the first scene of the first episode of the program. In the opening of the pilot "Everything Changes," the team arrives on the scene of a murder, the latest in a string of similar stabbings. They plan to use an artifact they have recovered and dubbed the resurrection gauntlet (though Ianto refers to it as the risen mitten) to temporarily resurrect the victim, in hopes of identifying his killer. When he cannot help them, the team wonders what to do with the few seconds the man has to live. Jack kneels and ask him, "What was it like when you died? What did you see?" The man becomes frantic and shouts, "Nothing. I saw nothing. Oh my God, there's nothing!" and then dies again, as the power of the gauntlet fades.

This notion runs throughout the show, particularly through the characters of Jack, Suzie, and Owen. For example, as a result of a series of incidents during his adventures with the Doctor, Jack gains an inability to die or, more specifically, an inability to remain dead. He is actually killed several times throughout the course of seasons one and two, always waking, usually just a few seconds later. He views this longevity as a curse and implies that he wants to find a cure, so he can finally die and stay dead. Because of his situation, he feels great sympathy toward others who want to die, as in the episode "Out of Time," when he sits with a man from the early 20th century who has fallen through the rift and wants to kill himself. Jack only warns him that when one dies "it just goes black." He sits with the man, holding his hand, as the latter dies of carbon monoxide poisoning.

On the other hand, Suzie, who was an original member of Torchwood before her replacement by Gwen, is capable of doing anything to stay alive. Three months after her suicide, the Torchwood team resurrects her using the gauntlet because they need help with a case (in the episode "They Keep Killing Suzie"). It becomes apparent, however, that Suzie set up their case months in advance, in the event of her death, so that they would need to resurrect her. Furthermore, the gauntlet has created a link between Suzie and Gwen, slowly draining Gwen's life energy for Suzie's benefit, in effect killing the former and healing the latter. Suzie's motivation emerges through the following conversation with Gwen, who asks her what happens when you die:

> GWEN: So what's up there?
> SUZIE: Nothing, just nothing.
> GWEN: But if there's nothing, what's the point of it all?
> SUZIE: This is, driving through the dark, all this stupid, tiny stuff. We're just animals howling in the night, 'cause it's better than silence. [...] Creatures clinging together in the cold.
> GWEN: So when you die, it's just, it's just—
> SUZIE: Darkness.

Later, when Jack asks Suzie why she is, in effect, killing Gwen to stay alive, she says, "Because life is all [...] I'd do anything to stay, anything."

Like Suzie, Owen is also shot and killed (in the episode "Reset"), and, also like Suzie, he is resurrected through use of the gauntlet, but only so the team can say their goodbyes. However, through chance, in the following episode "Dead Man Walking," Owen is brought back somewhat permanently, without draining the life force of someone else as was the case with Suzie. He also admits that death is "nothing [...] darkness."

As shown, every character who has a brush with death reports the same thing—nothingness and darkness, an absence of an afterlife. There is no bright light, no pearly gates, and no loved ones waiting. Owen even jokes about this at one point when asked, saying, "There was a light, a tiny speck of light, and I was rushing towards it, like down a corridor. And it glowed brighter and brighter, and suddenly there were these gates ... these big pearly gates. And there was Saint Peter, and he said, 'You've been a very naughty boy.'"

Also noteworthy is the implication, as seen from Suzie's quotation above, that the traditional Western idea of an afterlife, with its fluffy, white clouds, harp-playing angels, and reunion with loved ones, is a sign of immaturity. Not only does the show make such an extraordinary claim about what happens to human beings when we die, but it also seems to dismiss as childish commonly believed alternative.

Two. Existentialism and Christian Symbolism (NEIGHBORS)

However, both Suzie's and Owen's accounts of the afterlife seems to undermine the notion that no afterlife exists, that there is only nothing. In fact, there seems to be a *consciousness* of darkness, of being alone, and of nothingness. This is acknowledged through the continued references throughout the series to something "moving in the dark,"[3] an apparent reference to either the demon Abaddon who emerges from the rift to terrorize Cardiff in the episode "End of Days" or to the embodiment of death who follows the resurrected Owen into the world of the living in "Dead Man Walking." This consciousness, or continued personal existence, after death implied by both Suzie and Owen does not indicate the absence of an afterlife. On the contrary, it shows that one exists, even if it is only an unsatisfactory one. The apparent contradiction may arise, however, from the inherent inability to realize a cessation of our own consciousness.

These are just the major examples pointing to the lack of an afterlife (or existence of a nontraditional, unacceptable one) in the *Torchwood* universe. There are many other minor examples, such as the explaining of apparent haunting through scientific means in the episode "Ghost Machine," and the screen suddenly fading to black in "Random Shoes" when the point-of-view character Eugene truly dies. Portraying a lack of an afterlife is an interesting stance for a television show to take, particularly one with so many other fantastic elements, especially when similar shows with similar worldviews, such as *Buffy the Vampire Slayer* (20th Century–Fox Television, 1997–2003, U.S.), take a more traditional stance. Still, however extraordinary this position is for a contemporary television show, it is also somewhat conflicting, or at the very least puzzling, when its consequences are considered.

First and most straightforward are the consequences to morality. If "life is all" as Suzie proclaims in "They Keep Killing Suzie," then there is no reward waiting after death for good deeds, and without a promised reward, moral acts must find new motivation. They must be performed for their own sake and must have intrinsic value, or at least, if nothing has intrinsic meaning, a value that is attributed to them. This casts a new light on everything done by Torchwood throughout the course of the show.

In addition, without an afterlife, the question of an existential "meaning of life" arises, or as Gwen puts it, "But if there's nothing, what's the point of it all?" Suzie answers that "this is," meaning "life" is the point or, to put it somewhat paradoxically, life is the meaning of life. However, this idea is where the consequences of the show's existential stance becomes somewhat confusing.

In many ways, life in the *Torchwood* universe (and life in the real world by association) is portrayed as nothing but misery. Each of the characters go through some form of hell during the course of the show. For instance, both Ianto and Owen lose loved ones. After dealing with yokel cannibals in the episode "Countrycide," Gwen becomes unable to cope, begins an affair with Owen, and comments that what she has witnessed while working with Torchwood has "chang[ed] how [she] sees the world," presumably for the worse. In addition, through her ordeal with a pendent that allows the wearer to read minds in "Greeks Bearing Gifts," Tosh questions how she can even go on living.

> TOSH: I can't stand it anymore, the weight of it, the depravity, the fear. It fills me up.... It feels like there's nothing. I can't forget the things I've seen, the things I've heard [...] I had hope that I'd see something, a little random act of kindness [that would] make me think we were safe, some essential good in us. There isn't. We're frightened, and we're callous, and I can't be a part of that any longer.

This reasoning can be summed up in a line from the poem "The Stolen Child" by Yeats, which is quoted in the episode "Small Worlds." It reads thus: "For the world's more full of weeping than you can understand." Nonetheless, Suzie claims that life is the point, even though series one portrays it as nothing but sadness and cruelty. The series even describes life in the same language it uses to describe death — nothingness, darkness, and isolation. However, this portrayal of life is mitigated to a certain extent in season two, after certain Christian symbolism is inserted into the show.

Ironically, while in the midst of contesting religious ideology, *Torchwood* has an abundance of, often jarring, Christian symbolism. For example, in the episode "Adam," Jack passes "communion" to his team as they gather around a table, reminiscent of the Last Supper, but their bread comes in the form of amnesia pills to defeat a mind-altering alien. Also, to prove that he has died, Owen has the suicidal woman from "A Day in the Death" touch his gunshot wound, a la the interaction between the resurrected Jesus and Saint Thomas. This encounter "saves" her from committing suicide. However, the most glaring example of Christian symbolism in the show is found in "End of Days." Jack acts as a Christ-figure through his willful self-sacrifice and subsequent resurrection. He confronts the satanic figure of Abaddon, as the only one who can possible stop it, but the encounter costs him his life. The team, his disciples, wait patiently for his resurrection, but it doesn't occur in a few seconds as is normal. In fact, it takes him several (possibly three) days to resurrect. His reunion with the team resembles Jesus' return to his disciples who had all betrayed him prior to the event, particularly with Jack's hugging of Owen, who, during their last meeting, shot him. The forgiveness of Owen's betrayal by Jack seems to parallel the forgiveness of Saint Peter's betrayal by Jesus.

This last sequence of events seems important because following it and throughout season two, the characters begin to experience a transformation, or as some may argue, a sort of redemption, and the negative portrayal of the existential worldview in the show is in some ways diminished.

For instance, each major character achieves some positive circumstance in their life during season two, a change directly opposed to his or her struggles from the first season. Jack finds a renewed sense of purpose in life and knowledge of what it means to be human during his further adventures with the Doctor[4] in between the first and second *Torchwood* seasons. Gwen overcomes the guilt from her affair with Owen to marry long-time boyfriend Rhys in the episode "Something Borrowed." She also comes to grips with her new job at Torchwood and is even able to tell Rhys specifics about her work, albeit against Jack's wishes ("Meat"). In addition, while Tosh struggled with loneliness during season one, a trait used by an alien to take advantage of her, in season two she legitimately falls in love with a soldier from World War I ("To the Last Man") and is even able to tell Owen how she has felt about him since the beginning of the program ("Dead Man Walking"). Also during season one, Ianto suffered the loss of his girlfriend after she was turned partially into a Cyberwoman ("Cyberwoman"), but during season two, he is able to move on, even to begin a relationship with Jack. Owen perhaps undergoes the biggest change of all, when, through his death, he minimizes his cynicism and sees more than darkness in life ("A Day in the Death").

It is through this last transformation that the negative view existentialism of *Torchwood* is most mitigated. For example, when Martha Jones, a recurring character in the *Doctor Who* and *Torchwood* universe, asks Owen what death is like, he responds, "There was nothing, not that I can remember." ("Dead Man Walking") Here is the first time in the program that a statement about death being "nothing" or "darkness" is qualified. This qualification allows for something more after life, far different from an afterlife's strict non-existence during season one. It leaves open the possibility that those who have died and returned simply are incapable of remembering what it is like to be dead, what the afterlife is truly like. As Owen states, he's "not sure the living should [even] know" what death is like.

Not only is the possibility of an afterlife suggested in season two, but also life is portrayed as not being completely filled with misery, as opposed to its portrayal in series one. This is most apparent during the Owen-centric episode "A Day in the Death." During the episode, Owen confronts a dying man who the team believes holds an alien bomb, and Owen also talks with a woman who plans to commit suicide by jumping from a building. The man believes the device is keeping him alive, but Owen tells him that "it's hope. That thing, it's just hope." He continues, "You're just scared of the darkness. Join the club. Trust me, I know how shit everything can be." The dying man says that he needs "to know that there is more out there, that this isn't all there is."

Owen's experiences, namely dying and resurrecting, give him the ability to comfort the dying man. He even implies that though both life and death have their own undesirable qualities, both have some positive traits and neither are to be feared. Shortly after the dying man gives Owen the device, the man dies, and Owen believes the strange, pulsing thing is going to blow up. He braces himself to die once again. However, an interesting thing happens. The device turns out to be a message from a distant alien race, responding to the probes sent into space during the 1970s, introducing themselves with a beautiful and colorful light show. Something Owen assumed contained destruction turned out, instead, to contain beauty.

Owen recounts this story to the woman on the rooftop. He says, "The alien device] sang to me. It gave off light in the darkness. You see, sometimes it does get better."

Owen goes on, in complete defiance of the tone from the first series:

> OWEN: You've got a choice. If you think that the darkness is too much, then go for it. But if there is a chance, just some hope — it could be having a cigarette or that first sip of hot tea on a cold morning or it could be your mates — but if there is even a tiny glimmer of light, then don't you think that's worth taking a chance?

Owen has come to acknowledge that some aspects of beauty exist in life, and he has come to value living. Ironically, it took his own death for him to realize this.

One may be inclined at this point to suggest that the show takes a step back from its earlier position, that in some sense the Christian symbolism of Jack's sacrifice and role as Christ figure redeems the Torchwood team, lending credence to that ideology and the ideological state apparatus that produced it. However, that is not the case. The presence of Christian symbolism in *Torchwood* only points to how thoroughly the symbols saturate our cultural mythos; it does not promote the ideology. In addition, the shift in tone between the two seasons is more likely due to the move of Torchwood from BBC 3 to BBC 2 — and a shift to being more family-oriented — than to any sacrificial happenstance in the content of the show itself.

Throughout the series, the existential worldview of *Torchwood* is never abolished. In fact, the positive tone of the second series even serves to make existentialism more appealing as an alternative to religion. Thus, while few shows attempt to question traditional religious ideology, *Torchwood* stands as an example of challenging, thoughtful, and entertaining programming.

Notes

1. Louis Althusser, "Ideology and Ideological State Apparatuses: Notes towards an Investigation January — April 1969," in *Lenin and Philosophy and Other Essays*, trans. Ben Brewer (New York: Monthly Review, 1971), 127–186.
2. Jean-Luc Comolli and Jean Narboni, "Cinema, Ideology, Criticism," 1969, rpt. In Gerald Most, Marshall Cohen, and Leo Brandy, eds., *Film Theory and Criticism* (New York: Oxford University Press, 1992), 682–689.
3. See the episodes "They Keep Killing Suzie" and "Dead Man Walking."
4. See the *Doctor Who* episode "Utopia" (BBC, 2007, UK).

THREE

Policing the Rift:
The Monstrous and the Uncanny
Susan J. Wolfe
& Courtney Huse Wika

What do you think the truth will do to them? We've seen what comes through the rift. I don't want mom and dad living in fear of what's prowling around in the sewers.
— Gwen, "Something Borrowed"

    Much is at stake for Torchwood, the organization whose members police the Rift to protect the citizens of Cardiff and their "mundane" lives. It exists, as the opening voice-over states, "Outside the government, beyond the police," and has its secret headquarters — cavernous, filled with daunting technology and a few body parts in jars — beneath the sidewalks of the Millennium Centre. Torchwood's mission, known only to a few, is more than top-secret, for if the public were to learn of the Rift and the space/dimensional flotsam and jetsam it deposits, mass hysteria would undoubtedly result. The contrast between Torchwood's dimly lit interiors and hidden existence and the city it guards is highlighted in every episode. We are shown aerial shots of the city at night, its lights twinkling in the dark, during the opening voice-over, and action scenes are often intensified by cut-way views of the city. The horrors of individual episodes are juxtaposed by banter between protagonist Gwen Cooper and her fiancé Rhys as he fixes dinner or watches sports on the television. The differentiation between the two worlds of Torchwood can be analyzed by Ernst Jentsch's and Sigmund Freud's theories of the Uncanny,[1] which explore tensions between the familiar and the unfamiliar, the known and the unknown, and these theories can be extended to the binary which is at the heart of Torchwood's mission, the human and the monstrous.

    Sigmund Freud argues in his 1919 essay "The 'Uncanny'" that the uncanny is "undoubtedly related to what is frightening — to what arouses dread and horror" and is "that class of the frightening which leads back to what is known of old and long familiar."[2] Freud, in an attempt to move "beyond the equation 'uncanny' = 'unfamiliar,'" investigates the definition of the uncanny in a number of languages. He focuses mainly on the translations of the German word *Heimlich* from Daniel Sanders's *Worterbuch der Deutschen Sprache*, 1860. He finds *Heimlich* to mean "not strange, familiar, tame, intimate, friendly," and "belonging to the house or the family, or regarded as so belonging," and "restfulness and security as in one within the four walls of his house."[3] The meaning, however, changes and comes to mean also that "which is concealed, kept from sight, so that others do not get to know of or about it, withheld from others" and as "deceitful and malicious."[4] Freud concludes from this analysis that "what interests us most [...] is to find that among its different shades of meaning the word *heimlich* exhibits one which is identical with its opposite, *unheimlich*."[5] Thus, the uncanny arises when the barriers between the binaries are traversed, such as when the monstrous comes through the rift, disrupting the safety and security of life in Cardiff, or when the human becomes monstrous, breaching the very definition of human.

This infringement of boundaries is not a welcome one, as it gives rise to "intellectual uncertainty." Ernst Jentsch's 1906 article "On the Psychology of the Uncanny" posits that "intellectual uncertainty" is its principle manifestation, as "it is an old experience that the traditional, the usual and the hereditary is dear and familiar to most people, and that they incorporate the new and the unusual with mistrust, unease and even hostility (misoneism)." These negative reactions are caused largely by the subject's inability to cognitively identify the new thing; in other words, there is great difficulty in the "intellectual mastery" of it.[6]

Jentsch's argument of uncertainty not only corresponds to the anxiety of duality (am I human, or am I monstrous?) in the members of Torchwood, but it also encompasses the anxiety inherent in the threat of the unknown and Other eclipsing the familiar space of home and human identity, respectively.

In the show, the uncanny manifests whenever the boundaries between familiar/unfamiliar, known/unknown, human/monstrous is violated. While these boundaries are traversed by the many categories of monster presented on the show, they are also navigated by the Torchwood members, for in order to effectively police the Rift and protect the ordinary citizens from the horrors of the unknown, they must willingly invoke the uncanny. However, they do so at the risk of becoming the alien Other they seek to contain — of becoming monstrous themselves.

Torchwood consciously plays two definitions of the "monstrous" against one another, for creatures whose forms are bizarre or grotesque are sometimes harmless while both creatures taking human form and humans themselves are found to be malevolent. Of course, those outside Torchwood are not privy to the existence of aliens and, attempting to incorporate their strange appearances within a familiar framework, fail to recognize creatures for what they are. The opening episode of the first season, "Everything Changes," shows us how ordinary people react initially to the uncanny. Policewoman Gwen Cooper chases a mysterious figure in a greatcoat up a flight of stairs; she enters a hallway sealed off with packing plastic, sees an upright biped at the other end of the hall, and approaches to interrogate it. Though its face is horribly distorted and its hand terminates in loose-skinned, clawed digits, both Gwen and the custodian who follows her through the barrier mistake the monster, a Weevil, for a masked human. In fact, Gwen chides the monster for failing to provide answers when she interrogates it, and the custodian proclaims the "disguise" to be "brilliant." The Weevil simply stands there, digits twitching, until the custodian attempts to touch it. Then it suddenly lunges for him, and several jets of blood spurt from the neck of the shrieking man. At this moment, Gwen confronts the uncanny; clearly her "witness" is not human but something quite unknown.

We, the audience, are able to identify the being as a monster once Gwen is close enough to question it and thus find the reactions of Gwen and the custodian humorous, as we would if a Martian were asking directions of a fire hydrant. But the creature's sudden violence and the realistic-looking blood are not funny at all. Unanticipated changes in mood and action occur continually in the series so that, like Gwen, we are kept continually off-balance by shifts between the humorous and the horrible, the ordinary and the eerie, the human and the monstrous, and discomfited by the fact that little enough seems to separate them.

In fact, such dichotomies constitute the structure of "Everything Changes." An opening scene that introduces Gwen for the first time shows her beside another police officer at a crime scene; standing in a downpour and wearing yellow slickers, they chat about a weekend get-together. To Gwen's query about the corpse's identity, the cop replies, "I dunno. Some bloke," and both appear to be calm, undisturbed by the apparent murder. Gwen's complacency is shattered, however, once the Torchwood crew arrives and uses a metallic glove to revive the dead man.

Later, masquerading as a pizza delivery person, Gwen enters Torchwood's headquarters through an entrance disguised as the wall of an ordinary-looking office. The headquarters' interior is huge, easily several stories high; amidst laboratory equipment and computer screens are two glass jars containing a disembodied hand and head. As she looks around, Gwen is startled by a pterodactyl which glides overhead, screaming. Here, too, the ordinary is juxtaposed against the eerie.

Gwen is shown the killer Weevil, now confined and subdued. It is no longer terrifying, however, and not just because it has been sedated. As Gwen looks into the eyes of the Weevil, we, like Gwen, cease to attribute its violence to a vicious nature. It is merely an animal, one whose eyes reveal a level of intelligence, and it appears as puzzled by humans as we are by them. As Jack explains that the Weevil, normally inhabiting the city sewers, accidentally came to the surface, the moment of intellectual uncertainty ends; knowledge of the heretofore unknown has been assimilated and the mystery behind an urban legend (of monsters in the sewers) revealed.

The Weevil is the first monster (other than the pterodactyl) we are introduced to in the series, and thus establishes the human/monstrous dichotomy for the rest of the episodes. While its appearance is horrifying and it represents the sort of monster we believe we are *supposed* to fear, in some ways it is among the least frightening of the monsters we encounter. Predictable in its animalistic behavior, once its identity is known and the "intellectual uncertainty" is transcended, it no longer invokes the uncanny. Hence Jack is rather cavalier about the Weevil when he informs Gwen that it is the murderer. He shows a similar nonchalance in communicating with extraterrestrials whose spaceship has appeared in earth's atmosphere; he greets the aliens, but requests that they please "get the hell out of our atmosphere; they're spooking the locals."

Other alien creatures seem positively gentle, such as the behemoth lying captive and motionless in "Meat"; its size may be monstrous, but its eyes suggest kindness. It seems unconscionable that human beings are carving the living, sentient being to sell as steaks and roasts. Because of the vast size of the creature, people wielding chainsaws and wearing miners' helmets enter its cavernous body in order to butcher it, perhaps symbolizing our immersion in the consumerism of late-stage capitalism or our unethical insistence on consuming meat. Certainly we understand the Torchwood team's moral outrage at the creature's suffering. This is not the only instance that the human or human-like disregards the understood system of ethics and morality, and traverses the boundary of the monstrous.

As Shakespeare observes, "The devil hath power [to] assume a pleasing shape," and many of *Torchwood*'s monsters do just that.[7] Some of its monsters are all the more frightening because they appear as human beings. In "Greeks Bearing Gifts," Torchwood's computer genius, Toshiko Sako, is addressed by an attractive, vivacious blonde in a pub. Mary is, of course, nearly two centuries old, but the alien which has inhabited her has kept her young and pretty. Her alien body is no less unpleasant than her human one — humanoid, though floating gracefully and glowing like an illuminated moon jellyfish — but Tosh is completely unaware of Mary's true nature. Thus, though Mary quickly puts Tosh at her ease, we are uncomfortably aware of her duality; she is an entity concealing the unknown beneath the familiar, the alien within a human façade.

At the beginning of the episode, we witness the alien force, in the form of embodied light, possess Mary. Previously we see a young woman in terror, pursued by a soldier bent on killing her; once inhabited by the alien, however, she ignores the bullet hole in her body, zips effortlessly over to him, plucks his still-beating heart from his chest, and takes a hearty bite of it. Hence we are on tenterhooks when Tosh succumbs to her charms and becomes her lover. But once she is exposed as an alien, Mary's motives for seducing Tosh seem all too familiar and quite human: she has enjoyed herself while at the same time using sex to get what she wanted. Owen Harper, Torchwood's doctor-turned-agent, may be horrified at Mary's indifference and the fact that she has survived for decades on a steady diet of human hearts, but the episode places greater emphasis on Tosh's sense of betrayal. Mary may not have eaten Tosh's heart, but she certainly breaks it.

Several other *Torchwood* episodes center on the human form which conceals an alien, or entities which embody both meanings of *heimlich*; appearing "familiar" and "friendly," even "intimate," they use a human body as a façade, concealing the unfamiliar and the monstrous beneath it. In "Day One," for example, a gaseous energy cloud from outer space enters a young woman who has been ditched by a date. Since the host body appears to be only a sexually aggressive young woman with pheromones to die for (literally, it turns out), when she enters a nightclub she immediately locates a willing man with whom to have intercourse. Sex begins normally enough (albeit in the bathroom of a nightclub), but to our horror, at the moment of her partner's orgasm he disintegrates into a pile of dust as she ingests his energy. A club bouncer who voyeuristically watches the entire sex act and its fatal consequence on closed-circuit television predictably declares the victim's destruction to be "impossible." Not even the Torchwood members are immune to the alien's charms, despite knowing that something monstrous lurks beneath the surface. In fact, Gwen is seduced by the entity, who is confined in the Torchwood hub. Paralleling the bouncer, the rest of the members, both shocked and enticed, watch Gwen's "snogging" session on the closed-circuit television, until the alien rejects Gwen because she is not of the "right" human sex.

Likewise, Tosh is ensnared by "Adam" the antagonist in an episode of the same name, who looks at first like a harmless young man but is a stranger to the audience. It is not clear to us where he has come from, though the rest of the team seem to have established relationships with him. Gwen, however, validates the audience's unease and confusion when she, too, is startled by the presence of the stranger in their headquarters. But Adam quickly implants into Gwen's mind "memories" of their first meeting, for he cannot survive unless he exists in the minds of the humans around him. Adam manipulates the minds of everyone in Torchwood, firmly ensconcing himself among them and disrupting their lives in the process. Gwen is alienated from her fiancé Rhys; her memories of him have been removed, so Rhys, not Adam, seems like the threatening interloper. Tosh is affected as well, as Adam has implanted memories of a long-term relationship between the two of them, and in the end, though the façade is finally revealed, she clearly has a difficult time accepting that what she thought was love shared with a boyfriend was only a manufactured reaction to a parasitic alien being.

In "Sleeper," the happily-married Beth learns that she is really one of a number of aliens planted on Earth to gather data in preparation for an alien invasion. Beth's discovery of a mechanical implant buried in her forearm reflects a particularly postmodern version of the uncanny, the sense that the boundary between the human and the mechanical has been breached. According to N. Katherine Hayles, we now live in a post-human era in which "there are no essential differences or absolute demarcations between bodily existence between bodily existence and computer simulation, cybernetic mechanism and biological organism, robot teleology and human goals."[8] Donna Haraway concurs, stating that we had moved into the post-human by the end of the twentieth century, when "machines [had] made thoroughly ambiguous the differences between natural and artificial, mind and body, self-developing and externally designed."[9] Haraway heralds the advent of the cyborg for its liberating potential, seeing in its boundary transgressions the possibility of replacing humanist, essentialist models of identity with more open-ended ones, for cyborgs "make very problematic the statuses of man or woman, human, artifact, member of a race, individual entity, or body."[10] However, she also recognizes that the cyborg is viewed by many as a means for the "final imposition of a grid of control on the planet," a technological advance created in post-industrial society to further an ideology of war.[11]

It is the latter, dystopic vision of the cyborg that dominates the plot of "Sleeper." Alien cyborgs are not free; rather, they are programmed to perform specific acts of destruction upon receiving a hidden signal. Their right arms suddenly terminate in knives they use to kill the people closest to them, people they have loved, before engaging on a number of suicide missions intended to reduce Cardiff to rubble. Unlike the other alien cyborgs, Beth struggles to retain her humanity, in both senses of the word "human": she wishes to retain her individual personality, including emotional ties to her husband, and to retain her compassion for others. The alien Other thus represents conformity to a group identity, loss of individuality, and the ruthless pursuit of an objective dictated by the group.

"Cyberwoman" is equally pessimistic about the results of transgressing the boundary between the organic and the mechanical; this episode speculates that Cyborgs may become contemptuous of human frailty and take action to eradicate it, even at the expense of human lives. Ianto, in love with the cyberwoman, Lisa, conceals her in the basement of Torchwood headquarters and dabbles with technology, hoping he can preserve her long enough for him to convince someone to convert her back to a fully human person. At first, Lisa, in love with Ianto, is overjoyed at the prospect of becoming human so that she can be with him. When a doctor enables her to breathe on her own, she is at first delighted to be alive. Soon, however, her cybernetic self takes over; she determines that she is superior to ordinary humans. Declaring to the doctor who revived her, "The human race is weak; I can make you strong," she places him in a device in order to give him cybernetic implants. When he dies instead, Lisa, by then convinced that human beings are inferior, weaker than cyborgs, attempts to "upgrade" a man with cybernetic implants, killing him in the process. When Ianto comes upon the doctor's corpse, a cybernetic implant projecting from one bloody eye socket, he realizes that he can no longer protect the woman he loves, for she no longer really exists; instead, Lisa is now almost fully Other, a monstrous entity whose actions he can neither understand nor condone. Unlike the Torchwood team's reaction to the Weevil, Ianto's knowledge of what she has become does not eliminate his intellectual uncertainty; for in this instance, while she may indeed look and sound like his Lisa, her actions and behavior do not mesh with what he knows as "human." Intellectual uncertainty ensues and suddenly Lisa — as well as their relationship and its history — becomes a site of the uncanny. Their verbal exchange confirms his fears. Her voice now largely mechanical, Lisa calmly states, "His upgrade failed," and when Ianto pleads, "Tell me you didn't do this," she replies that she "wanted to repay him for helping me by removing the weaknesses of his humanity."

One of the episode's visuals seems to be a homage to Mary Shelley's *Frankenstein*,[12] which is, as Michèle and Duncan Barrett observe in *Star Trek: The Human Frontier*, "the ubiquitous earliest reference-point of the monster who exceeded the expectations of his creator and got out of hand" (although Frankenstein's monster initially sought to be accepted by human beings).[13] After Lisa places the doctor in the cybernetic-implanting machinery, electrical flashes illuminate the room like lightning bolts, back-lighting her half-mechanical form. Like Shelley's story and unlike Haraway, "Cyberwoman" does not celebrate the cyborg as a liberating force but rather as a monstrous technology which threatens human existence.

Nevertheless, *Torchwood* does not confine its exploration of the uncanny to cyborgs and aliens; one of its eeriest episodes, "Countrycide," does not involve monsters who emerge from the Rift but rather those living in rural Wales. As Joan Gordon and Veronica Hollinger state in *Blood Read: The Vampire as Metaphor in Contemporary Culture*, the boundaries between the human and the monstrous have become blurred: "At the present postmodern moment, it seems that even our monsters have become transformed, as the boundaries between "human" and "monstrous" become increasingly problematized in contemporary narratives."[14] *Torchwood* writers seem to concur, but add that humans, too, are sometimes transformed, perhaps succumbing to primordial desires that usually lie buried in the subconscious (in "Countrycide"), perhaps to greed (in "Meat").

"Countrycide" has all the trappings of a very conventional horror movie; the first thirty minutes of the episode are filled with predictable if frightening visual and sound effects. A woman is driving alone down a dark, deserted country road loses her telephone service and then sees what appears to be a human body lying across the road. The "body" is only a decoy, and mysterious, hooded figures break into the parked car and capture her. Torchwood arrives to investigate, because the woman kidnapped the previous night was only the most recent victim; seventeen people have gone missing in the general area.

Owen and Gwen discover a human body which can scarcely be termed a corpse because it has been stripped of all flesh and bodily organs; there is, as Owen states, "nothing left but a carcass." All of the Torchwood people hike to the nearest town, the only one within thirty miles, and once they arrive, a hooded figure spies on them through tree branches. The town is apparently deserted (of course), but there are recently dead barnyard fowl nailed to the principal building (and the camera cuts periodically from shots of the Torchwood team to these fowl); the cawing of rooks and violin music in a minor key accompanies the group as they canvass the area. Ianto and Tosh, searching outside, are soon separated by stone walls, and Tosh disappears without warning. When Jack, Gwen, and Owen seek safety in a pub, they wall off the outside door (which is rattled from the outside) but forget the basement, the source, as any horror fan knows, of inhuman dangers.

Owen, who is a trained physician, and Gwen, who was a police constable, cannot suppress their horror and revulsion upon discovering corpses in varying stages of decay and mutilation. Owen is nauseated by the first carcass they find, and Gwen nearly vomits at the sight of the third, still recognizably female although covered in blood and missing her abdominal wall. "We're meat," she declares.

Torchwood does not know of the village's custom of culling passing strangers for consumption and thus the group is understandably convinced they are dealing with an alien involvement. Upon discovering one of the mutilated bodies, concludes that they're facing an alien threat. When Tosh finds a room with human bodies wrapped in plastic and hung like sides of beef, she too, assumes that the killers are not human. But a villager replies, "How else are we gonna look?" exposing the occupants of the village as the cause of all the recent deaths, and we the audience are as horrified as Ianto to discover that in this episode, perhaps the most uncanny in the first two seasons of *Torchwood*, villagers of very ordinary appearance are quite strange, the monsters which must be guarded against all too human.

It is at the end of "Countrycide" that Gwen, gazing out at the lights of Cardiff through the glass panels enclosing Owen's apartment, says, "All these things are changing me, changing how I see the world. And I can't share them with anyone." Yet Gwen's encounters with the uncanny change her less than such encounters alter other members of the Torchwood staff, most of who are shown transgressing the boundary between human and monster. Their hybrid state results in part from their constant exposure to frightening entities and events; as Jack tells Tosh, there are some things we (humans) are not meant to know. But the necessity of isolating themselves from the rest of the human race so as to maintain secrecy also affects them; we see that affect in the relief Tosh feels when confiding in Mary ("Greeks Bearing Gifts").

Gwen serves as the conscience of the group, maintaining the boundary between her life above ground in the world Torchwood attempts to protect, and her "other" life as a Torchwood agent (although it seems that these reverse positions and her life with Rhys becomes her "other" life quite quickly). The constant struggle she endures to maintain this boundary is highlighted in "Something Borrowed" where images of Gwen's bachelorette party and its drinking, dancing, and strippers are spliced with images from earlier that night of her chasing a shape-shifter through dark streets and alleyways. The shape-shifter manages to bite her before he is killed, and we see the bandage soaked with blood as she is standing in the bathroom gossiping with her friends. While it seems to be just a minor bite, Gwen wakes up the next morning pregnant with the shape-shifter's "razor-toothed" spawn. But Gwen refuses to postpone the wedding, despite the fact that the birth will kill her, and when asked why, she replies, "I need stability."

Though Gwen is able to sustain that stability, however tenuous it may be, the other members of Torchwood are far more affected by the corruptive influence of alien technology. Ianto literally embraces it, as he considers it his only opportunity to save Lisa, the woman he loves. He secretes her and the cyberconversion unit away in the depths of the hub, and refuses to see the implications of her cyborg status. He believes that with the right technology, he can restore her to the woman he once knew, and even when she begins attempting to "upgrade" others, killing the hapless humans who cross her path, he tells Lisa more than once that "she didn't mean to do this," and proclaims to the others, "She's not a monster." While he acknowledges the repercussions of his actions, admitting, "This is my fault; I am responsible for this," after finding the body of the doctor, his inability to objectively view Lisa's status and her subsequent actions costs more than one life and risks the lives of the rest of the team, including Gwen, whom Lisa attempts to upgrade. Yet he still cannot bring himself to harm Lisa in the end; the rest of the team must do it for him.

Tosh's experience with the amulet in "Greek Bearing Gifts" invokes the uncanny motif of telepathy. Despite the warning in Mary's admission that the amulet "changes how you see people," Tosh willingly wears it more than once. Throughout the episodes we see the Torchwood members willingly becoming monstrous through alien technology in order to suppress the alien Other or the monstrous human. But while the amulet allows her to prevent a family murder-suicide, she uses it most of the time to spy on her fellow Torchwood members. The control she thinks she has over her use of the amulet is short-lived, as she later admits, "What I did was an invasion. I wasn't in control." While Tosh is eventually able to distance herself from the technology enough to destroy it, something Ianto was not able to do, it seems the damage to her relationships with her fellow team members is already done, because, as Jack comments at the end of the episode, "There are some things we're not supposed to know."

If Ianto and Tosh are used to illustrate the result of momentarily losing sight of the boundaries, Suzie is an example of what happens when the boundaries are no longer visible. Obsessed with the resurrection glove, Suzie has no qualms about killing innocent humans in order to test its powers. The audience is horrified to discover that the murders being investigated at the opening of the series are her work, and that the very humans that Torchwood's mission is to protect have become her own personal experiment in death and immortality. Not only does she sacrifice innocent Cardiff citizens, but she unflinchingly puts a bullet through Jack's head when he threatens to take the glove from her. While she first garners from the audience what is perhaps a sliver of sympathy, as Ianto did, because we are led to believe that she is hoping to save her cancer-riddled father's life, the true motives behind her actions — that of immortality — are revealed in full in "They Keep

Killing Suzie." Jack's comment "It's the glove; I told you they get hooked" is a comment not only about the resurrection glove, but the danger of moral and ethical deformity that alien technology poses.

Another victim of the resurrection glove is Owen, who, like Suzie, is brought back to life with its power. Even before his resurrection, however, Owen displays monstrous tendencies, due in part to his widening alienation and disconnect as a result of his frequent exposure to uncanny entities and events. In fact, in "Fragments" we see him as a different person, before he became a Torchwood agent. Even in the midst of his struggles with an ailing fiancé, we see him as somewhat happy, and obviously compassionate and loving, a far cry from the distanced and sardonic Owen of Torchwood, and the Owen who willingly climbs into a cage with a Weevil and cows him with a growl. After his transformation he becomes the King of the Weevils and for a short while he harbors (and then momentarily defeats) Death itself. But perhaps the uncanniest element of his change is his "unnatural" monstrousness; he is the walking dead in every sense of the word, as his body is unable to heal. Slice him in half, as the jagged piece of glass threatens to do in "Fragments" and he remains that way forever, living but not alive.

At the end of "Cyberwoman," Ianto, grieving the loss of Lisa, tells Jack, "You like to think you're a hero, but you're the biggest monster of them all." Jack is similar to a cyborg: his pheromones are too strong, and he cannot be killed. He's been biologically modified in ways we are not privy to. He's the counterpart of Owen's "living death"—neither should be walking around because the one is a dead human, and the other is an immortal human. Throughout the episodes we see Jack's death played out in manifold ways: he is shot, pushed off a skyscraper, and buried alive, among others. Not even Abaddon, ruler of the demons, whose very shadow brings death, can fell Jack. Since mortality is one of the principal differences between man and machine, Jack, like Abaddon, has crossed the boundary to the monstrous. What is more, Jack, like Owen, presents as uncanny, as other humans cannot tell that either of them has crossed the line until presented with evidence.

Jack's monstrosity has to do not only with his immortality, but with his individual system of ethics, which differs from the rest of his team's. Jack is a Utilitarian, willing to kill individuals, monsters, and humans for the greater good, while the members of his crew are not. And he is willing to do so because, with his fifty-first century perspective, he knows that "everything changes" in the twenty-first century.

This disparity in belief systems is presented as a conflict in many episodes, such as "Small Worlds" when Gwen is aghast at Jack's permitting the malicious fairies to take the small child to their world, or in "They Keep

Killing Suzie," when, despite her unconscionable acts, the team still hesitates to kill her. Gwen asks Jack, "Could you, though, kill her?" And Jack replies, "Oh yeah." The season two opener presents the same issue: a fish-headed alien holds hostage a suburban family, some of whom have already been killed, and although the team outnumbers him three to one, they still do not shoot. Only Jack, reappearing suddenly after vanishing at the end of season one, can manage to shoot the alien without a moment's hesitation.

It is Gwen, however, who functions as the group's conscience, protesting brutality and murder, and maintaining the boundary between the human and the monstrous, the familiar and unfamiliar, the known and unknown. Ultimately, *Torchwood* is an allegory of what can happen when we cross those boundaries completely. The "normal" monsters, the Weevils, are in some ways the least disturbing of all the monsters presented. They are savage but easily distinguishable from the human and not very bright; they fit easily in the category of "beast" and may be frightening to the characters because violent, but they're not terribly frightening to the audience. The truly frightening monsters are those who seem "familiar," but who are revealed to be the opposite. These are monsters posing as aliens, or humans who have transgressed the boundary into the monstrous, both of which defy the ethical and moral systems that define the human; they are the monsters living among us. *Torchwood* explores the unstable nature of human identity and the postmodern anxiety which arises due to its fragility. This anxiety manifests as the uncanny, but in post-modernity, the uncanny is particularly disturbing because we can no longer distinguish ourselves from the machine — the era of the cyborg — and because we are immersed in the consumerism of late-stage capitalism. It is precisely the secret that Torchwood protects that allows us to maintain the notion of human superiority/dominance on the one hand and, more subtly, the queasy feeling we will get once we realize we no longer really know who *is* human — the feeling of the Uncanny.

Notes

1. See Sigmund Freud, "The 'Uncanny,'" in David H. Richter, ed., *The Critical Tradition: Classic Texts and Contemporary Trends,* 3d ed. (Boston: Bedford/St. Martin's, 2007) and Ernst Jentsch, "On the Psychology of the Uncanny," *Angelak* 2 (1996), 7–15.
2. Sigmund Freud, "The 'Uncanny,'" in David H. Richter, ed., *The Critical Tradition: Classic Texts and Contemporary Trends,* 3d ed. (Boston: Bedford/St. Martin's, 2007), 514–515.
3. *Ibid.,* 516.
4. *Ibid.,* 516–517.
5. *Ibid.,* 517.
6. Ernst Jentsch, "On the Psychology of the Uncanny," *Angelak* 2 (1996), 8.
7. *Hamlet* II, ii 628–29. William Shakespeare, "Hamlet," in Craig Hardin, ed., *The Complete Words of Shakespeare* (Chicago: Scott Foresman, 1961), 898–943.

8. Katherine N. Hayles, *How We Became Posthuman: Virtual Bodies in Cybernetics, Literature, and Informatics* (Chicago: University Chicago Press, 1999), 3.
9. Donna Haraway, "A Cyborg Manifesto: Science, Technology, and Socialist-Feminism in the Late Twentieth Century," in *Simians, Cyborgs and Women: The Reinvention of Nature* (New York: Routledge, 1991), 149.
10. *Ibid.*, 178.
11. *Ibid.*, 154.
12. Mary Shelley, *Frankenstein or the Modern Prometheus: The 1818 Text* (New York: Oxford University Press, 2009).
13. Michèle Barrett and Duncan Barrett, *Star Trek: The Human Frontier* (New York: Routledge, 2001), 120.
14. Joan Gordan and Veronica Hollinger, eds., "Introduction," *Blood Read: The Vampire as Metaphor in Contemporary Culture* (Philadelphia: University of Pennsylvania Press, 1997), 5.

Four

Touching the Other: Alien Contact and Transgressive Touch

RIA CHEYNE

An aerial shot of Cardiff frames the distinctive white form of the Altolusso apartment buildings, the city's tallest residential structure. The camera swoops down toward a lone figure on the rooftop's edge: Captain Jack Harkness. Cutting to medium close up, then an extreme long shot, the camera's eye circles around Jack — watching him as he watches over the city — then rapidly pulls back into an aerial shot, Jack's figure dwindling from view.

This scene from the premiere episode "Everything Changes" encapsulates some of the key themes and motifs of *Torchwood*, including anticipation, surveillance, and insignificance in the face of a larger world. In particular, it stresses isolation: high up and alone over the bustling city, Jack's location suggests that he is in the human world, but not of it. One of the distinctive features of *Torchwood* is its constant exploration of themes of isolation and separation, connection and contact, from its links with parent show *Doctor Who* to the honeycombed hexagons of the team's logo. The rift in time and space over Cardiff is a point of contact between human and alien worlds, but the Torchwood team struggle to make meaningful connections with each other and the human world around them. Touch is one of the key ways in which this struggle to connect is presented, with skin contact frequently used as a kind of shorthand for the creation or affirmation of deeper bonds.

The significance of touch is, of course, not limited to the fictional world. "Caresses and blows express profoundly and instantly what language labors over at length. A kiss is worth a thousand words. Touch precedes, informs and overwhelms language."[1] Many of our terms for emotional connection are based around notions of touch: an affecting narrative is "touching," we "touch base" with others, or exhort them to "keep in touch." While moments of human touch may have widely differing meanings — think of the difference between a kiss, a handshake, and a slap — they are united by the fact that touch is always a two-way process. One cannot touch another person without being touched in return; as Field writes, "Touch is our most social sense. Unlike seeing, hearing, smelling, and tasting, which can generally be done alone, touching typically implies an interaction with another person."[2] It is this mutuality — the fact that it always involves a bringing-together of self and other — that lends touch its larger significance.

Given the show's much-vaunted "adult themes," sexual contact is perhaps the most obvious form of touch in *Torchwood*, and the emphasis on the sexuality of the characters is one of the notable differences between *Torchwood* and *Doctor Who*. In terms of touch, though, sexual contact is only one element of a larger signifying system used to express the themes of contact and connection (and the failure to connect) that are so important in the show. In different ways, all of the Torchwood team struggle to make contact with others. A man out of his own time, Jack has seemingly lost the ability to empathize with others, to see people as people, rather than things. Owen Harper's casual sexual encounters are no substitute for meaningful human contact. In season one, the team members are so out of touch with each other that they are unaware that a heartbroken Ianto Jones is hiding his girlfriend, a half-converted cyberwoman, in the basement, in the hope that she can be made human again. Technical expert Toshiko Sato is a different kind of cyberwoman, a genius with machines who never goes anywhere without her laptop; but her adeptness with technology is matched only by her ineptness at personal relationships. She nurses a hidden passion for Owen, while claiming that work at Torchwood leaves no time for a partner. Owen's comment on relationships in "Day One" — "I can get all the grief I need here" — confirms that he too views Torchwood as a substitute for or alternative to significant romantic relationship; they can have one or the other, but not both.

New recruit Gwen Cooper's real role in the Torchwood team, then, is not to act as a replacement for Suzie Costello or as a liaison to the police, but to bring the members of the team back into touch: with each other, with the human world outside Torchwood, and with their own humanity (though Jack's "human" status always remains ambiguous). In "Everything Changes," Gwen is offered, and accepts, a position at Torchwood, in a dialogue that takes place as she and Jack stand on top of Cardiff's Millennium Centre. The rooftop setting and sweeping aerial shots in this scene recall the images of Jack alone (discussed above, and seen by the viewer just ten minutes earlier), but this time Gwen stands with him, both literally and figuratively. Though the two of them do not actually touch, the implication is clear: Jack is no longer alone. However, this moment of unity is fleeting. While the aerial shots of Jack on the Altolusso building, as well as other images of him alone on Cardiff's rooftops, are repeated throughout the first season, these shots of Jack and Gwen never reappear, leaving the primary associations of his character — loneliness and isolation — unchallenged.

While connection through meaningful touch is valued in *Torchwood*, E. M. Forster's famous dictum "Only connect..." does not straightforwardly apply.[3] In the twenty-first century world of *Torchwood*, Forster's epigraph to *Howards End* (and maxim for an increasingly fragmented and divided twentieth century) becomes problematic. The science fictional context opens up new possibilities for contact and connection, but also new dangers. Too close a connection with the alien world may mean falling out of touch with the human one, as illustrated by the fate of Gwen's predecessor and double, Suzie. Seduced by the alien technology of the Resurrection Gauntlet and associated knife — "You've got to get inside this stuff, surrender yourself to it. I did" ("Everything Changes") — Suzie loses touch with the human world, killing with the knife in order to have the chance to use the gauntlet. While Gwen's ability to get in touch with others is a valuable asset to the team, it brings with it the danger of harm or death (as illustrated in "They Keeping Killing Suzie"), as well as the larger danger of losing her own humanity.

The parallels between Gwen and Suzie are confirmed in "They Keep Killing Suzie" not only by Gwen's resurrection of Suzie using the gauntlet (previously wielded by Suzie herself), but also by the revelation that Suzie, like Gwen, had sex with Owen. In *Torchwood*'s symbolic system of touch, Gwen's affair with Owen is a seduction away from the human world, as represented by her boyfriend Rhys, and into the alien world of Torchwood. (Gwen's other possible lover, Jack, is neither fully of Torchwood nor of the human world; his status remains ambiguous.) Gwen's choice of Rhys, then, is a choice not just of him as an individual over other lovers or potential lovers, but a placing of the human world and human contact ahead of Torchwood. It is a rejection of the isolation that choosing Torchwood would ultimately bring. When it appears that Rhys is dead, Gwen says "This is what happens here, we all end up alone" ("End of Days," Season 1, Episode 13). Gwen's choice of Rhys and the human world is repeatedly affirmed in the show's second season, perhaps most explicitly in "Meat" (Season 2, Episode 4), where she threatens to leave Torchwood rather than betray Rhys: "You all think it's cold and lonely out there, but it isn't for me because I have him."

Though she remains connected to the human world, Gwen's attempts to bring the Torchwood team back into touch with each other and the world beyond the Hub are only partially successful. Though the team (minus the absent Jack) is united under her command at the start of the second season, this state of affairs is only temporary. Virtually every episode emphasizes the loneliness or isolation of one or more characters. All of the central team take a turn, as well as most of the significant guest characters, many of whom function as doubles for members of the main cast: Eugene in "Random Shoes" (Season 1, Episode 9), Tommy in "To the Last Man" (Season 2, Episode 3), Henry Parker and Maggie in "A Day in the Death" (Season 2, Episode 8), Jonah in "Adrift" (Season 2, Episode 11), and Captain John Hart.

The use of touch to express these themes of isolation and connection is particularly well illustrated in "Random Shoes," an episode notable for its central focus on a character outside the regular cast, and for its stylistic and thematic similarities to "A Day in the Death" (discussed below). In "Random Shoes," Eugene awakens to find he is lying on a road, and discovers his own dead body and the Torchwood team investigating. No one, it seems, can see him or hear him, and when he tries to touch Toshiko, his hand goes right through her. Unable to remember the two weeks leading up to his death, Eugene stays with Gwen as she breaks the news to his family and investigates his death.

Eugene's ghostly presence in death is a literalization of his inability to connect with those who meant the most to him in life. Given an alien eye as a child on the day his father left for good, his longing for his father became displaced onto and mingled with dreams of alien contact, leading to a lifetime spent waiting for both the alien and his dad to return for what was left behind. Growing up into an ET enthusiast, Eugene is aware of the existence of the Torchwood team, and in particular Gwen, whom he adores, but his attempts to talk to them are failures. Dismissed by the team as a crank, he "couldn't quite make contact." In death, though, with the assistance of the alien eye, Eugene becomes increasingly connected with both human and alien worlds. He realizes how much his friends and family cared for him. He is able to get into the Torchwood base, spend time with his heroes, and confirm that his belief in alien life and in the authenticity of the eye is justified. In particular, he comes into closer and closer contact with Gwen as she investigates his death. Gwen's ability to connect with others is reaffirmed by her increasing awareness of Eugene's presence as the episode progresses: she insists there is something strange about his death even when the others are uninterested, orders Eugene's regular lunch at a café, and seems to intuit his suggestion that she call his best friend. Discovering Eugene's absent father is still in Cardiff, she is about to go and speak to him, but changes her mind when Eugene protests, responding to his "I'm sorry" with "It's okay." It is Gwen who literally brings Eugene back into touch with the world. When Gwen's life is threatened, Eugene is able to rematerialize to push her out of the way of a speeding car, saving her from meeting the same fate as him — both on the literal level of dying in a car accident, and the symbolic level of living a life out of touch. The bond between the two is confirmed with a kiss. Eugene's father finally acknowledges his presence (he is visible to the friends and family gathered nearby) and returns to parent his younger brother. Finally achieving contact with those who mean the most to him but whom he was unable to reach in life, Eugene is able to move on.

Alien Contact and Transgressive Touch

While touch between humans is important in *Torchwood*, the science fictional context also allows for the exploration of touch between humans and aliens (and other non-human others). Always carrying an emotional charge — hence the prominence of the fingertip contact between E.T. and Elliott in the promotional materials for Spielberg's *E.T.: The Extraterrestrial* (1982, U.S.) — this type of touch transgresses the norms of human contact, the types of touch that are routine and accepted. While the touch between E.T. and Elliott signifies a moment of connection, this kind of mutually desired contact between human and alien is virtually non-existent in *Torchwood*. Owen's comment on the apparent discovery of a new alien race, "Well, let's hope they're friendly then" ("Fragments"), is laden with irony because the aliens in *Torchwood*— assuming we exclude Jack from this category — are *never* friendly. Though the seemingly benevolent message from an alien race in "A Day in the Death" hints that a different type of relationship might be possible, the aliens in Torchwood most often appear in the role of villains or, less frequently, victims (as in "Combat," "Meat," and "Reset").

Two separate scenes in *Torchwood* echo the moment of hands' touch between human and alien in *E.T.*, but with very different implications from the contact in Spielberg's film. In "Reset," Gwen stretches out a hand toward a suffering and imprisoned alien being — but though the alien appears to reach back toward her, the glass prevents them touching, and Gwen is unable to make contact. In "Greeks Bearing Gifts," Toshiko's lover Mary is revealed to be alien rather than human, and there is a moment of contact between them when Mary is in her true form. Though the image of the human and alien hands reaching toward each other is clearly seen by the viewer, the camera angle changes just before Toshiko and Mary touch, rendering the momentary fingertip contact between them barely visible. The obscuring of this key moment of contact, de-emphasizing it, hints at the true state of their relationship, which is built upon lies and deceit rather than being a genuine two-way bond.

Mary describes human culture as "a culture of invasion" ("Greeks Bearing Gifts") but in *Torchwood* it is always the aliens who are the invaders: Mary penetrates the bodies of her human victims to pluck out their hearts, and even the pendant she gives Toshiko allows Toshiko to perceive the thoughts of others, an act Toshiko characterizes as an "invasion." This theme of invasion is reflected in the way touch between humans and aliens is depicted in the series, which borrows much from body horror, involving not just skin-to-skin (or skin-to-whatever) contact, but an invasion of the human body, a touch that violates the secure boundary of the skin. Steven Connor writes that "when, in contemporary horror fiction and films, the frail containing envelope of the skin is torn, dissolved, melted and lacerated, this is perhaps an apprehension in a violent mode of the growing fluidity of relations between the self and its contexts and secondary instruments, a condition in which the skin is no longer primarily a membrane of separation, but a medium of connection or greatly intensified semiotic permeability, of codes, signs, images, forms, desires."[4] In *Torchwood*, the skin may no longer function properly as a "membrane of separation" between human and alien other, but these Transgressive touches beneath the boundary of the skin serve only to highlight the fundamentally hostile nature of the relationship between humans and alien others in the series. The emotional charge associated with skin contact between human and alien is intensified in this type of profoundly intimate touch. The associations of possession and invasion that come with it imply a touch-relationship of inequality; an invader and an invaded, rather than a meeting of equals.

Aliens invade human bodies and minds repeatedly in *Torchwood*, from Mary's taking possession of the human body she wears in "Greeks Bearing Gifts" to the mind-controlling alien in "Adam." In "Day One," on her first day as part of the Torchwood team, Gwen accidentally releases an alien being. The alien takes possession of the body of a young woman by entering through her nose and mouth. As the alien feeds on "orgasmic energy"— though apparently only the male orgasm will do — its victim Carys is driven to have sex with strangers, who dissolve into dust at the moment of climax. In a moment of lucidity, she pleads with the Torchwood team, "Please, get it out of me." The invasion of Carys's body is clearly meant to be understood by the viewer as a form of rape (powerfully evoked by images of a naked Carys crying in the shower), but whatever form the alien invasion takes, the consequences are always negative for the humans involved: Owen's fiancée dies from an alien parasite in her brain (as shown in flashback in "Fragments"), Martha nearly dies in "Reset," and Gwen's life is threatened by her alien pregnancy in "Something Borrowed."

Touching Hands

If Jack standing alone on the rooftops of Cardiff is one of the iconic images of *Torchwood*, the severed hand is one of the iconic objects. A crossover item from *Doctor Who*, the hand is immensely precious to Jack, presumably because it will signal to him that the Doctor has returned for him. Sealed in a jar and part of the furniture of the Torchwood hub, the hand appears in several episodes in the first season. The importance of the hand to Jack is demonstrated in "Day One," when Jack chooses to let Carys, still possessed by the alien, escape rather than risk harm to the hand, a decision criticized by Gwen. He is willing to risk Carys's life before he will sacrifice his connection to the Doctor. For Jack, the hand is a symbol of the connection he has with others (or an other) akin to him — but at the same time, the fact that it is severed indicates his own isolation in twenty-first century Cardiff. In "Day One," despite Jack's efforts, Carys smashes the jar containing the hand; a visibly moved Jack cradling the still-twitching hand in his own is one of the most striking (as well as the strangest) representations of his isolation in the series.

The hand survives to appear in further episodes, eventually crossing back over to *Doctor Who* at the end of season one, but its inclusion is only one example of something of an obsession with hands, particularly the touch of hands, in the first two seasons of *Torchwood*. Hands are the part of the body used to "reach out" toward another person, the primary mediators of touch: "Somewhere in the chain of evolution the hands took over the function of the cat's whiskers and became the principal organs of the sense of touch."[5] Though the sense of touch is the property of the entire skin, the hands and in particular the fingertips are amongst the body parts with the most nerve endings[6] and which are therefore the most sensitive to touch. In *Torchwood*, hands play an important role, indicating a person's ability to connect with others.

The viewer's attention is repeatedly drawn to hands and moments of hands' touch (or failure to touch). In "Greeks Bearing Gifts" and "Reset" the touch of hands signifies the nature of the relationship between humans and aliens, the inability to make genuine contact. During Owen's interrogation of Ed Morgan in "Ghost Machine," close-ups of both men's hands are intercut with close-ups of their faces, the play of emotions in this scene expressed as much by the hands as by facial expressions. In "Out of Time," one of the emotional high points is the clasp of hands between Jack and his double John Ellis; both are men literally out of their own time, struggling to adapt to the new world they find themselves in. The touch of hands can signify a powerful bond, but it can also be used to harmful ends: villain Billis gets Gwen to hold his hands before showing her a false image of Rhys, dead, in the season one finale "End of Days"; the mind-control in "Adam" is effected through a hand's touch; and the alien technology which can resurrect the dead (and which causes so much trouble in season one and two) takes the form of gauntlets to be worn on the hands.

However, the key focus on hands comes in season two, in parallel storylines involving Jack and Owen. No sooner has the severed hand disappeared, than a new association between Jack and hands takes its place. In "Kiss Kiss, Bang Bang," the first episode of season two, Jack has a flashback, an image of clasped hands parting, at the mention of his brother Gray. Four episodes later, in "Adam," the story behind this is revealed in an extended flashback sequence. As a child, Jack was tasked with keeping his younger brother safe during an alien invasion, but in the confusion "I let go of his hand. It was the worst day of my life." The image of clasped hands parting is repeated, and figures not just for the loss of his brother, who Jack never found despite years of searching, but for the loss of the rest of his family and his home. When the grown-up Gray returns in the season two finale, he too explicitly figures Jack's abandonment in terms of hands' touch. Detailing his unhappy fate after losing Jack, tortured by aliens and wishing for death, Gray says to Jack that everything that happened did so "Because you let go of my hand" ("Exit Wounds"). Losing hold of Gray's hand was the defining moment of Jack's life, but with his atonement and absolution complete at the end of the episode, the story arc is concluded.

Owen's narrative in the second season is about an even more profound loss of touch. After Owen is shot and killed in "Reset," Jack (perhaps unwilling to lose another brother-figure) steals a Resurrection Gauntlet, the partner to the one used in season one, and uses it to bring Owen back. Whether because this glove has different qualities or because Jack is the one who wields it, Owen is resurrected permanently rather than temporarily, but brings something alien back with him: "I'm not the same, Gwen. I came back different" ("Dead Man Walking"). Though whatever it is that has invaded Owen's body is dispatched by the end of the episode — the only side effect being that he is now feared by the Weevils, vicious aliens who dwell in the sewers — Owen is still dead, and still different from how he used to be, living a kind of half-life, conscious but with all bodily processes stopped.

In "A Day in the Death" Owen details his life from this point onwards, in an episode that echoes "Random Shoes" in its use of flashback, voiceover, and focus on an isolated young male figure. Like Eugene, Owen's status is uncertain; both figures disrupt the binary opposition of life and death. Owen has lost more than just the ability to breathe, to eat and drink, and to have sex (no blood flow means that he cannot get an erection). He has also lost the ability to get in touch with others. Significantly, this is explained after Owen injures his own hand—an injury which will never heal because his dead flesh will not knit back together. As Martha stitches the wound, he tries to convey to her what his new existence is like: "I can't feel anything. I can't feel the needle or thread. Can't feel your hands on mine. I can touch things, I can hold them. I know they're there. I just can't feel anything. I'm numb." The purely physical element of touch is still there, but the emotional element of it, the part of touch that involves *feeling*, is gone. The injury to Owen's hand symbolizes his inability to form meaningful relationships with others in his new state. However, the means by which he acquires it suggests that his inability to make contact and subsequent isolation is at least partly self-willed: the injury is both accidental and self-inflicted (he cuts himself while repeatedly throwing and catching a scalpel). This is confirmed by his rejection of Toshiko in the same episode. Immediately prior to his death in "Reset," Owen had finally agreed to go on a date with her; in "Dead Man Walking," Toshiko, thinking his resurrection was temporary, told him she loved him. In "A Day in the Death," Toshiko rather ineptly tries to reconnect with Owen, though it is unclear whether her aim is friendship or a romantic relationship. Owen rounds on her, accusing her of wanting to be with him because a "safe" (i.e., non-sexual) relationship is the only kind she is comfortable with: "Maybe you want somebody who's as screwed up as you, who's twisted and screwed-up like you are." Asking "Do you want to see broken?" he breaks his own finger as tangible evidence that he cannot have a relationship with her—though it is clear that his anger is directed as much at himself as it is toward her.

Despite his rejection of Toshiko, Owen's self-inflicted injuries—kept prominent in the viewer's mind by highly visible bandages—actually serve as a reminder of his kinship with her. At the end of season one, Toshiko has an injured hand and sports a similar bandage (in "Captain Jack Harkness" and "End of Days"). Though her injury is also self-inflicted, the motivation behind it is very different from Owen's: stranded with Jack in the 1940s, Toshiko cuts her own hand so she can write a message in blood for the rest of the team. While Owen's wound indicates his inability to connect with others, for Toshiko it offers a way to get back in touch; her wounded hand heals, while his will not. Owen admits that even before he was shot, he and Toshiko "sort of missed each other," but takes the responsibility for this ("Exit Wounds"). With the possibility of developing a relationship with Toshiko seemingly ruled out, Owen's post-resurrection status is perhaps best indicated by the striking image which concludes "A Day in the Death": Owen stands on a Cardiff rooftop, one hand clasping an alien artifact which emits beautiful streams of light, the other holding the hand of Maggie, to whom he has narrated his story. Maggie is human, but was on the roof to jump; as a potential suicide she, like Owen, is no longer fully a part of the human world, existing somewhere between life and death. The alien artifact in Owen's other hand demonstrates that he is also something other than human, its presence indicating Owen's connection with an alien world rather than the human one.

Conclusion

Touch, and particularly the touch of hands, plays a significant role in *Torchwood*, used to indicate developing relationships and emotional bonds, the disjunction between human and alien worlds, and the ambiguously human status of some of the characters. Yet the touch of the alien other is ultimately rejected in the series, with humans and aliens segregated. Like the transformed human victims returned by the rift in "Adrift," they are kept apart, at the same time as touch between those who are unambiguously human is valued and foregrounded. Norman Autton writes that "In our technological and impersonal culture perhaps we need closeness and physical intimacy more than ever. No symbol can be as powerful as a gesture of friendship; no action as meaningful as a dimension of commitment and trust."[7] Here we find the reason why human touch is so valued and so emphasized in *Torchwood*: living in a world of high-tech machines and alien others, a world which constantly threatens to seduce them away from human contact, the Torchwood team need human touch not just to maintain their connections with the human world, but to preserve and assert their very humanity.

Notes

1. Constance Classen, "Contact," in Constance Classen, ed., *The Book of Touch* (Oxford: Berg, 2005), 13.
2. Tiffany Field, *Touch* (Cambridge, MA: MIT Press, 2001), 19.
3. E. M. Forster, *Howards End* (1910; rpt. London: Penguin Books, 2000).
4. Steven Connor, *The Book of Skin* (London: Reaktion Books, 2004), 65–66.
5. Roy Sheldon and Egmont Arens, "Make It Snuggle in the Palm," in Constance Classen, ed., *The Book of Touch* (Oxford: Berg, 2005), 426.
6. Tiffany Field, *Touch*, 81.
7. Norman Autton, *Touch: An Exploration* (London: Dalton, Longman and Todd, 1989), 3.

Five

More Than Just a Hero's Journey: Harry Potter, Frodo Baggins, and Captain Jack Harkness

VALERIE ESTELLE FRANKEL

One magazine described the "celestially promiscuous Harkness, who has bedded at least one female member of his Torchwood crew, one male member, various comely outer-space creatures, and a smoochy 'Time Agent' played by guest star James Marsters (*Buffy the Vampire Slayer*)."[1] But Jack Harkness is more than a second James T. Kirk, seducing every female alien he meets. Throughout the first two seasons of *Torchwood*, Jack grows as a person and as an archetypal hero traveling the mythic path.

While most science fiction explores the human condition, confronting such controversial issues as racism and the rights of the individual, the greatest offers more. Some also carries viewers through the hero's journey, in which the hero battles death itself to defeat his evil shadow-self. Thus the hero gains responsibility and maturity while becoming a true leader of men. Captain Jack Harkness travels on this very quest, but through a world of as much fantasy as hard science, thrusting us into a compelling semi-urban narrative more suited to Middle-earth or Hogwarts than to typical science fiction.

Jack Begins His Journey

On his first appearance in *Doctor Who*, Jack lacks the concern for human suffering that consumes the semi-mythical Doctor and especially his companion Rose Tyler. Jack is lurking in 1941 not to save lives but to disguise his "self-cleaning con" in a flurry of bombing. A self-confessed criminal and con man, Jack only cares about flirting with Rose and pawning off "space junk" on the Time Agency. Jack remorselessly pilots a stolen ship and abandons Rose and the Doctor when faced with danger, though he eventually returns for them. His final speech to his computer reveals his playboy personality perfectly: "Last time I was sentenced to death, I ordered four hypervodkas for my breakfast. All a bit of a blur after that. Woke up in bed with both my executioners. Lovely couple. They stayed in touch. Can't say that about most executioners."[2] While critics describe him as "a little bit Han Solo, a little bit Jack Sparrow, with a touch of Tom Cruise,"[3] he clearly has an edge, with a willingness to kill in cold blood. His sonic blaster seems especially nasty beside the pacifist Doctor's gentler screwdriver.

At the same time, his criminal behavior reflects a void in Jack's life, a deep maiming that consumes him: Two years are missing from his memory. Thus Jack is fragmented, missing a part of himself that the rest of us take for granted. This literal condition reflects a deeper theme: Jack is uncertain who he is. Many other heroes grow up with a great lack: Luke Skywalker longs to be a hero, Harry Potter longs for a proper family, as do Coraline, Lyra Belaqua, Peter Parker, and many others. In science fiction hero's quests, such as *Babylon 5* (Warner Bros. Television, 1994–1998, U.S.), *Hitchhiker's Guide to the Galaxy* (BBC, 1981, UK), or *Dark Angel* (20th Century–Fox Television, 2000–2002, U.S.), the hero grows up with missing memories, like Jack, and must grow into a leader by learning what he's lost.

The hero's journey is predominantly a quest for identity, and shallow Jack, burying himself in innuendo and humor, can be as frivolous as he likes: "I try never to discuss business with a clear head," he says, drinking champagne and teasing Rose with psychic paper.[4] In fact, his Emergency Protocol 417, initiated when death is certain, involves a martini. He continues to flirt with everyone, despite constant admonitions that "there's a time and a place."[5] Most importantly, Jack disavows responsibility for his actions: "I don't know what's happening here, but believe me, I had nothing to do with it," he protests repeatedly, as an alien virus from the ship he swears is "harmless space junk" overruns 1941 London and threatens total destruction of humanity.[6]

Clearly, Jack is a rogue, thief, conman, and trickster, who charms himself out of sticky moments. On the one hand, Jack seems incorrigible. On the other, a change is already taking place. "Take a look around the room. This is what your piece of 'harmless space junk' did," the Doctor chides.[7] In reality, the medical equipment from Jack's crashed Chula warship is misdirected nanobots, busily rewriting human DNA into a monstrosity. The Doctor forces Jack to realize what he's done, and then uses "psychology" on him, until the cheeky con man willingly sacrifices himself to stop a bomb from falling on innocents.

As Christopher Vogler, author of the mythic exploration *The Writer's Journey*, explains, "Mentors in stories act mainly on the mind of the hero, changing her consciousness or redirecting her will."[8] These mentors, like Gandalf, Obi-Wan, or Merlin, have an esoteric wisdom. They are magicians, forces for change in the surrounding world, with power or technology the inexperienced hero has never imagined. Dumbledore, the greatest spellcaster of the wizarding world, can make himself invisible even without Harry's magic cloak.[9] Kosh, of *Babylon 5*, boasts an unheard-of organic ship, telepathic like the heart of the TARDIS. He teaches the human captain John Sheridan to "fight legends," and understand himself through a series of cryptic dreams and lessons.[10] Whether wizard, alien, or grizzled old man, these mentors guide the hero to become a better person, acting as conscience and advisor through the struggle.

In this way, the Doctor travels selflessly through the galaxy to combat exploitation and ensure history follows the proper course. As he invites conman Jack to travel in the TARDIS, Jack experiences a new type of behavior and grows through it. As one reviewer puts it, Harkness turns "from a cheesy jerk into a likable champion."[11]

"Jack, don't you dare," the Doctor says, when Jack pulls his gun on an angry mob.[12] The Doctor's lessons continue, mainly through example: In Cardiff, the Doctor plans to deliver a female Slitheen to her execution, but when the heart of the TARDIS regresses her into an egg, the Doctor drops her on a Slitheen colony, allowing her to restart her life from infancy. In the following episode, "Bad Wolf," he saves the innocent girl he's promised to protect, no matter the odds. And then, finally, he sends Rose to safety, an action formerly selfish Jack applauds. As Rose puts it, "The Doctor showed me a better way of living your life ... you don't just give up, you don't just let things happen."[13]

Jack remains cheeky on the journey: "The pleasure was all mine — which is the only thing that matters in the end,"[14] he glibly tells the female droids who strip him and treat him as a fashion model before he decapitates them. Still, in season one's final episode he willingly sacrifices his life, and the entire human race, to stop the Daleks. "I wish I'd never met you, Doctor," Jack says. "I was much better off as a coward."[15] Though he utters this in his brash, teasing tone, he's clearly aware of how the Doctor has altered him. He steps up as a leader, speaking to the noisy crowd with heart and "psychology" just as the Doctor would, encouraging them to join the fight. Series producer Russell T. Davies observes, "He comes under the Doctor's influence, under the wing of a much better, much cleverer, a much more compassionate man and learns off him."[16]

Jack dies bravely, sacrificing himself so the Doctor can save the universe. Still, Rose returns to rescue them both, embodying the TARDIS heart and saving them through a burst of pure love. Here we see her as the mythic goddess on the hero's journey, protecting him through the power of the unconscious: emotion over rationality or technology. She is his heart, his vitality. As Joseph Campbell describes it, "The mystical marriage with the queen goddess of the world represents the hero's total mastery of life; for the woman is life, the hero its master and knower."[17] Saved by his "Lady of the Lake," Jack awakes, mysteriously alive in the year 2001, but he realizes the Doctor has abandoned him, aching with questions. As Davies says, "I've always been fascinated by the fact that he [the Doctor] is a man who always leaves. And when the Doctor does go, it's the people who are left behind who have to pick up the pieces."[18]

Indeed, the mentor always leaves once the hero is set on his path: While the Doctor flits in and out of Jack's story like Gandalf or Aslan, he gives Jack space to grow as a person. Thus abandoned, Jack indeed picks up pieces of his life, traveling to 1892 Earth, only to discover he's immortal. "Thought it was kind of strange," he comments about waking from getting shot in the heart.[19]

With his new godlike immortality, Jack is well-started on the hero's path, able to defeat sexy aliens and monsters all with his unquenchable life-force. Still, he's plagued with questions, and a hundred years of solitude to ask them: As Julie Gardner, *Torchwood*'s executive producer, speculates, "How does it affect a character if they can't die? Is that a great glorious wonderful exciting thing? Or is it a terrible curse as well? And the loneliness of that, and what does it mean?"[20] Thus struggling, Jack eventually joins the Torchwood Institute, while always remembering the power the heart can offer, beyond any of his alien knowledge or charm.

Jack and Gwen

As actress Eve Myles comments, "There's an instant connection between Gwen and Jack. From the first moment that Jack sees her spying over onto the dead body."[21] More than that, they complement each other. She has the inquisitive nature and wonder that jaded Jack needs, soulful where Jack is shallow, caring for the human element even as he dwells on the alien. "The two of them work so well as partners because what she lacked as a leader he had in abundance and vice versa," Eve Myles adds.[22] They complete each other, in a way they perfectly summarize as early as the first episode "Everything Changes":

GWEN: I'm a bit tired of following you.
JACK: No you're not. And you never will.

In *Pretty Woman* (1990, U.S.), *My Fair Lady* (1964, U.S.), and even *Annie* (1982, U.S.), the authoritative hero shows the heroine how to shine in his world of mysterious rules and customs, educating and training her. In turn, she reveals the hero's lack: the inner world of emotion and spirit. She shows him how to heed others and enjoy life. And thus as Jack teaches Gwen about aliens, she teaches him about humanity.

Teamwork

Jack certainly needs more training in the human element: His obsession with finding the Doctor over working for Torchwood has clearly halted all promotion: he only takes charge in 1999 as an incredibly long-delayed "reward for a century of service," as discussed in the episode "Fragments." As head of Torchwood, Jack still can't comprehend that his team needs to trust him. "Who are you? What are you doing here?" Gwen asks in "Day One," voicing the team's perplexity. "You think knowing the answers would make you feel better?" Jack replies with his usual enigmatic smile, and quickly changes the subject. He never explains why the only "Captain Jack Harkness" on record vanished in 1941. Setting aside his off-the-cuff reference to his past pregnancy, he won't even reveal to which gender he's the most attracted (aside from the obvious answer of all of the above). His team doesn't know he can't die until "End of Days."

Worse than this mystery is his total blindness to the team's personal problems. Jack neglects Ianto, who has an entire lab devoted to his secret cyber-girlfriend, whom he cannot bear to entrust to the team. Tosh, too, has a hidden relationship with an alien female ("Greeks Bearing Gifts"). This one Jack catches in time, but he only comforts and offers advice after killing Tosh's lover in front of her. A single reprogram sends the alien into the center of the sun: "It shouldn't be hot," he says glibly. "I mean, we sent her there at night and everything." Jack's neglect is most apparent in the case of Owen, who starts fighting Weevils as an outlet for all his anger.

"I'm tired of living with Jack's secrets — we don't even know who he is," Owen cries ("Captain Jack Harkness"). He is their leader in name, but mistrust between teammates provides a shaky foundation that eventually crumbles.

This fractured team reflects Jack's own fractured self, with every impulse within him warring for control. He's torn between his duty at Torchwood and need for the Doctor, his need for relationships and his guilt and uncertainty over living forever. In a psychological reading, other characters symbolize parts of the self, like Hermione's intellect and Ron's emotion guiding Harry Potter through the series. Captain Kirk gets similar support from crewmates Spock and McCoy. However, by the end of series one, Jack's teammates are increasingly disobeying him, implying a complete dissolution of both team and identity.

The war finally turns external: Owen's rage and frustration culminate in "End of Days" when Jack refuses yet again to confide in the team. But this time Owen's had enough: "If you're not even a real person, then why the hell should I follow your orders?" Jack lashes out in return, firing Owen. Though teammates Gwen and Tosh plead with him to back down (again indicating his inner conflict), Jack can't accept Owen's defiance. Just as Jack realizes his leadership has been an illusion, the entire team rebels, determined to open the chaotic Rift and (as they think) rescue their loved ones. Jack's insults and blanket demands for trust fail, showing how little a foundation their trust had in the first place.

Heroism

The episode "End of Days" sees the world ending. Death incarnate walks the earth, stomping it with his skyscraper-tall feet. He devours everything in his path. His disciple walks before him, proclaiming, "The whole world shall die beneath his shadow." This is Abaddon, whose name meant "realm of the dead" in the Old Testament. In the New Testament, he's "the great destroyer," arriving at the end of days to bring about the Apocalypse.

The street is soon littered with corpses as people fall under his shadow and instantly perish. Abaddon is indeed the force of entropy, loosed upon the everyday world. Weak from his latest death, Jack knows he's humanity's only chance: "Abaddon is the bringer of death. Let's see how he does with me. If he feeds on life and I'm an all you can eat buffet." Confronted with evil incarnate, there is only one choice, and so this battle strengthens him. In this moment, he feels no conflict or fragmentation. He faces the beast across an empty field, as it advances on him, "come to feast on life." An angelic light pours from Jack as he screams, louder and louder. The beast is drowning in this crippling light of immortality, its antithesis, until at last it crumples to the ground and perishes. Life has vanquished death.

Still for weakened Jack, allowing the creature to devour him is a sacrifice, casting him, apparently forever, into death. "No one can go through an experience at the edge of death without being changed in some way,"[23] warns hero-myth scholar Christopher Vogler. Even for ordinary humans, after a near-death experience, "colors seem sharper, family and friends are more important, and time is more precious. The nearness of death makes life more real."[24] In myth, this death-journey is a time for great arcane wisdom, the answers Jack has sought through the entire first season. As with Harry Potter or Frodo Baggins, Jack's sacrificing his life leads to a meeting with his mentor, returned from a great distance to give him the truth he seeks.

Self-Knowledge

The Doctor has been Jack's obsession for over a century on Earth. He hoards the Doctor's severed hand through the entire first season of *Torchwood*, like a crystal ball or magic amulet. The moment he hears the TARDIS in "End of Days" Jack abandons all responsibility to chase after it, all the way to the universe's collapse. This is the one quest that outweighs his budding responsibility and honor: the chance to discover what he is.

They reunite awkwardly, as the Doctor finally reveals why he abandoned Jack: his godlike regenerative power makes him an abnormal part of the universe. He is more than mere mortal—he is a demigod, condemned to live apart. These magical powers and miraculous conception appear in just about every myth and hero legend, from Merlin to Moses, but Jack hasn't yet accepted them. "Do you want to die?" the Doctor asks him.

"I thought I did. I dunno," Jack hesitates.[25] Jack has more to live for than he's admitted—his responsibility as leader of Torchwood, his friends and protégés he's left there. Jack follows the Doctor, teamless, through a year of horrors inflicted by the Master, a Time Lord gone hideously mad. At last, Jack and his friends manage to rewind time, leaving only those at the epicenter of events aware of what has occurred. After suffering through this isolation and torture, Jack explains to the Doctor that he's most missed his duties as head of Torchwood: "I had plenty of time to think that past year, the year that never was, and I kept thinking about that team of mine. Like you said, Doctor, responsibility."[26]

The Doctor's influence is even clearer when we find Jack has reformed Torchwood for him, "in your honor,"[27] as Jack puts it. In fact, Jack's year of seclusion gives him more than a mission: he comes to terms with being an "impossible thing," unable to die, but endowed with gifts that can save the world in every crisis.

Facing the Self

As actor John Barrowman notes, "Jack is different [in season two]. He's come back having resolved all his issues with the Doctor, and he's much more like the guy we initially met.[28] On the surface he hasn't changed, cockily striding back to Torchwood and taking charge without a word of explanation (in the episode "Kiss Kiss, Bang Bang"). In fact, he spends the episode dodging questions about the Time Agency, the Doctor, his past, and his brother Gray. Still, he's more comfortable in himself. He asks out Ianto, finally breaking down that barrier between himself and one of his team. Clearly he's accepted who he is, or at least his new talents and position of responsibility. "I came back for you. All of you," he says, and he means it. When the team's memories are threatened in "Adam," he cradles them all paternally and comforts them. He sees what's best in their memories and coaxes it out, and speaks of "pride and warmth" for them, able to express a deeper level of feelings at last. He saves Gwen's wedding, and welcomes Martha Jones to Torchwood. But now that his frantic quest for identity is concluded, he has a darker fight ahead, against the most menacing reflections of his inner self.

The first takes place in season one, carrying him back to the 1940s to encounter the "true" Captain Jack Harkness, in the episode of the same name. This man is modest, loving, self-sacrificing, shy, and frightened — the parts of himself our Jack suppresses. "Captain Jack Harkness is really the hero that this Captain Jack would love to emulate himself to be," Barrowman observed.[29] As one critic notes:

> The Captain Jacks both share the same name and are quite similar in physical appearance, thus literalizing the homo-ness of the situation. Through the time-travel device this points to a narcissistic self-fascination, the old cliché that homosexuality is the love for sameness.[30]

But this isn't just homoerotic love, it's egoist love, the love of the self: Captain Jack Harkness. As the producer jokingly puts it, "Who was the one man that Captain Jack is going to fall in love with, and that's himself."[31] "There's nothing I can do for him," Jack moans, knowing this quieter doppelgänger is doomed, but he offers the other man what he can't have himself: a wonderful night of true love as he kisses his girl goodbye.

The relationship Jack (or both Jacks) undertakes is a way of healing the self, of reconciling missing parts. One Jack gives in and crosses 1940s taboos to dance with another man, and the other abandons temptation to stay and help his counterpart. Thus, this meeting lets both discover unseen positive qualities in themselves: it's a method of growth. When they dance together, both with blissful smiles, they reintegrate: our Jack gains responsibility while the other gains the recklessly brazen homo-romantic displays that define Torchwood's captain. "It's about two people connecting," said Tosh-actress Naoko Mori, claiming their memorable kiss was "not sexual."[32] This moment of wholeness prepares Jack for his life-shattering encounter at the End of Days; the next doppelgänger won't be nearly so altruistic.

This man is Captain John Hart, a fifty-first century flirt and ex-time agent. They have similar names and ranks, similar period military dress, and similar taste in lovers. Captain John is a "compulsive liar"—where have we heard that? He's Captain Jack all over again but darker, twisted. "In seeing John you see the way Jack could have gone, and probably did, for a little while. Jack, in his experiences with the Doctor and Torchwood, made a very conscious decision to move away from that behavior," the scriptwriter comments.[33] John Hart is also exaggerated, displaying attraction to poodles and murdering teammates in cold blood, a step beyond where we've seen Jack travel.

Like the 1941 doppelgänger, John Hart is Jack's shadow, his unexpressed or rejected aspects made manifest. The writer describes John Hart saying, "What the show needed—and what Captain Jack needed—was a proper nemesis, somebody to really test him, to push him, and to reveal something about Jack's character."[34] In time, every mythic hero faces his dark alter-ego: "The qualities we have renounced and tried to root out still lurk within, operating in the shadow world of the unconscious," as Vogler puts it.[35] It is the shady part of ourselves, the fears and regrets that haunt us. For Frodo, the greatest adversary isn't the dark lord Sauron; it's turning into the wasted Gollum, last victim of Frodo's ring. Harry's unusual abilities like parseltongue come straight from Voldemort, while Luke Skywalker in *Return of the Jedi* (1983, U.S.) acknowledges how his Jedi powers derive from his evil father. "Kill him and take his place at my side," the emperor orders, and Luke must accept that he could be the next dark lord, if he chose. Only then can he understand Vader and redeem him.

Captain John especially manifests this temptation by coaxing Jack back to his way of life, reminding him of their "old routine" where they could travel the stars "just like before" in the episode "Kiss Kiss, Bang Bang." Jack has returned to his team, respectability, duty. But this younger, shallower side of himself arrives to entice him: "I want for you to come to your senses," John says. "Join me, Jack." Some part of Jack remembers his irresponsible old self and misses the glamour and adventure of space. Actor Burn Gorman, who plays Owen, adds, "Captain John Hart is in three words immoral and slippery and sexually questionable. In a number of ways he's like Captain Jack: he has this own understanding of morality but all in all a pretty addictive personality to be around."[36] Still, as Jack faces this mocking, shallow past, he also remembers how he's grown into a leader. He kisses John goodbye and firmly tells him to leave forever.

However, past selves aren't dismissed so easily: With the words "I've found Gray," John Hart offers an even deeper allurement: the opportunity for Jack to fix his greatest mistake. "I searched for Gray for years," Jack reveals, guilt-ridden for allowing his brother's hand to slip from his. Gray is inextricably bound with temptation: When the alien nemesis Adam bribes him with memories, Jack sobs, moved beyond words by a single family recollection. Gray is his childhood, his innocence, the cherished part he gave up more than 150 years before: On that day, he lost father, brother, and safe family life forever. The inner child is a compelling enticement: the innocent bundle of desires and self the hero has repressed for so long.[37] "This too is a powerful metaphor for the idea of saving the child Self, the soul-self, from being lost again in the unconscious, forgetting who we are and what our work is,"[38] mythologist Clarissa Pinkola Estés explains of this tenuous inner voice.

Since Jack "lost" Gray, he has buried everything about him, even the memories: "It was the worst day of my life. It's the last thing I want to remember," he says, in "Adam." Now, Jack's growth forces him to remember this separated part of himself and finally confront it as Gray, brought to Cardiff by John Hart, proceeds to demolish Jack's carefully-constructed world of safety. Gray is another double like John Hart, as this lost boy shares Jack's childhood and the past that could have been his. At the same time, he's "gray," morally cloudy, like all shadows. In fact, Gray is a murderer, twisted and lost: the most terrifying alter-ego yet to appear. He's determined, in "Exit Wounds," to "take Jack's life, destroy it from the inside out." Psychologically, he represents Jack's self-destructive impulses. "The only strength I have is my hatred for you. I begrudge you everything. I want to rip it all from you," Gray says, echoing the little voice inside Jack's heart. "I want your life."

"If I could swap with you, I would," Jack says, full of remorse at inheriting the better, daylit world as Gray suffered through hidden torments and alien torture. Gray drags him back in time and then buries him alive, forcing him to die over and over for a thousand years. As we discover in *Doctor Who*, Jack fears dying and aging unceasingly.[39] Here is the function of the shadow, to make Jack examine his hidden self, to acknowledge the darkness deep within, the parts of himself he rejects rather than exploring.

Jack willingly lets John Hart and his brother bury him, slaying him untold times: "It was my penance," he says later. This death is "a relief," a way to atone for separating from the dark side of himself. This is the hero's descent into the innermost cave: the realm of death where he must confront the shadow-self he lost years before and reintegrate it into his personality. By welcoming burial, Jack willingly gains knowledge through the realm of death, as do Odysseus, Hercules, Orpheus, and all the great classical heroes. In this way, Frodo succumbs to the Witch-King's stab and a primordial spider-bite, both times sinking into temporary death. Harry Potter descends into underground caverns, graveyards, and more, at the climax of each of his seven books. *Babylon 5*'s Captain Sheridan, like Jack, embraces death willingly, hurling himself from a balcony rather than succumbing to the malevolent Shadows: Beyond death he finds a mystic mentor and the chance to rise again. This descent is like regressing to the most primitive self, the child-self Jack lost so long ago. He becomes Gray, tortured for millennia, but this same ordeal doesn't warp Jack: it makes him stronger.

In fact, he becomes a pair of Jacks existing simultaneously in order to outmaneuver his younger brother. "I've crossed my own timeline," he reveals when Torchwood rescues him. The two Jacks demonstrate his understanding of his own duality: light and dark, savage and leader. One has been shut away all this time, hidden in the darkness of Torchwood's vaults, until Jack can reintegrate all these parts of himself. "I forgive you," he tells Gray, gripping him, embracing him, acknowledging him as part of himself. "I give you absolution. Now do the same for me." Jack realizes he has to reconnect with his missing self, to become whole. Though Gray refuses, Jack embraces him and finally freezes him in stasis, guarding this dangerous part of himself, just as Jack was immobilized for a century. This moment echoes Luke's forgiveness of Darth Vader, transforming him from technological monster into benevolent ghost. Jack's innocence has been destroyed, and while he can come to terms with this, he cannot regress to that boy on the beach. Though he cannot release this dangerous murderer part of himself, he can't destroy it either. It sleeps there, loved, forgiven, and accepted, dormant. As Joseph Campbell puts it, "Atonement (at-one-ment) consists in no more than the abandonment of that self-generated double monster"; by abandoning the self, the hero manages to reconcile his good and evil selves into a cohesive whole.[40]

Future Echoes

So what's in store for Jack Harkness (or whoever he really is)? The next stage in the hero's journey is to become a father and guide for the next generation of heroes, often complicated by an evil child or parent. This appears in King Arthur, *Star Wars*, and so many more. To Jack, Gray represented this evil child, his responsibility, his heir, his enemy. But perhaps Jack is ready now for a real child, and the struggle of increased responsibility that entails.

Beyond that, the last stage of the hero's journey is becoming a mentor and sage to future generations, before ascending to the realm of the spirit like Obi-Wan or Dumbledore, never to return. As it is, Jack's journey has taken many centuries to build him into a true hero and leader of men: it will take far longer before Jack grows to be as wise as the Doctor.

Fans are intrigued by a tantalizing hint in the *Doctor Who* episode "Last of the Time Lords": "I used to be a poster boy when I was a kid in the Boeshane Peninsula," Jack says. "The first one ever to be signed up for the Time Agency ... the Face of Boe, they called me." Companion Martha Jones and the Doctor regard each other, stunned. Can this charming rogue truly become the galaxy's most ancient font of wisdom, a "god"? Even after a thousand years buried alive, Jack hasn't gained the maturity to marry and settle down. And how can the incredibly physical Jack manage without a body? Still, five billion years might be enough time for Jack to grow up.

What are the implications here? The Face of Boe is a disembodied head, craggy and wise-looking. He has evolved to the point of total intellect: no limbs or torso. In fact, his fishbowl-like container separates him from others. He sings telepathic ancient songs and prophesizes, like an oracle. As seen in the episode "New Earth," he has such mental power that he can will himself to teleport, without need for visible technology. He is indisputably at one with the universe.

A curious parallel emerges as the Face becomes the Doctor's mentor in turn. "You are not alone," he tells the Doctor.[41] A plot point, certainly, but also a reminder to trust his companions, the ones who stay with him on all his journeys. As long as he has Rose, and Martha, and all the others, he is part of a team, the lesson Jack learned long ago. Most significantly, legend tells that just before dying the Face will reveal his greatest secret to "one like himself." This, we find, is the Doctor, "the man without a home: the lonely god." So the Face, too, is homeless (Jack often alludes to this in himself) and has become a sort of deity, the final stage in the hero's path. The Face of Boe, after his long existence, is more than the Doctor's advisor; he has grown into the Doctor. Time Lord and Time Agent are one.

Before this can happen, Jack has far more challenges to confront, on *Doctor Who* and *Torchwood: Children of Earth*. Still, he has managed an incredible amount of growth, all the while remaining the beloved "Captain of Innuendo" and uncontainable flirt that inspired Russell T. Davies to build an entire series around him. After confronting his longevity and his demons, what's next? Can he ever treat love as more than a game? Will he find the missing piece of his memory, and what will he learn from it? Whatever transpires, Jack's future will mix irrepressible charm with something far deeper: growth along the hero's path.

Notes

1. Ken Tucker, "Work That Bawdy," *Entertainment Weekly* 981, March 7, 2008, 79. *http:// galegroup.com.mill1.sjlibrary.org*
2. "The Doctor Dances," *Doctor Who* (BBC, 2005, UK).
3. Melanie McFarland, "On TV: BBC America's Hot 'Torchwood' is a Cool Place to be Saturday Nights," *Seattle Post-Intelligencer*, 12 September 2007. *http://seattlepi.nwsource.com/tv /330634_tv07.html*
4. "The Empty Child," *Doctor Who* (BBC, 2005, UK).
5. "Bad Wolf," *Doctor Who* (BBC, 2005, UK).
6. "The Doctor Dances."
7. *Ibid.*
8. Christopher Vogler, *The Writer's Journey: Mythic Structure for Writers*, 2d ed. (Studio City, CA: Michael Wiese Productions, 1998), 121.
9. J. K. Rowling, *The Tales of Beedle the Bard* (New York: Scholastic, 2008), 97.
10. "Hunter, Prey," *Babylon 5* (Warner Bros. Television, 1993, U.S.).
11. McFarland, "On TV."
12. "Utopia," *Doctor Who* (BBC, 2007, UK).
13. "The Parting of the Ways," *Doctor Who* (BBC, 2005, UK).
14. "Bad Wolf."
15. "The Parting of the Ways."
16. "Episode Eleven — Ello Ello Ello," *Doctor Who Confidential* (BBC, 2007, UK).
17. Joseph Campbell, *The Hero with a Thousand Faces* (New York: Princeton University Press, 1973), 120.
18. "Episode Eleven — Unsung Heroes and Violent Death," *Doctor Who Confidential* (BBC, 2005, UK).
19. "Utopia."
20. "Jack's Back," *Torchwood Declassified* (BBC, 2007, UK).
21. "Bad Day at the Office," *Torchwood Declassified* (BBC, 2007, UK).
22. Eve Myles, "S2 Episode 1: Inside Look 5," *BBC America—Torchwood, http://www.bbc america.com/content/262/index.jsp*. Gary Russell, *The Torchwood Archives* (London: BBC Books, 2008), 105.
23. Vogler, *The Writer's Journey*, 30.
24. *Ibid.*, 164.
25. "Utopia."
26. "Last of the Time Lords," *Doctor Who* (BBC, 2007, UK).
27. "The Sound of Drums," *Doctor Who* (BBC, 2007, UK).
28. John Barrowman interview by Katie Campling, *The Huddersfield Daily Examiner*, 14 January 2008.
29. "Blast from the Past," *Torchwood Declassified, Torchwood—The Complete First Season*, DVD, produced by Russell T. Davies (2007; U.S.: BBC Warner, 2008).
30. Glyn Davis and Gary Needham, *Queer TV* (New York: Routledge, 2009), 153.
31. "Blast from the Past."
32. *Ibid.*
33. Neil Wilkes, "Chris Chibnall Talks 'Torchwood,'" *Digital Spy*, April 1 2008, *http://www. digitalspy.co.uk/tv/a92590/chris-chibnall-talks-torchwood-lo-london.html#yourviews*
34. *Ibid.*
35. Vogler, *The Writer's Journey*, 71.
36. Burn Gorman, "S2 Episode 1: Inside Look 3," *BBC America—Torchwood, http://www. bbcamerica.com/content/262/index.jsp*
37. Midori Snyder, "The Armless Maiden and the Hero's Journey," *The Journal of Mythic Arts*, The Endicott Studio (Winter 2006), 3. *http://www.endicottstudio.com/rdrm/rrHJourney3.html*
38. Clarissa Pinkola Estés, *Women Who Run with the Wolves* (New York: Ballantine Books, 1992), 449–450.
39. "Last of the Time Lords," *Doctor Who* (BBC, 2007, UK).
40. Campbell, *Hero with a Thousand Faces*, 130.
41. "New Earth," *Doctor Who* (BBC, 2006, UK).

SIX

Screwing Aliens and Screwing with Aliens: *Torchwood* Slashes the Doctor

RICHARD BERGER

In summer 2004 an independent study of the BBC's web provision was published. The Graf Report stated for the first time that the BBC's web content should be now viewed as the corporation's third medium — alongside radio and television. In addition the report put the case for what it called "360 degree commissioning" whereby content was produced across the BBC's platforms, simultaneously. The effect was almost immediate, with the BBC shutting down some of its many websites and reorganizing its new media division as elements of existing departments, rather than an adjunct to radio and television output. At the same time discussions were already underway for the revival of a television franchise which had been largely ignored for 16 years, despite having an almost fanatical following.

At first glance the re-launched *Doctor Who*, in 2005, seemed to embody the BBC's new cross-platform policy. The new series came with a raft of merchandise, novelizations, comic books and its sister "commentary" series *Doctor Who Confidential*. The accompanying website hosted games and other downloads and this was followed by the more "adult" spin-off, *Torchwood*, in the fall of 2006 and then *The Sarah Jane Adventures* from the beginning of 2007. The *Doctor Who* series has always been surrounded by an array of texts, some official, most not, since its inception in 1963, so this was nothing new. What *was* new, however, was the dialogic relationship between the new *Doctor Who*, and the other "utterances" such as *Torchwood*. There had been a series of official *Doctor Who* novels complementing the series, right through the franchise's 16-year hiatus. Up until 1991, these publications were novelizations — that is, reworked stories and scripts from the original TV show. From 1991, however, the novels were largely new stories produced by a new generation of writers. Many of these writers had grown up with the original *Doctor Who* series and were self-confessed fans. Mark Gatiss wrote the original *Who* novels *Roundheads* in 1997 and *Last of the Gaderene* in 2000. These new stories featured the second and third Doctors, respectively. Gatiss would graduate to write for the revised *Who* television series from 2005, but these spin-off novels were vaguely canonical and were not dialogically linked to *Who* diegesis. *Torchwood* would be very different. In this chapter, I aim to show how the revived *Doctor Who* series, and *Torchwood*, has its origins in the fan communities and activities that had taken place during the show's hiatus between 1989 and 2005. Fans of the franchise, an aggressively passionate and committed constituency, had kept the series in cultural circulation by writing their own fan fiction. These fan produced writings would have a significant influence on *Doctor Who*, and a more Transgressive form, slash fiction (or slash) strategies would be ignited and enacted by *Torchwood*.

The Dialogics of Torchwood

Fan fiction (or fanfic) is a form whereby fans of a novel, film or television program, write their own stories, publish them in fanzines ('zines) and online. Fanfic writers can develop minor characters in a well-known text or provide sequels/prequels to major literary, filmic or televisual works — which can clearly be seen in *Torchwood* with the furthering development of the Captain Jack Harkness' character. Both Russell T. Davies and Mark Gatiss were *Doctor Who* fanfic writers, before Gatiss' "profic" (officially sanctioned stories). However, as with the *Who* novels from 1991, it is rare for fanfic, or profic, to become part of any "canon" so traditionally such texts sit outside and beyond the reach of "official" sources.

When television became a mass medium from the mid–1950s, fanfic soon followed, and a new generation of fanfic writers began to provide episodes of their favorite TV shows, such as *Star Trek*, *The Man from U.N.C.L.E.* and *Starsky & Hutch*. So, fan writing is synonymous with fan culture and fanfic acts as a type of cultural virus in the way it can mutate and evolve to suit new media. Fanfic can refashion television into what Roland Barthes would call a "writerly" text[1] as it allows for more participation, and therefore engagement, by audiences. However, most *Who* fanfic adhered to broadly canonical structure — unlike the "official" spin-off novels — and rules were quickly established whereby writers had to adhere to canonical aspects of a series, character or setting, mediated by *Who*'s increasingly passionate fan-base. Fanfic that synchronically departed from the rules of the diachronic source text were generally considered to be poor. The trick was to maintain a significant level of fidelity while at the same time exploring new plots and developments. In this way minor characters in a canon would become popular with fanfic writers because they offered more scope for exploration, but still within the recognizable diegesis of a TV series.

The 1960s saw a boom in fanfic, generally in the science fiction genre, and the fledgling *Doctor Who* series was no different. The *Who* diegesis provides a great deal of scope for the fanfic writer as the countless regenerations, companions and time travel possibilities allow the type of artistic freedom and expression that adhering to a *Star Trek* narrative, for example, would not provide. This decade also saw the emergence of a splinter-genre of fanfic which would deliberately frame itself as non-canonical. In fact this was its virtue. Slash fiction — so called because of its denotative "slash" in advertising a Transgressive non-canonical coupling — was a more aggressive form of sexually explicit fan writing. Slash fic writers would imagine sexual relationships between characters in largely mainstream television programmes which weren't portrayed or explored in the original text.

Apart from the misfire of the 1996 television movie — which perhaps went too far in exploring the Doctor's sexuality — and a few radio productions, *Who* fans had been starved of content for almost two decades. Despite this, the BBC continued to generate a great deal of income from merchandising. *The Doctor Who Magazine*— its earliest incarnation beginning in 1979 — provided fans with information and interviews with former cast members, writers and crew. The magazine also featured largely non-canonical stories, but I would argue that the general strategy was for nostalgia, which was the permanent state of the *Who* fan and spin-off industry. The magazine continued — as a monthly publication — throughout the series' enforced television hiatus. A regular comic strip would feature previous Doctors, but would align itself with the current incumbent from 2005, in a broad attempt at fidelity. Back stories for characters such as the Cybermen were explored by a series of writers. So, it was clear that the fans not only demanded more from the *Who* diegesis, but they were willing to go the extra step and write their own stories for an increasingly global audience online. Fanfic writing allows for fans to be in constant conversation with a text. Readers are often writers too, and the climax of the narrative is delayed as it is a never ending unclosed process which blurs the boundaries between writers and readers. Slash writers further subvert this process by reimagining the relationships in the progeny series, particularly between the tenth Doctor and Rose Tyler.

The popularity of the web would extend slash fic's reach and would create a vibrant fan community, whereby consumers of texts elsewhere could debate their merits with like-minded audiences. There is an instantaneity about fan writing, and often readers are very vocal for writers to continue a particular narrative. As Susan Clerc suggests: "The most primal instinct a fan has is to talk to other fans about their common interest"[2] and *Who* fans had had 18 years to discuss their favorite text within their own creative productivity. Since the 1960s, fan culture had become increasingly participatory, as John Fiske observes: "Fans produce and circulate among themselves texts which are often crafted with production values as high as any in the official culture."[3]

However, these spheres of cultural reproduction are increasingly dialogical. *Who* has always been intertextual: the new series made overt references to not only its own back-story and history but also to other texts such as Douglas Adams' *Hitchhiker's Guide to the Galaxy* series and even the Disney film *The Lion King*. With the addition of *Torchwood* to the franchise, these intertextualities deepened to a new level of dialogism as the new spin-off series obliquely referenced its "parent" series: Episode 3 not only established the eponymous "Ghost Machine" (further developed in *The Sarah Jane Adventures*) but graffiti hinted at "The Rise of the Cybermen" *Who* episode; UNIT gets a mention in Episode 7, "Greeks bearing gifts"; there is more "Bad Wolf" graffiti in Episode 12, "Captain Jack Harkness"; former companion of the eighth Doctor, Samantha Jones, gets a name check in Episode 19, "Reset" as well as the revelation that Harkness is The Face of Boe, and so on. *Torchwood* was first conceived by Russell T. Davies in 2002, as a UK version of *Buffy the Vampire Slayer*. It was reconfigured as a *Doctor Who* spin-off in 2005, and seeded into the *Who* episode "Tooth and Claw." The Doctor's "hand in a jar" became a key narrative device, and the character Gwen Cooper was worked in as a descendent of the Gwyneth seen in "The Unquiet Dead." *Torchwood* then becomes an utterance of the *Who* universe, engaged in a dialogical relay with the older series. For Michael Holquist, dialogism "is a way of looking at things that always insists on the presence of the other, on the inescapable necessity of outsidedness and unfinalizability."[4] So, in this sense, *Torchwood* is much more than intertextual.

Dan McKee argues that the web has allowed fan communities to form more quickly and these fans therefore display "agency in their everyday media consumption."[5] Again, for Henry Jenkins, "an alternative conception of fans as readers who appropriate popular texts and re-read them in a fashion that serves different interests, as spectators who transform the experience of watching television into a rich and complex participatory culture."[6] Similarly Clerc, writing about television fans, suggests, "Fans, whether online or off, discuss characterization [and] speculate about what would have happened if some feature of a story had been different.... Fans try and fill in the gaps left by writers and form connections between episodes."[7]

In mainstream television, the biggest "gaps" in texts are often about sexuality — *any* sexuality. So, slash fic writers had a rich ground to explore and develop in any number of non-canonical reconfigurings, because "fanfic happens in the gaps between canon. The unexplored or insufficiently explored territory."[8] The difference here though is that *Torchwood*'s explicit sexual storylines were canonical.

Fan and slash fiction then can be read here as a commentary on the "official" culture, and this commentary — just as with the texts it seeks to comment on — has changed a great deal. Adaptation theorists such as Geoffrey Wagner[9] have often cited a text's re-purposing as having the potential for commentary, but this dialogue is little more than a conversation between an adaptor and an adapted work. Fanfic, and its sub-genres, is a far more interactive, visible and therefore plural process, and *Torchwood*'s relationship to *Doctor Who* embodies this.

So, I am suggesting that fanfic is a genre, and like any such genre, it is by no means a fixed or closed system. Rather it undergoes fundamental change and development in its life-cycle; in this case a hegemonic cycle whereby the subversive elements of slash are reworked, albeit in a neutered way, back into mainstream culture. What Pugh[10] calls the "democratic genre" seeks to fill in what Fiske,[11] Jenkins[12] and Clerc[13] all call "gaps" left by television programs. Now slash communities have formed online and new fanfic canons have emerged. These communities have provided nurturing spaces where a contributor's work is commented on, and feedback is given. In short, slash can be conceived of as a subversive form of appropriation, where the source text is opened-up to subversion for the purposes of a sexual and often political agenda. *Torchwood* enacted slash strategies from the start, subverting its parent series, by being far more explicitly violent and sexual.

Fanfic now, thanks to *Doctor Who* and *Torchwood*, has a veneer of authenticity, mirroring the forms it seeks to comment on. Slash is no longer just a commentary on a text but it is a commentary on the medium of television itself. Fanfic is largely concerned with television, and is an extension of what John Ellis[14] calls the medium's "working through": fanfic authors take an idea, theme, or issue of concern and works through it in communion with a favorite television character or text. Slash merely takes this into a more playful realm of sexual desire.

Slashing the Doctor

The advent of the world wide web in the early 1990s shaped fanfic in a number of ways: it provided a new space far beyond the reach of fanzines and conventions; it facilitated more sophisticated routes of anonymity; it made fanfic more visible; it allowed fanfic writers to form online communities and slash would join with other forms of sexually explicit content online. This period was a dialogical era for fanfic and their writers. Slash writers could now be in more open conversation with the texts they were commenting on and with each other. Some sites, such as slashfanfiction.com, began to archive material from the 60s and 70s, introducing the genre to a new audience who would go on to write their own stories.

Interestingly, slash has provided problems for literary and cultural studies scholars, particularly when attempting to define the term. As Mark McLelland notes, "Slash ... is an underground fandom and many English-speaking people, including academics working in cultural studies, seem unaware of the extent of the genre or its longevity."[15] Hutcheon[16] argues that fanfic is certainly not a type of adaptation and I would agree. Rather fanfic and slash writing is more of a conversation, where fans are in communion with an array of texts, which they already find a great deal of pleasure in.

In 1991 the first original *Doctor Who* novels emerged, which did not explicitly adhere to any canon. The popularity of the web a few years later would further encourage *Who* fanfic, and at the time of writing, www.whofic.com has 21, 648 stories written by 2777 authors. Over 3000 of the stories in this archive are *Torchwood* fics. In the late 1990s, Russell T. Davies' television series *Queer As Folk* (Channel 4, 1999–2000, UK) broke new ground in its portrayal of gay relationships and characters, and pushed the boundaries of what could be shown on television. Davies' revival of *Doctor Who* was notable for its treatment of sexuality. The Doctor has always been asexual and non-violent, and Davies' new Doctor largely adhered to this model as *Doctor Who* is a "sacred" text. However Davies and his writing team did populate the series with sexual tension and a subtly more explicit treatment of sexuality. Rose Tyler, and later Martha Jones, clearly had romantic feelings for the Time Lord, but so did Captain Jack Harkness, a bi-sexual Time Agent. Played by musical theatre star, John Barrowman, the character brought a cheeky campness to a mainstream television audience.

From the start *Torchwood* was billed as an "adult" spin-off and Harkness was the show's central character. Indeed, the first *Star Trek* slash story, "A Fragment out of Time" by Diane Marchant — published in the fanzine *Group* in 1974 — imagined a sexual relationship between the two principle male characters Kirk and Spock. As McLelland notes, "Like Western slash fiction writers, the authors took heterosexual, heteronormative narratives and 'queered' them by imagining sexual relationships between the male characters."[17]

So, *Torchwood* serves to develop a character in a similar fashion to the ways in which fanfic does in enacting almost slash-like strategies, and like slash, in a far more sexually explicit way. *Torchwood* is the "profound" text to *Doctor Who*'s "sacred" one, and the relationship between the two is what Mikhail Bakhtin would call "carnivalesque." Fanfic writing is itself carnivalesque as Bakhtin further argues that "carnival ... does not acknowledge any distinction between actors and spectators."[18] For Simon Dentith, this carnival is "an aesthetic which celebrates the anarchic body-based and grotesque elements of popular culture, and seeks to mobilize them against the humorless seriousness of official culture."[19]

In a sense, from the late 1990s, fanfic had "remediated"[20] television drama and this new dialogue legitimized slash to an extent. *Torchwood*, then, continues the conversation with *Doctor Who*, which had been established by fan writers originally. The first episode, "Everything Changes"— the only one of the first two seasons written by Davies — is almost painful in establishing its adult credentials with a police officer disclaiming, "It's a fucking disgrace" in the first few minutes, but it is the series' treatment of sexuality and relationships which reveal *Torchwood*'s slash-like dialogism.

In Episode 2, "Day One," a promiscuous alien adopts a female host body and prowls Cardiff searching for men to have sex with. This episode is problematic in that we are witness to the unwitting self-abuse of a woman, much like an extraterrestrial rohypnol attack. In one scene we see the woman take a shower, similar to the way rape victims are depicted in film and television. In the same episode, Gwen is overcome and is seduced by the alien too. From then on, sexual relationships are developed between the residents of Torchwood 3. In Episode 4, "Cyberwoman," we meet Lisa, Ianto's girlfriend who is a Cyberwoman from Torchwood 2. In Episode 6, "Countrycide," Gwen sleeps with Owen, and Toshiko and Mark sleep together in Episode 7, "Greeks Bearing Gifts." Jack and Ianto's relationship begins in Episode 8, "They Keep Killing Suzie," and Gwen discovers them both having sex in Episode 24, "Adrift." Owen and a character from 1953, Mary, get romantically involved in Episode 10, "Out of Time," and Toshiko falls tragically for Tommy Brockless in Episode 16, "To the Last Man." Season two is notable for its significant ramping up of *Torchwood*'s exploration of heterosexuality, homosexuality and bi-sexuality, as the show steps out of the long shadow of the TARDIS, and defines itself more as an science fiction series for grownups which deals with some very real (and therefore human) issues.

There are also unconsummated attractions too, not just the ongoing frisson between Toshiko and Owen, but between Jack Harkness and Captain John Hart and between Harkness and the *real* Captain Jack. I would argue here that this is precisely what slash fiction does: it fills the gaps in pre-existing material, usually with more sexually explicit material, thereby reconfiguring a text into a more Transgressive form of commentary. It's clear that, as fans and fan writers themselves, the creators of the revived *Doctor Who* deliberately enacted slash strategies in creating a narrative which was so much more than an intertexually bound spin-off. The spin-off novels, comic books, animations and radio series are vaguely canonical by virtue of their intertexuality, but *Torchwood*, by enacting these slash fic strategies, is firmly canonical.

Continuing the Conversation...

Unlike the "official" *Who* spin-off novels, *Torchwood*, like a great deal of fanfic, is at pains to establish itself as an integral part of the *Who* canon and universe. If both series were to be arranged along a timeline, then Captain Jack Harkness' regular sabbaticals from The Hub always chime with his appearances in the TARDIS. This dialogic pollination continues with the tenth Doctor's companion, Martha Jones, joining *Torchwood* for three episodes in the second season and all the members of *Torchwood* appearing in the *Doctor Who* season finale, "The Stolen Earth/Journey's End."

When *Doctor Who* began in 1963, it was created as an educational series for children and written by veterans of British science-fiction novels and television. In many ways, the original series reflected their concerns. Writers such as Terry Nation, Terrance Dicks and Douglas Adams were contemporaries of British science fiction writers such as Arthur C. Clarke, Brian Aldiss and J. G. Ballard. Russell T. Davies, Stephen Moffat and Mark Gatiss however, were *Doctor Who* fans. Not only that, but they had written *Who* fanfic, and in Gatiss' case, profic. So, it's not surprising then to note that the resurrected *Doctor Who* is very much a fan text, and it clearly and overtly enacts carnivalesque fanfic strategies. However, for Bakhtin, the carnival was always a temporary state and both *Doctor Who* and *Torchwood* give the "sacred" and the "profane" a permanence across all forms of popular culture, and the fan writers themselves contribute to and reshape this ongoing carnival.

The new *Doctor Who* fills in the gaps left by previous versions and stories. It is able to playfully revisit and rewrite aspects of the *Who* canon, and to establish itself as a source text for the development of *Torchwood*. One way a new version of a much cherished — and "sacred" — narrative can establish itself is to serve as an influential source for more dialogically linked texts. So, the revived *Doctor Who* is a fan commentary on the original series, characters and storylines. This in turn is commented on by a new generation of fans, some of whom now write their own stories.

All genres are subverted eventually, and fanfic is no different. *Torchwood* is *Doctor Who*'s slash fic, however its parent series rewires it as a canonical text and *Torchwood*'s exploration of Transgressive sexuality is now very much part of the *Doctor Who* diegesis. Sexuality is implicit in *Who*, but explicit in *Torchwood*. This link with fan writing and fan culture allows the series to constantly adapt and reshape its structure. This is most obvious with the single-story arc of the third season of *Torchwood*, exhibited over five consecutive nights in 2009. This structure is interesting as it could be argued that this season is a commentary on the first two seasons: the third season is season one and two's fanfic.

The increasing amount of *Torchwood* (as well as *Doctor Who*) fanfic gives a good indication of the series' enduring popularity. If *Torchwood* doesn't continue beyond its third season, the fan writers and slash writers will use their *Torchwood* stories to keep open an unending conversation with their favorite text and a continuing commentary on the *Doctor Who* universe. A mainstream television program that appropriates the conventions of fan writing is a bold and imaginative idea. Taking this to the next step and producing a slash version of a staple of the BBC's family entertainment output is a feat of exceedingly brave commissioning by a team of creative people who in many ways are not only paying their respects as fans, but who also recognize the dialogical relationship some fans have with a television series. In *Torchwood*'s case, it is a strategy that has paid off, because far more than being just another intertextual spin-off, *Torchwood* deepens our involvement in *Doctor Who*, and *Torchwood* deepens our understanding of *Doctor Who* and its audiences.

Notes

1. Roland Barthes, *S/Z* (Oxford: Blackwell, 1974), 4.
2. Susan Clerc, "Estrogen Brigades and 'Big Tits' threads: Media Fandom on-line and off," in *The Cybercultures Reader*, ed. David Bell and Barbara M. Kennedy (London: Routledge, 2001), 216.
3. John Fiske, "The Cultural Economy of Fandom," in *The Adoring Audience*, ed. Lisa A. Lewis (London: Routledge, 1992), 39.
4. Michael Holquist, *Dialogism* (London: Routledge, 2002), 195.
5. Alan McKee, "Fandom," in *Television Studies*, ed. Toby and Andrew Lockett Miller (London: BFI, 2002), 67.
6. Henry Jenkins, *Textual Poachers: Television Fans and Participatory Culture* (London: Routledge, 1992), 23.
7. Clerc, *The Cybercultures Reader*, 216–7.
8. Sheenagh Pugh, *The Democratic Genre: Fan Fiction in a Literary Context* (Bridgend: Seren Books, 2005), 92.
9. Geoffrey Wagner, *The Novel and the Cinema* (Cranbury, NJ: Associated University Press, 1975), 222–223.

10. Pugh, *The Democratic Genre*.
11. Fiske, *The Adoring Audience*.
12. Jenkins, *Textual Poachers*.
13. Clerc, *The Cybercultures Reader*.
14. John Ellis, *Seeing Things: Television in the Age of Uncertainty* (London: I. B. Tauris), 91.
15. Mark McLelland, "Local Meanings in Global Space: A Case Study of Women's 'Boy love' Web Sites in Japanese and English," *Mots Pluriels* 19, October 2001, 9.
16. Linda Hutcheon, *A Theory of Adaptation* (London: Routledge, 2006), 9.
17. McLelland, *Mots Plurals*, 6.
18. Mikhail Bakhtin, "Folk Humour and Carnival Laughter," in *The Bakhtin Reader: Selected Writings of Bakhtin, Medvedev, Voloshinov*, ed. Pam Morris (London: Arnold, 1993), 198.
19. Simon Dentith, *Bakhtinian Thought: An Introductory Reader* (London: Routledge, 2003), 66.
20. Jay David Bolter and Richard Grusin, *Remediation* (Cambridge, MA: MIT Press, 2000).

Part II

Character and *Torchwood*

SEVEN

The Eternal Vigil: Captain Jack as Byronic Hero

G. TODD DAVIS

The lamp must be replenish'd, but even then
It will not burn so long as I must watch.
My slumbers — if I slumber — are not sleep,
But a continuance of enduring thought,
Which then I can resist not: in my heart
There is a vigil, and these eyes but close
To look within; and yet I live, and bear
The aspect and the form of breathing men.
But grief should be the instructor of the wise;
Sorrow is knowledge: they who know the most
Must mourn the deepest o'er the fatal truth,
The Tree of Knowledge is not that of Life.

Lord Byron[1]

To say that the most popular phenomenon of the English Romantic Movement and the figure with the most far-reaching consequences for nineteenth-century Western literature was the Byronic Hero is no overstatement of the case.

Peter L. Thorslev Jr.[2]

The Byronic Hero has been an indelible and pervasive component of our literary culture since its inception. Even though Peter L. Thorslev Jr.'s *The Byronic Hero: Types and Prototypes* was published in 1962, it still stands as the definitive work on the characterization and genesis of Byron's hero. Other critics have used this book as a foundation for their own work, most notably Atara Stein in her *The Byronic Hero in Film, Fiction, and Television*, published in 2004.[3] Stein connects the Byronic Hero with a wide-ranging collection of individuals in popular culture, some of which include: Eric Draven from *The Crow*, Q from *Star Trek: The Next Generation* (Paramount

Television, 1987–1994, U.S.), the Terminator from *Terminator 2* (1991, U.S.), and Angel from *Buffy the Vampire Slayer* (20th Century–Fox Television, 1997–2003, U.S.) and *Angel* (20th Century–Fox Television, 1999–2004, U.S.). In my own "Fictions of Byron: An Annotated Bibliography" on *Romantic Circles*,[4] over one hundred novels, short stories, poems, plays, movies and television shows showcase Byronism, which the author defines as the perpetuation of the Byron legend, a process of refashioning that has been effected by both Byron himself and by authors who alter, expand, or moderate this discourse. That project focuses more broadly on Byron's image and character in fiction, constructed from autobiography and biography and refashioned in various forms throughout the nineteenth and twentieth centuries in such specific guises as the vampire, the ghost, the madman, and the queer.

For this chapter, though, the focus is more specifically on the Byronic Hero, and the way in which Captain Jack Harkness exemplifies the traits and personality of this persistent and pervasive heroic character. As suggested by Thorslev,[5] the Byronic Hero did not emerge fully-clothed from Byron's mind as did Athena from Zeus's hewn head. The Byronic Hero's myriad predecessors helped to cast and shape him into the familiar form he inhabits. In addition to some of the more obvious sources, such as Milton's Lucifer, Prometheus, Faust, Cain, and Ahasuerus, Thorslev also suggests that such heroic types as the Child of Nature, The Hero of Sensibility, The Gothic Villain, and The Noble Outlaw help to form the character and the persona of the Byronic Hero. This is not to say, however, that Lord Byron doesn't deserve the credit for melding these various parts into a codified and interwoven mélange. Byron brilliantly fused the components into the instantly recognizable form we still acknowledge with his name today. We can easily identify this development and fulfillment in Child Harold, Manfred, Lara, the Corsair, and in other heroes of Byron's imagination.

As for the traits themselves, we have a number of them to delineate and elucidate before we can determine whether or not Captain Jack qualifies as one of their own. The Byronic Hero is highly intelligent and cynical, with a superiority complex. While the Enlightenment period disdained *hubris* as a transgression, an attempt to transcend a sacrosanct boundary that determined the Great Chain of Being between God and humanity, the Romantic tended to embrace *hubris* as a laudable and virtuous endeavor. In this regard, then, the Byronic Hero's arrogance sets him apart from common humanity in a commendable and even enviable fashion. His disdain for the ordinary and mundane bolsters him against the ravages of mediocrity. He disparages the crowd because of their softness, their stupidity, their insensitivity, and ultimately their inability to make the hard choices.

By standing apart from the crowd, the Byronic Hero buttresses his own individuality. As Thorslev suggests, he tends toward a "positive and passionate assertion" of himself as an individual, which leads to a "self-assertion which makes impossible any wholehearted commitment to dogmas or to absolutes outside of oneself," and which eventually takes the form of "a lust for violent emotional experience, even for suffering — any psychic activity which will heighten and make more acute a sense of self-awareness and self-identity."[6] This heightened sense of individualism, of a belief in his own superiority, leads him to ridicule and deride creeds or doctrines that enchain the mind and spirit in what William Blake in "London" described as "mind-forged manacles."[7]

This independence allows the Byronic Hero to disavow an allegiance to either heaven or hell. Manfred, for example, refuses to bow down to any source outside of himself. He refuses to acknowledge that either the Abbott or the demon has any power over him. He stays autonomous and self-sufficient, divorcing himself from the powers of good or evil. Thorslev says: "The Romantic hero types ... are invariably solitaries, and are fundamentally and heroically rebellious, at first against society only, and later against the natural universe or against God himself."[8] The Byronic Hero takes this one step further, by refusing to align himself with anyone or anything. He believes only in himself, confident in his ability to enact change according to his own rigid standards of protocol and conduct.

As such, the Byronic Hero sins without expectation of repentance and salvation because he rejects the idea that morality exists outside of himself. He formulates his own moral codes and beliefs, and strictly adheres to them. He doubts and questions everything while surrendering to nothing. He is guided by a destiny that only he can perceive, but a destiny nonetheless that drives him compellingly forward into dangerous and often life-threatening situations. He cares little for his own life, and in the case of Manfred, seeks death as a way to end his interminable and insufferable grief.

This grief is often the result of a hidden and private guilt that pervades the hero's consciousness. Thorslev says that the Byronic Hero has "a self-inflicted and all-consuming guilt from some nebulous origin, usually an unbearable loss that creates a mental, moral, and spiritual anguish for which he is unable to forgive himself."[9] While this guilty secret is frequently alluded to, it is almost never revealed. That would strip the guilty secret of its power to impel the Byronic Hero to new heights of self-loathing. In the opening lines of *Manfred*, the eponymous hero suggests that he must suffer with a "continuance of enduring thought" and that there is a vigil in his heart that must be constantly attended to and maintained. He goes on to the say that "grief should be the instructor of the wise; / Sorrow is knowledge: they who know the most / Must mourn the deepest o'er the fatal truth, / The Tree of

Knowledge is not that of Life."[10] He subsumes himself within and even luxuriates in the power of his guilt. It becomes the driving force behind his larger-than-life personality. Because he has experienced the most sorrow, he has therefore become the wisest. Because he has mourned the deepest over the fatal truths, he has therefore risen to heights beyond which most mortal men can only aspire.

This super-abundance of knowledge and experience tends to be depicted in a heightened supernatural or even superhuman fashion. Manfred, for example, has the ability to summon spirits and converse with the Witch of the Alps, Nemesis, the dreaded Destinies, and even Arimanes himself.[11] In some of the modern versions of the Byronic Hero, the character is superhuman or possesses supernatural powers. As suggested by Atara Stein, this can even lead to an omnipotent being such as Q in *Star Trek*. They become allegorical and even mythical, especially when drawing upon the prodigious capabilities of a Titan such as Prometheus as their genesis. This, of course, only feeds their superiority complexes, preventing them from adjusting to any society they inhabit. As Thorslev suggests, "They either go down to glorious defeat, cursing God and dying, or they commit their lives to transforming the world."[12] There is rarely any middle ground for a Byronic hero: it is almost always all or nothing.

Consequently, the Byronic hero often acts ruthlessly, culling the individual to save humanity. He is passionate and revolutionary, and his embrace is almost always fatal. While he loves absolutely and without reservation, his passionate intensity is almost too bright for any mere mortal. He tends to incinerate them, which only adds to his guilt and his determination to remain separate from those he deems inferior. Still, as Thorslev suggests, they consistently maintain two inviolable tenets: "The concern for individual liberty, and the concern for society, the brotherhood of man."[13] These heroes are "thoroughgoing rebels, they invariably appeal to the reader's sympathies against the unjust restrictions of the social, moral, or even religious codes of the worlds in which they find themselves."[14] Because of their own demand to remain free from any allegiances to either heaven or hell, they incessantly fight for that same inherent right for all humans.

We turn now to the ways in which Captain Jack Harkness embodies the Byronic Hero. For the physical description, Thorslev compiles his depiction from both the Gothic Villain and the Noble Outlaw. He says that the hero is always striking and frequently handsome, with a tall, manly, stalwart physique coupled with dark hair and brows. He usually has a pale and ascetic complexion with all-seeing, dark, and terrifying eyes that command attention. He tends to be aristocratic, partly for the power and partly for the air of the fallen angel. Frequently, a mystery surrounds his birth and upbringing, and there tends to be an aura of past secret sins. He has a commanding voice of authority that demands unquestioning loyalty.[15] It could also be suggested that Lord Byron's own description tends to correspond to the above listed attributes, which only perpetuates the connection between Byron and his heroes.

Clearly, the actor John Barrowman fits the physical profile as listed above in the synopsis. Once he gets into character, Captain Jack Harkness seems to exude the characteristics even more completely as a result of his melancholic, brooding behavior, and the way in which he tends to dress in dark, muted colors, complete with black leather jackets or garb that resembles the soldier's uniform. Moreover, he sustains an aristocratic air that only accentuates his powerful voice and flashing eyes. The audience has only been given bits and pieces of Jack's biography, which frequently remains shrouded in mystery. We don't even know his real name, as Captain Jack Harkness is only an assumed identity based on Jack's respect for and perhaps even love of the real Captain Jack Harkness. Be that as it may, he wears the persona easily and thrives within its margins.

That Jack is intelligent is manifest by his ability to cheat death even before Rose Tyler makes him essentially immortal in "The Parting of the Ways."[16] He delights in the guise of an interplanetary rogue until he becomes a Time Agent. After he discovers the loss of two years of his memory, however, he leaves the Time Agency to become a conman, complete with psychic paper and spaceship. At one point in the eighteenth century, he steals a copy of a lost Shakespearean play and attempts to sell it in the twentieth century. He even attempts to con Rose Tyler and the Doctor, by trying to convince them that the Chula ambulance he has been towing is actually a warship. We can see from these various stunts and swindles, all of which are essentially harmless in that he wasn't attempting to sell weapons or biohazardous material, that Jack is simply trying to "survive" before his transformation into an immortal being. His lust for life and his yearning for new experiences allow him to move beyond the confines of the typically mundane life.

It is only after his death at the hands of the Daleks, and his miraculous resurrection as a result of Rose's intervention by taking the power of the TARDIS into herself, that he becomes a Byronic Hero. Before this point, he was merely a shrewd tactician, with the ability to get what he wanted by working the system. After his modification, however, he enters the realm of the supernatural and superhuman. While he feels pain, and while he will continue to age, he continually cheats death. He dies but continues to be reborn. In fact, we learn in "Fragments," that he has died at least 1,392 times. In "Day One," we learn that he has the ability to give of his life-force to save others, and in "Ghost Machine," we learn that he is unable to sleep. He eventually becomes the Face of Boe, a huge head enclosed in a large glass tank. We have a nice allusion here to his home world, the Boeshane Peninsula, and his poster boy status as a child. As the "Face of Boe," he was witness to the end of the Earth in the year 5 billion in "The End of the World,"[17] and he was briefly nursed by the Cat Nuns in "New Earth."[18] He is neither omnipotent nor omniscient, but his immortality allows him to amass a tremendous amount of information. As a giant head, he symbolizes the embodiment of the analytical being, an entity whose eternal thirst for knowledge eventually annihilates his still human body and allows him to become a quintessential intelligence. He does eventually die, but only through his own choice of giving his life-force to save the trapped drivers in the motorway of New York in "Gridlock."[19]

His death is a conscious choice on his part rather than some random act of chance. He cheats death until the very end, when he chooses the place and time of his demise. He remains beholden to no one, and he refuses to align himself with any particular dogma or creed. He remains free from any allegiance to heaven or hell, and dies on his own terms, giving his own life to save humanity once again. This recurring motif permeates his actions both in *Doctor Who* and *Torchwood*. We see it again when he fights against the biblical demon Abaddon in the "End of Days." The question of what happens when an unstoppable force meets an unmovable object is answered for the audience in the final moments of this episode. Abaddon sucks the life-force out of individuals, feeding on it in much the same way that Galactus the Destroyer feeds on worlds in the Marvel Comic Books. Abaddon's hunger is seemingly unquenchable and yet Jack's life-force is seemingly without end. Jack is unsure whether or not he will survive the encounter, and yet he willingly surrenders to the inevitability of the situation and the possibility of his own demise. In an act of pure altruism, he is perfectly willing to martyr himself to save the human race. As we see from this episode, Abaddon continues to feed off Jack until the demon literally expires from an excess of life. The unstoppable force has been stopped by the unmovable object.

This immortality does tend to feed Jack's superiority complex. He often remains austere and arrogant, separating himself from the crowd and from the joviality that permeates the offices at Torchwood headquarters. Within the various episodes, the audience can see his struggle to adjust to a changing society and to assimilate. More often than not, he retreats to his office, surrounding himself with mementoes from the past or future, and listening to the big band sounds of Glenn Miller. He remains hyperaware of his self-identity as an outsider and as a supernatural being. This reclusive isolation and loneliness does tend to exert itself occasionally in the form of cynicism, skepticism, and sarcasm. He tends to view society from a contemptuous and scornful position of a man who has seen too much and experienced the illicit and repulsive ills that societies can produce.

One of the few times that Jack has shown anything akin to joy is when the Doctor arrives. He watches the severed hand like a hawk, and when, on those rare occasions it starts moving, Jack immediately halts what he is doing, and runs out of the offices to find his Doctor, whom he seems to love. It is more than just love, however, that prompts this effusive reaction. The Doctor is one of the few individuals for whom Jack feels an abiding respect and even awe. As a Time Lord with a seemingly infinite ability to regenerate, the Doctor stands as the closest associate with whom Jack shares a supernatural affinity. With the Doctor, Jack is no longer an outsider or an anomaly, even though the Doctor finds Jack's immortality unnatural and somewhat distasteful. Still, Jack finds his presence soothing, and in more than one episode longs for his return.

Sometimes, though, this feeling of isolation leads Jack to question everything while surrendering to nothing. He occasionally finds it necessary to act ruthlessly and cull the individual in order to enact the greater good and save the community or the larger human race. In "Small Worlds," he allows a young girl to become a fairy while silently suffering under the pleas and protests of the young girl's mother and Gwen Cooper. The fairies have marked the young girl as one of their own, and they will only retreat from their promise to harm a significant number of humans if Jack will allow the transformation. He makes the difficult decisions out of concern for society. As Thorslev says of the Byronic Hero, Jack "is not a fatalist. He accepts the burden of his conscience willing, even defiantly; ... he does not attempt to evade his moral responsibility."[20] Additionally, as Thorslev says of Manfred, Jack, in these decisions, demonstrates an "aristocratic air of authority."[21] We see this again in "Adrift," wherein Gwen discovers that Jack is keeping a number of rift victims concealed within a sanctuary (or asylum, depending on the victim). Gwen adamantly demands that a rift victim be allowed to receive visitors, which only ends up causing irreparable emotional harm to both individuals. These are only two examples of many that point to Jack's ability to make the difficult decisions that, in the short run, may result in the death of an individual, while, in the long run, will serve to perpetuate the greater good.

Jack often transfers this "aristocratic air of authority" to the personal relationships and sexual interludes in which he partakes. While his embrace is frequently fatal, he still remains sympathetic to the viewer because of his heightened sense of personal morality and his scorn for any particular society's social mores. As has been said of the Byronic Hero, Jack loves absolutely, and he sins without expectation of redemption. Jack enjoys flirting and remains above the heterosexual or homosexual divide. We might suggest that Jack is omnisexual, or in the parlance of contemporary critical theory, queer, which suggests a highly fluid, incessantly mutable sexuality. Jack enjoys playing sexual games with Ianto Jones while mooning over and pining after Gwen Cooper. While in the privacy of his office, he fondly gazes at a picture of himself with his wife, while at the same time keeping an eye on the severed hand of the Doctor for his relentlessly expected arrival. In "The Empty Child,"[22] he quips that both Rose Tyler and Archie have "excellent bottoms," and ends up kissing both Rose and the Doctor in the "Parting of the Ways."[23] He doesn't restrict himself to humans, either, as he attempts to charm Chantho in "Utopia."[24]

He does have a special place in his heart (or perhaps another of his organs) for soldiers. In one of the most tender scenes in the entire program, he slow dances and then shares an extended kiss with his namesake in "Captain Jack Harkness." He remains poignantly aware that the young soldier is going to his death, and yet for this brief space of time, the two men dance and kiss as if they were the only two individuals left in the world. Jack also enjoys a bit of roughhousing with his sexual partners. After engaging in a bit of hide-and-seek, Gwen interrupts Jack and Ianto in a rather delicate moment, and instead of apologizing, Jack suggests that Gwen might join them. Moreover, when Captain John Hart, Jack's former partner and lover in the Time Agency, makes his grand appearance on the scene, they first engage in a violent brawl before falling into each other's arms for an extended kiss in the appropriately named "Kiss Kiss, Bang Bang."

Unfortunately, like most Byronic Heroes, Jack suffers from a guilty secret that he keeps hidden from his associates. When he was just a child, he was given responsibility for his younger brother Gray when a horde of violent aliens attacked his home world. As they were running away from the destruction, Jack happened to let go of his younger brother's hand while they were escaping. He searched but was unable to locate his younger brother, whom we learn later, was captured by the aliens and relentlessly tortured. We finally learn that Captain John Hart has been forced into his villainous behavior by Jack's brother Gray, who was the mastermind behind the scenes. Eventually Gray kidnaps Jack and buries him alive in 27 A.D. Jack submissively acquiesces to this punishment, accepting it as his penance for letting go of Gray's hand. He remains buried until 1901, when he is exhumed and placed in suspended animation in Torchwood's headquarters until 2008.

In this way, Jack enacts what Thorslev says of the Byronic Hero: "He has a self-inflicted and all-consuming guilt from some nebulous origin, usually an unbearable loss that creates a mental, moral, and spiritual anguish for which he is unable to forgive himself."[25] Even after being buried alive for almost nineteen hundred years, he still finds it difficult to forgive that moment of powerlessness and the inability to serve as protector for his younger brother, who had been given into his care by their father. As such, he uses this guilt and this incident as an impetus to persistently engage in fighting the good fight and in endlessly placing himself in dangerous situations to save humanity. This embodies his more extensive penance: to fight for both the individual's freedom and the safety of the larger community.

In his book, Thorslev summarizes Aristotle's concept of the hero: "First of all the hero must be 'bigger than life'; he must be above the common level, with greater powers, greater dignity, and a great soul. He must have the qualities of an ordinary mortal so that we can see ourselves in him, but he is an idealization, a man whose capacities have been multiplied and enlarged so as to make him a giant among men. Furthermore, in spite of his tragic flaw, he must be 'better,' more 'virtuous,' than the average man."[26] He then goes on to show how the Byronic Hero embodies and embraces this description. In just such a way, then, so too does Jack. He is perceptibly larger than life, especially as he transitions into his extended life as the Face of Boe. His immortality grants his greater powers that allow him to face dangerous situations without thought for his own mortality. In fact, he often uses his immortality to fool his enemies into thinking that he is dead, as he does with the Daleks in "The Stolen Earth."[27] However, he still has all-too-human flaws, which allow the audience members to see themselves within him. He definitely, though, emerges as an idealized hero, whose "capacities have been multiplied and enlarged." In spite of, or perhaps as a result of, his secret guilt over his brother Gray, he strives to always act in a virtuous although sometimes ruthless fashion to further the evolution of and protect humanity.

As we can see from the preceding examples, Captain Jack Harkness more than amply qualifies as a Byronic Hero. In the first instance, as suggested by Thorslev, Jack "is always first a victim of, and only then a rebel against society; his sins, if not completely exonerated, are at least palliated by reference to his innate gentleness of nature."[28] While Jack will ruthlessly cull the individual to serve the greater good, he never seems to forget his principal objective: to allow humanity to unfold in the fullness of time while making certain that particular factions or individuals don't circumvent or even derail that evolution. In this way, Jack embodies some of the characteristics of Cain and Ahasuerus. He is somewhat doomed to eternally wander while also retaining the protean capability of being all things to all individuals. He remains isolated from society and perpetually misunderstood.

By the same token, however, he also exemplifies the most prominent traits of the Titan/God Prometheus. He becomes apotheosized and mythological as the Face of Boe. Even at the very end of his seemingly immeasurable life, he chooses to give the last of his life force to save a world that would otherwise remain enslaved to an endless loop of driving within a confined and smoggy thoroughfare — a rush-hour Möbius strip, if you will. According to mythology, Prometheus valiantly rebels against Zeus's tyrannical and authoritarian strictures, preferring to have his internal organs ripped out on a daily basis by a vulture than reveal the secrets that will allow Zeus to continue his despotic reign. For the Romantic Period, both Prometheus and Lucifer from Milton's *Paradise Lost*, become heroes rather than villains in their defiance against a repressive and brutal sovereign. Jack, too, wages war against tyranny, despotism, and enslavement. He remains valiant and heroic even though he often exists outside the boundaries of humanity. In homage to Byron, Thorslev says: "Byron may in some sense have become his hero after the fact, but his hero was no mere outgrowth of the poet's personality. Byron did not project life into literature nearly so much as he projected literature into life."[29]

If there is one final and clarifying thought that *Torchwood* presents, it is this projection of literature into life. Captain Jack Harkness radiantly embodies the characteristics of a Byronic Hero, thereby aligning him with such literary heroes as Milton's Lucifer, Prometheus, Faust, Cain, Ahasuerus, and Byron's Manfred among others. As for modern-day heroes, we have the Crow, Q, the Terminator, and Angel, again only to name a few. Jack's legacy will live on, even if *Torchwood* does not. He takes his place in a long line of heroic figures that exist to show humanity the heroic in all of us.

Notes

1. Lord Byron, *The Complete Poetical Works*, Jerome J. McGann, ed. (Oxford: Oxford University Press, 1980–93).
2. Peter Thorslev, Jr., *The Byronic Hero: Types and Prototypes* (Minneapolis: The University of Minnesota Press, 1962), 3.
3. Atara Stein, *The Byronic Hero in Film, Fiction, and Television* (Carbondale: Southern Illinois University Press, 2004). Her death from multiple sclerosis on March 21, 2008, at the relatively young age of 48, was a blow to Byron scholarship and the Byron community. Her wit and passion will be sorely missed.
4. G. Todd Davis, *Fictions of Byron: An Annotated Bibliography*. See *http://www.rc.umd.edu/reference/byron-fictions/index.html*
5. Peter Thorslev, Jr., *The Byronic Hero: Types and Prototypes* (Minneapolis: The University of Minnesota Press, 1962).
6. *Ibid.*, 89.
7. See William Blake, "London," in David Damrosch, Peter J. Manning, and Susan Wolfson, eds., *Longman Anthology of British Literature, Volume 2A: The Romantics and their Contemporaries* (New York: Longman, 2002).

8. Peter Thorslev, Jr., *The Byronic Hero: Types and Prototypes*, 66.
9. *Ibid.*, 8.
10. See *Manfred*, I, I, 1–12 in Lord Byron, *The Complete Poetical Works*, Jerome J. McGann, ed. (Oxford: Oxford University Press, 1980–93).
11. As suggested in the *Longman Anthology of British Literature*, Arimanes is derived from Ahriman, the principle of evil in Zoroastrianism. See David Damrosch, Peter J. Manning, and Susan Wolfson, eds., *Longman Anthology of British Literature, Volume 2A: The Romantics and their Contemporaries* (New York: Longman, 2002).
12. Peter Thorslev, Jr., *The Byronic Hero: Types and Prototypes*, 66.
13. *Ibid.*, 108.
14. *Ibid.*, 22.
15. This description is compiled from various sections in Thorslev's book, which run between pages 51 and 83.
16. "The Parting of the Ways," *Doctor Who* (BBC, 2006, UK).
17. "The End of the World," *Doctor Who* (BBC, 2005, UK).
18. "New Earth," *Doctor Who* (BBC, 2006, UK).
19. "Gridlock," *Doctor Who* (BBC, 2007, UK).
20. Peter Thorslev, Jr., *The Byronic Hero: Types and Prototypes*, 164.
21. *Ibid.*, 89.
22. "The Empty Child," *Doctor Who* (BBC, 2005, UK).
23. "The Parting of the Ways," *Doctor Who* (BBC, 2006, UK).
24. "Utopia," *Doctor Who* (BBC, 2007, UK).
25. Peter Thorslev, Jr., *The Byronic Hero: Types and Prototypes*, 8.
26. *Ibid.*, 186.
27. "The Stolen Earth," *Doctor Who* (BBC, 2008, UK).
28. Peter Thorslev, Jr., *The Byronic Hero: Types and Prototypes*, 22.
29. *Ibid.*, 12.

Eight

Gwen's Evil Stepmother: Concerning Gloves and Magic Slippers
Valerie Estelle Frankel

Magic World

Gwen Cooper has an excellent life. She's a strong, confident beat cop with a loving boyfriend named Rhys and a pleasant flat. Still, it's not enough. Like many women seeking success in what could still be considered the male-oriented job world, juggling work and family while being "one of the boys," she seeks to prove her intelligence and dedication. "Everything is geared to getting the job done; climbing the academic or corporate ladder; achieving prestige, position, and financial equity; and feeling powerful in the world," as Maureen Murdock explains in her psychological study, *The Heroine's Journey*.[1] Yet when many women accomplish all this, they still feel a lack. Murdock notes that, having attained all their goals, they find themselves seeking the next hurdle, the next challenge. More, each heroine feels an empty place inside herself, one which must be filled with more activities, more challenges, lest she notice this imbalance. As Murdock adds, "She has learned how to get things done logically and efficiently but has sacrificed her health, dreams, and intuition. What she may have lost is a deep relationship to her own feminine nature."[2] Women are traditionally insightful, creative life-givers — the nurturers and builders. This fundamental lack leaves the woman brittle and incomplete; thus, she begins her journey of growth.

In fantasy, the heroine ventures into a magical world, where sidekicks and villains reflect aspects of herself and force her to explore her deepest nature. *Torchwood*, despite its urban setting and science fiction base, offers the same form of escape: As Producer Russell T. Davies says, "The point about Torchwood is that it's the real world in which fantastic things happen."[3] There are magical talismans like Suzie Costello's resurrection glove, holding the power to bring back the dead. There are ancient goddesses and fairies and ghosts and irrationalities because that's the side of herself Gwen has never explored. In fact, our cop dressed in asexual bright orange has repressed many aspects of herself, and Torchwood is determined to change that....

In the premiere episode, appropriately titled "Everything Changes," a random victim's violent death plunges Gwen into the world of the unconscious. There, magic is commonplace and frightening monsters stalk the streets. The rainy, dark atmosphere and grisly murder offer an aura of mystery. Into this walk the shadowy Torchwood team, who circle the corpse in a ritualistic fashion and revive him. At this moment, Gwen's safe world vanishes forever. She flees back to her cozy, secure flat, but can't dismiss the images. She craves the supernatural knowledge she's been lacking: the knowledge of something *more*.

Her senses now heightened, Gwen investigates Torchwood and its Captain Jack Harkness but discovers only more mystery. Her first alien, the Weevil, attacks her in the hospital. As Julie Gardner, executive producer, states, the Weevil is "the bridge from her normal life into her extraordinary life," the moment she can't dismiss.[4] Worse, this sewer-dwelling creature represents all that is dark and frightening in the subconscious. It is a guardian, threatening Gwen in her safe world. "Do you really want to know?" it seems to ask. "This is the world you're investigating: terrors and nightmares you've never confronted. Are you strong enough to probe deeper? Or will you go home, give up, retreat to your safe little mundane world?" In the parlance of *The Matrix*, she can take the blue pill and none of this will have been real. Or she can take the red pill and discover the truth behind Cardiff and all it holds.[5]

To enter Torchwood, she vanishes down the elevator into a subterranean world. There, Jack forces her to confront her fear, by showing her the Weevil that so shocked her: "It's alien. Look into its eyes.... It was born on a different world. And it's real." Gwen's expression, wide-eyed with shock and wonder, shows how total this transition is: Even an amnesia pill can't erase this encounter from her mind.

Jack finally offers her a job, and Gwen can't resist this chance to explore the hidden world. Now she can never turn back.

On The Path

Torchwood is a world more alien than Gwen imagined, where murders are covered up and false witnesses planted in a total subversion of the police procedures she lives by. They suspend civil liberties by keeping databases of every face in Britain and tracking people through every camera in Wales.

They hoard the bodies of the dead. Gwen protests at one point that her co-workers can't just fake a man's death, but that's exactly what Torchwood does — and now she's part of it. This first assignment "throws Gwen right into the action: alien on the loose, death and disaster, and we see how Gwen finds her feet," explains Russell T. Davies.[6]

When a meteor hits ("Day One"), we see Gwen throwing tools and bantering with Owen Harper, trying to feel like "one of the team" on her first day. "Not sweetheart," she insists. "Gwen. One syllable. Sure you can manage it." The soldiers outside have just called her "little girl," and, despite Jack defending her, she's determined to take her place among the guys and the (at this point) brainy but sexless Toshiko Sato. However, her attempt backfires, as on "the worst first day ever," as Gwen says, her thrown chisel frees a murderous alien, and there's no way to atone for that. Following the rules will no longer protect her.

Reading this psychologically shows a burst of pink, formless gas flitting around the city being unabashedly feminine and seductive ... and killing men. In fact, the alien-occupied victim, Carys Fletcher, seeks out an ex-boyfriend as condescending and callous as the guards who insult Gwen and kills him. Gwen can later be found pinning Owen to the wall, admonishing him for his thoughtless behavior, just before the alien seduces him out of his key card and leaves him naked and humiliated. This alien, released by Gwen from its formless, imprisoning meteor, reflects a feminine side of her, slighted, ignored, and vicious, longing to escape.

At the same time, Gwen finds herself passionately kissing a young woman after the alien pheromones take effect — here is the missing side of herself: affairs and homosexuality and the threat of death, rather than just a cozy night in with boyfriend Rhys. Jean Shinoda Bolen, feminist myth expert, speaks of the need to "know something in our bodies as well as with our mind and hearts" and explains this dimension is out of balance for modern women.[7] We concentrate today on ignoring the messages our bodies give us: demands for food, sleep, relaxation, pleasure, all in favor of control. Here Gwen discovers her body's messages resurfacing with a vengeance.

By the end of her first day, Gwen surrenders herself to the alien cloud completely, offering it her body. While this is, on the surface, a selfless gesture to save Carys, Gwen is also offering the alien a chance to consume her, to unleash this lost feminine presence and eroticism within herself. She doesn't want to be a "good little girl"; she feels ready to be a sexual hellion. However, Jack, representing the more rational part of her personality, intervenes and rescues her. She finds herself thanking him with a kiss: not ready to become an amorphous cloud of sexual climax, but not ready to abandon her first steps of liberation either.

At the same time, repressed Gwen meets far more extreme examples of herself, warning her of what the future may hold. Jack lives at the Torchwood base and Ianto Jones seems a fixture there, popping out from around a corner when anyone needs tea. Later we find he truly is "married to the job," as his cybernetic girlfriend is part of the basement. Toshiko and Owen aren't much better. For happily-in-love Gwen, this is another alien world, but also an indicator of where she's been heading when she leaves Rhys Williams the "special ops widow" at home with the television night after night. "Don't let the job consume you," Jack advises in "Day One," echoing the thoughts Gwen herself is having. "Go home, Gwen Cooper. Eat lasagna. Kiss your boyfriend. Be normal. For me."

Tosh and Owen are seen in the first episode smuggling tech out of the office and exploiting it in their free time, a clear sign that the tech has engulfed every aspect of their beings from Tosh's reading (intellect) to Owen's one-night stands (body). They are Torchwood: thus, they are Gwen's subconscious. In fact, if Ianto is steadiness and stability, each Torchwood operative represents a section of Gwen's personality, frequently squabbling and conflicted. Jack, of course, is the leader, the willpower who makes things happen. Clearly only one drive is lacking and uncontaminated by the tech: heart. Here is the niche Gwen can provide. As Davies explains, "The rest of them are full of the alienness of the world and the technology and the science and the background of it and the mythology of it all. And actually she's there for the people."[8]

When Jack hires her in the premiere episode, he explains he's doing it "because maybe you were right. We could do more to help." Gwen plunges right in, exclaiming, "You've been hidden down here too long, spending so much time with the alien stuff you've lost what it means to be human." "So remind us," says Jack, clearly aware of what they lack ("Day One").

As we find in "They Keep Killing Suzie," Torchwood has a reputation for being callous and leaving a trail of bodies. Only Gwen has a problem with this, linked as she is to the police and the outside world. "These murderers are happening because of Torchwood. So Torchwood has got to do something," Gwen says. "Greeks Bearing Gifts" finds her smiling comfortingly at Tosh, advising her not to give up on emotions because "love suited you." In "Adrift," Gwen reminds Jack of his responsibilities to reunite the families of Rift victims rather than leaving them suffering. She worries about the team as well, chiding Jack for being cruel to Owen and unfeeling toward Suzie: "Did you ever look at Suzie, did you even think what that glove would do to her?" she protests, in "They Keep Killing Suzie." Gwen throws herself into playing conscience and reminding the team what it means to be human in the twenty-first century.

As Gwen opens her heart, her teammates reflect her, striving to unearth their buried emotional sides: Owen falls in love with pilot Diane Holmes, opening himself to more than a shallow affair. When she leaves, he sulks, and then finally releases his rage by fighting with Weevils in a terrifying arena. Ianto reveals the cyberwoman he's hidden away in the darkest area of Torchwood and struggles to resuscitate her. Failing that (rather disastrously), he finally releases her memory and starts an affair with Jack. Toshiko starts "shagging a woman and an alien" in her own homosexual affair, in the episode "Greeks Bearing Gifts." Though she starts the episode as an intensely serious character ("Sometimes I think even that stick up your ass has a stick up its ass," says Owen), she transforms into someone who kisses her lover in public and finally sneaks her into the base. Though she protests that her lover's mind-reading pendant makes her feel "dirty and ashamed" she finds herself exploring beneath people's surfaces into their dark impulses, including her own feelings for Owen. These encounters represent risk, danger, and taboo-breaking, the opposite of the team's burying themselves in work far below the ground. They, like Gwen, are escaping their shells.

Jack and Gwen

The heroine's journey often involves finding her soul-mate, or worse, a choice of several as her impulses conflict. As such, Gwen is torn between Rhys, the sweet kind handsome prince, and Jack, the compelling trickster.

Lovers on the heroine's journey are frequently shape-changers, normal one moment and alien the next. This represents all the shifts in mood and perception that accompany infatuation. "Women complain that men are vague, vacillating, and unable to commit. Men complain that women are moody, flighty, fickle, and unpredictable," observes hero's journey expert Christopher Vogler.[9] More than this, Jack is an alien-born fifty-first century man in disguise, with an unclear agenda to promote. "Jack is dangerous ... sexy ... dark ... enigmatic,"[10] says Julie Gardner, executive producer. Jack maintains his inscrutability by telling his teammates nothing about himself: "Not who he is, not where he's from," as Owen complains in "Day One." They're not even sure of his sexual orientation except that "he'll shag anything that's gorgeous enough" The "Captain Jack Harkness" with which he constantly introduces himself is a false identity. This murkiness, of course, is what makes the shape-shifter compelling — what is Jack's past, who is he? Though unpredictable and unreliable, he is the ultimate animus: "the bundle of positive and negative images of masculinity in a woman's dreams and fantasies," as Vogler puts it.[11] Jack's mercurial nature comes to a head on

Gwen's wedding day: He flirts and leans in to kiss her ... and is an actual alien shape-shifter who usurped Jack's likeness! Gwen's shock at his alien guise shows how unsettled she is with him as a romantic adversary.

Rhys, by contrast, is a transport manager who spends season one completely clueless about Gwen's near-magical job. "I'm excited for you," he says (in "Day One"). "You'll be brilliant." Yet the compliments, like the attention, frequently seem unidirectional. "Am I boring you? Too grand to get over transporters now, are we?" he asks when she tunes out, daydreaming about Torchwood. "He's the only thing she's got that's normal," actress Eve Myles relates.[12] He's adoring, reliable, and domestic, incredibly so. Much of Rhys' time with Gwen appears in shops and around their flat, cooking and watching television. Their first kiss was in a supermarket. "I always worried that you'd just settled for me," he confesses to her in the episode "Adam." Gwen comes to him for comfort, but we see her shutting him out regularly. She lies to him over her affair with Owen and most of their calls involve her "working late." Clearly, as she brushes him off and takes him for granted at every opportunity, she's far too comfortable with Rhys.

Jack's arrival represents these insecurities, the repressed desire for sex and romance rather than tea and hotpot at the kitchen table. Part of her longs for the first kiss, the outrageous flirting, the unpredictability of a new relationship. Jack, once again acting out her innermost desires, obliges her. But they never take it beyond the romantic tension.

Eventually, Beauty comes to realize that her life with the Beast is a romantic fantasy, an impossibility. The beast is varying and inconsistent, a misfit who hasn't yet grown up. While the teen heroine can be swept away by him, as an adult, she craves stability, respectability. Fairytale analyst Joan Gould in her book *Spinning Straw into Gold* explains, "In a sense she outgrows the Beast ... by daylight, she wants a father for her children," someone she can take to parties, someone who will be a stable partner, not a shape-shifting playboy.[13] This is why the Beast transforms into a prince at the end of the tale, so that Beauty can marry him and start a real life with him: "This is what Beauties want — to domesticate the Beast"[14] Hence, Christine chooses Raoul over the Phantom of the Opera, and knights defeat dragons and carry off princesses. Captain Jack cannot transform into a steady prince for Gwen, not without a century or two more of maturity. As actor John Barrowman commented in an interview, if Captain Jack settled down with Gwen, "he'd have to commit completely" to her; this is why he never acts on his feelings for her, because although she would let him flirt with other people, he could "never afford to do anything more."[15] Rhys is "a perfect husband," as Jack finally puts it at her wedding in the episode "Something Borrowed." Loyal, brave, "and best of all he really loves you." Here is

Gwen's chance for a true relationship, with secrecy replaced by trust, and flirtation replaced by love. She journeys off on her honeymoon with only a moment's wistful regret.

Evil Stepmother

Nowhere is Gwen's battle with her inner self more apparent than when she faces Suzie Costello in "They Keep Killing Suzie." Suzie hates Gwen: Gwen has replaced her, from joining her spot on the team to having sexual relations with Owen. Worse, she is more talented with *her* glove, her project. Suzie covets Gwen's place and lifeforce and attempts to steal both over the course of the episode. "She replaced me and now I'm doing the same to her. Isn't that fair?" she asks. Still, she doesn't just want her own life back: she wants to be Gwen, and absorb everything she is. "There's a part of her that's now me," Suzie warns Jack. "I'm the last thing that's left of Gwen Cooper." She's like the jealous old witch-queen in Snow White, killing the upstart young princess so she can be "the fairest of them all." The devouring stepmother "through her jealousy and envy of her daughter's talents and potential freedom tries to imprison her," as Murdock notes.[16] Evil stepmothers of the fairy tales have gone from beauty to crone, fading into obscurity. Soon the daughters will star in dazzling Hollywood weddings, leaving their mothers with only memories of their own romantic triumphs, so long ago. Thus they force their stepdaughters into rags, desperate to outshine them and steal their desirability. These terrible stepmothers want, as Gould says, "to absorb their daughters' youth to make up for what they themselves have been deprived of, or once had and lost."[17] This is Suzie in a sentence.

Gwen has the vitality dead Suzie once possessed, and killing Gwen will lead to her resurrection. Suzie even implements a mass murder to resuscitate herself, like a vampire feeding off corpses. She'll do anything to preserve her own life, no matter how many bodies are required. She is, as Murdock puts it, "The devouring, destroyer aspect of the feminine, who is in the service of the death.[18] In fact, Suzie has arranged to return to life especially to murder her own father. "Bring me her heart and liver so I may feast on them," Snow White's queen commands in the uncensored Grimms. As the episode progresses, she likewise feeds off Gwen, drinking her life-force to reanimate.

Gwen and Suzie, like Harry and Voldemort, Arthur and Mordred, Lyra and Mrs. Coulter, and so many other hero-villain pairs, are inextricably linked. Though Suzie is draining Gwen of life, the invasion goes in both directions: Gwen invades Suzie at the episode's start, walking through all that remains of her, in the form of stored possessions: "That's all we are in the end. A pile of boxes," Tosh says. They explore the room, opening, inspecting, and reading. Finally, Gwen reaches into Suzie completely, dragging her back to life through the glove and binding them into physical symbiosis.

Gwen can use the resurrection glove because she's in tune with feminine power that she's nurtured as the conscience of Torchwood. While male heroes wield swords, heroines are most often associated with clothing, like crowns, rings, slippers, and, you guessed it, gloves. There's Dorothy's silver slippers, Andersen's red shoes, Cinderella's precious footwear, the cloaks of Red Riding Hood and Thousand-Furs, magical gowns, and more. A few Cinderella variants even feature gloves, such as *Phoenix and Ashes*. While swords represent war, the external world, and masculinity (the modern male symbol derives from the spear and shield of Mars), feminine symbols represent the womb and the interior world of the spirit. *Torchwood* conforms with this gender split: Jack and Owen fail with the glove, while Suzie excelled in its use, devoting herself so completely that its power consumed her. The glove relies on compassion and empathy, traditional feminine strengths that Gwen holds in abundance. "Just be yourself," Jack says, and Gwen pours so much of "herself" in that her empathy bonds her to Suzie.

"It's like a rope from my heart to the glove," Gwen explains. This "heart" is the source of feminine power, and why the glove adapts itself so well to empathic women. Of course, the glove alone can't bring Suzie back, just as emotion can't act without knowledge and will (the male, Captain Jack-like side of the partnership). To bring someone to life, the feminine glove and the masculine knife must be united, in a moment all Freudian scholars would recognize. Thus when Jack thrusts the knife into Suzie's stomach and Gwen pulses emotion through the glove, Suzie revives. Gwen, source of life, has "birthed" Suzie, the vampiric death crone.

However vicious Suzie is, she's also Gwen's mentor, whose use of the resurrection glove revealed Torchwood to her in the first place. She has dwelt in the land of the dead, and possesses the arcane knowledge Gwen must absorb to become a wise leader — only by completely surrendering to the unknown can the heroine transcend her existence, and become a leader of her community. "Until the demonic powers of the dark goddess are claimed, there is no strength in the woman to grow from daughter to an adult," comments the author of *Descent to the Goddess: A Way of Initiation for Women*.[19] Indeed, death is a part of existence that must be confronted, not buried or ignored. Gwen seems to sense this as she stays friendly and compliant toward Suzie, understanding on some deep level that Suzie possesses wisdom she will need ahead. Gwen even sneaks Suzie out to see her father, unaware that this sympathy will drag her to the brink of death.

Suzie begins the episode in a white shroud, and then advances to dark clothes that highlight her pale face as she slumps under shadowed lighting. Gwen, by contrast, bustles around in a red top and offers Suzie biscuits in a motherly manner. Her lively nature emphasizes their differences, making Suzie seem even more shadowed. As Gwen drives through the featureless night, a darkly-dressed Suzie slumped beside her, Gwen describes her vision of death as "a white light" and reunion with her beloved Gran, while Suzie rejects this naive "primary school" notion. Again, Gwen clings to life and love while Suzie shadows her, coaxing her to see the darkness lying before them. Fading quickly from Suzie's draining, Gwen asks about the afterlife, and Suzie replies that there was only an enveloping emptiness: "Nothing. Just nothing," she says. "We're just animals howling through the night." Yet her cryptic mention of something moving through the darkness foreshadows Gwen's encounter with Abaddon at the "End of Days," preparing Gwen for her greatest trial.

Suzie guides her unwilling disciple closer to death, forcing Gwen to share her fatal gunshot wound. Gwen bleeds from the head, and then collapses halfway up the pier at the same time as Jack and Owen pull up. As Gwen sinks into death, Suzie revitalizes, until they've completely switched places. At the episode's end, Suzie's abandoned her dark clothing and stands dressed all in white with healthy coloring, fully resurrected. She revels in the daylight, triumphant, with a dark-shrouded Gwen draped over her shoulder. Finally, Gwen slumps to the ground. She has literally journeyed into death, and only Jack sacrificing Suzie can redeem her.

With Suzie's demise, Gwen returns, far wiser. Once the heroine has visited the realm of the dead, she has the wisdom and duality of both worlds, life and death, mundane and magical: Psychologist and author of *Women Who Run With the Wolves*, Clarissa Pinkola Estés writes:

> This is our meditation practice as women, calling back the dead and dismembered aspects of ourselves, calling back the dead and dismembered aspects of life itself. The one who re-creates from that which has died is always a double-sided archetype. The Creation Mother is always the Death Mother and vice versa.[20]

This duality helps Gwen achieve enormous power and become a guardian for those around her.

Taking Charge

Series One culminates with "End of Days," as complete apocalypse descends upon the world. Foreshadowed by her near-murder, Gwen experiences deaths much more frightening than her own: those of both Rhys and Jack. Almost at once she loses both romantic ideals: her shapeshifting Beast and his alter ego, the dull but steady prince. In this moment of lost chances, she realizes whom she's always loved.

Every epic heroine has a moment at which she's completely alone, with no lovers, friends, or support. The Torchwood team surrounds her, but for both deaths, they have no magic solution: Gwen's technical expertise, impulsive passion, and steadiness are all impotent when she's lost both her heart and her spirit. She lashes out in blind fury over Rhys's death and tears down the Rift itself to regain him. Abaddon, the great devourer, ravages the land as a symbol of her fury.

This uncontrolled destroyer is too much, and will vanquish the world if not stopped. Gwen, as seen through her talent with the glove, is empathy and heart personified. Jack has a greater lifeforce than anyone in existence. Together they battle Abaddon the "great devourer," and their antithesis. Gwen tries to protect Jack, but as the hero of *Torchwood*, he sacrifices himself to stop the beast, descending on his own journey into death. Rhys and the orderly world are restored to Gwen; everything returns except the magical trickster Gwen once admired. Below the conscious level, Gwen has chosen and the proper lover returns to life: Rhys, not Jack. Still, this fantasy's death is a loss. Gwen has regained her heart, but not her spirit, perhaps never again. Suzie's guidance has prepared her, however, showing how to harness her empathy and love.

In Beauty and the Beast tales, Beauty returns to find her beloved unconscious. She has caused this, through mistrusting and defying him, through her lack of faith. This moment marks her true loss of innocence: she sees him now, not as frightening and unknowable, but pitiable. She can't love him in the same way ever again: he's like the humbug behind the Great and Powerful Oz's curtain. Still, she wants him restored, cherished nostalgically as an outgrown toy if not lusted after. Thus, the beast of fairytales "lies indoors in a trance, waiting to be roused like a male Sleeping Beauty, while the heroine, burning with her new consciousness, displays an energy as purposeful as any male hero's to save him," as Gould comments in her analysis.[21] At this moment, the heroine's undivided heart blazes stronger than it ever has before. With her decision made, the trickster can be reborn in his new role.

Though Gwen can't fix Jack, she maintains a vigil, telling her friends forcefully that she "wants to sit with him." Days pass; the team grows increasingly concerned for Gwen but she remains faithfully by Jack's side, watching and guarding. At last, Gwen's kiss awakens Jack in a Sleeping Beauty reversal: "As in many stories, the heroine heals and redeems the man, rather than the man rescuing the woman,"[22] Gould notes. Here, she becomes the healing mother symbolically saving her lover from death: As Barrowman puts it, "I think Gwen, by having that spark of life and love and joie de vivre in her, gives him the spark back, and that's what brings Jack back to life."[23]

At the sound of the TARDIS, Jack hurries off to find the Doctor and the answers he's always sought. Thus released from her mentor's guidance, Gwen finds herself managing Torchwood. The season ends with Gwen standing decisively, surrounded by her bewildered team. She is now in charge. Eve Myles comments:

> Gwen goes straight into the leader mode, so she's completely focused: she's direct, she's strong, she's brave. She's still very empathetic 'cause she still is the conscience of the group. She had a very short space to grow up quite a lot. She's not so wide eyed and naive about things, as upset. So she's stronger; she's incredibly brave. She's a match for Jack.[24]

She has become a symbolic adult and Jack's equal, no longer his student. In fact, Gwen is ready to mature in other ways too: when we next see her, she has accepted Rhys' proposal, even though, in goofy fashion, "he had a twinge in his back and had to lie on a settee. That's when he popped the question." ("Kiss Kiss, Bang Bang"). Gwen has progressed beyond the romantic dream and has accepted a man she can marry and grow old with. Moreover, she is ready to grow up herself. As Jack was king of the Torchwood Institute, by the end of series one, Gwen has passed her fearsome initiation and ascended to successor-queen. She is a whole woman now, integrated with all the parts of herself, with the Torchwood team of conflicting impulses now in service to her. Jack can hurry off on his own adventure if he wishes: she can handle Torchwood "just fine" now that the heroine's journey has been achieved.

Gwen's journey is one we all face, starting as a frightened child fleeing the monsters in her shadowed world of nightmares. From there, however, she embraces the knowledge of sensuality, forbidden passion, empathy, and lastly, death and loss, growing into a leader who defends Torchwood through every crisis. She discovers the dormant intuition within, and then embraces it within the darkest caves of her inner self. This is the hero's tale, but one not limited to men and not limited to epic fantasy: it is the irresistible dreams of our deepest psyche, brought into stunning realization.

Notes

1. Maureen Murdock, *The Heroine's Journey* (Boston: Shambhala, 1990), 6.
2. *Ibid.*, 7.

3. "Jack's Back," *Torchwood Declassified, Torchwood—The Complete First Season*, DVD, produced by Russell T. Davies (2007; U.S.: BBC Warner, 2008).
4. "Jack's Back."
5. Andy Wachowski and Larry Wachowski, *The Matrix*, DVD, performed by Keanu Reeves and Laurence Fishburne (1999; Australia: Warner Brothers, 2007).
6. "Bad Day at the Office," *Torchwood Declassified, Torchwood—The Complete First Season*, DVD, produced by Russell T. Davies (2007; U.S.: BBC Warner, 2008).
7. Jean Shinoda Bolen, "Intersection of the Timeless with Time: Where Two Worlds Come Together," Address to Annual ATP Conference, Monterey, Calif., 6 August 1988.
8. "Bad Day at the Office."
9. Christopher Vogler, *The Writer's Journey: Mythic Structure for Writers*, 2d ed. (Studio City, CA: Michael Wiese Productions, 1998), 67.
10. "Jack's Back."
11. Vogler, *The Writer's Journey*, 66.
12. "To the End," *Torchwood Declassified, Torchwood—The Complete First Season*, DVD, produced by Russell T. Davies (2007; U.S.: BBC Warner, 2008).
13. Joan Gould, *Spinning Straw into Gold* (New York: Random House, 2005), 166.
14. Gould, *Spinning Straw into Gold*, 185.
15. John Barrowman, interview by Benjamin Cook, "Fit But You Know It," *Doctor Who Magazine* 398 (2008): 26.
16. Murdock, *The Heroine's Journey*, 19.
17. Gould, *Spinning Straw into Gold*, 15.
18. Murdock, *The Heroine's Journey*, 126.
19. Silvia Brinton Perera, *Descent to the Goddess* (Toronto: Inner City Books, 1981), 41.
20. Clarissa Pinkola Estés, *Women Who Run with the Wolves* (New York: Ballantine Books, 1992), 33.
21. Gould, *Spinning Straw into Gold*, 182.
22. *Ibid.*, 230.
23. "To the End."
24. Eve Myles, "S2 Episode 1: Inside Look 6," *BBC America—Torchwood*, http://www.bbcamerica.com/content/262/index.jsp

NINE

Transgressive Torch Bearers: Who Carries the Confines of Gothic Aesthetics?
DANIEL J. RAWCLIFFE

Although *Torchwood* locates itself in 21st century Cardiff, the series is deeply embedded in longstanding Gothic notions of the uncanny, transgression and excess. Plagued by monsters, alien threats, corrupted technology and mental disintegration, Cardiff is marked as a liminal Gothic environment—that is, a space populated by myriad examples of hybrid figures (extraterrestrials, cyborgs) all of which share a close relation to the uncanny. Embedded within current discussions of the Gothic, this chapter hopes to provide a reading of how Gothic notions of the uncanny permeate the account of identity politics—with a particular focus on sexuality—in the series. Beginning with a brief description of the Gothic genre with a reading of the uncanny as present in the morally ambiguous fairies and Weevils, I move onto a reading of the 21st century science-fiction Gothic heroine, Gwen Cooper, and the 21st century science-fiction Gothic hero, Captain Jack Harkness. With Gwen, meeting her doppelgänger (in the form of Suzie Costello) and having her seemingly inherent virtue violently called into question foregrounds the ways in which the Gothic and the uncanny are used to contain the possible subversiveness which is usually ascribed to the science fiction heroine. Examples of this figure include Ellen Ripley in Ridley Scott's *Alien* (1979) and its sequels; or the more recent embodiment present in Kara "Starbuck" Thrace of Ronald D. Moore's reimagining of *Battlestar Galactica* (NBC, 2004–2009). These women are strong, they possess a strength of character that is emphasized by their location in what is usually an intensely masculine environment. As a consequence of this they are often shown attempting to reconcile notions of traditional feminine identity with a hardened (often seen as masculine) identity. At the same time, the Byronic wanderer Harkness is simultaneously dangerous and inviting — his moral ambiguity linked uncannily to that of such creatures as the Weevils and the fairies — and is able to resist the containment preferred by the Gothic. That is, despite the strength apparent in Gwen Cooper her character is constantly answerable to Captain Jack; his authority is immutable, unquestionable and felt throughout the Torchwood Institute. His masculinity — crucially an omnisexual queer masculinity — enables him to move beyond the confine of the Gothic. This essay concludes that femininity in the series remains controlled by Gothic aesthetics while masculinity is able to draw upon the strengths of the Gothic (particularly its use of the uncanny and liminal sexuality).

The Gothic situates itself from the eighteenth century onwards as a "writing of excess" and this tendency permeates much of the genre's narratives, characters and settings.[1] Early Gothic novels such as Walpole's *Castle of Otranto: A Gothic Story* (1764), Radcliffe's *The Mysteries of Udolpho: A Romance* (1794) and Lewis' *The Monk* (1796) all contain elements of what would later be referred to by critics as full-dress Gothic romances. The full dress Gothic narrative traditionally takes place in a foreign environment and this displacement serves to distance the narrative both physically and metaphorically. Narratives involving blood, sin and sex attained a modicum of acceptance so long as they remained very much in the realm of the distantly exotic. In constructing tales wherein "ornate and convoluted" narratives that gave voice to challenges to Enlightenment discourses,[2] the aforementioned writers gave birth to what is now known as the Gothic.[3] These stories usually contained typical Gothic conventions such as castles, medieval settings, supernatural occurrences, female characters falling prey to the psychological instabilities of patriarchs, and murder. Also inherent in early Gothic writing is the idea of sublime terror present in the natural world. A vast mountain range replete with bleak splendor often formed the backdrop for these stories, adding further resonance to the underlying idea of excess. These elements then, constituted many early Gothic texts; and to a large extent they remain, albeit in other guises, present in its later renditions of the genre. The influences of Gothic excess are visible in the sprawling Overlook hotel of Stephen King's *The Shining* (1980); or the uncanny strength of a teenage girl in Joss Whedon's *Buffy the Vampire Slayer* (20th Century–Fox Television, 1997–2003) and in the unending life of *Torchwood*'s Captain Jack.

The Gothic then is ultimately a genre centered around the concept of mutability; its ability to shift and adapt in order to reflect contemporaneous social trends is partly what has enabled it to remain popular. Since the late nineteenth century, the Gothic has undergone distinct changes in content and focus. Instead of the sublime terror envisaged in the natural world, emphasis centers instead on the terrors that exist within the urban environment. Fred Botting argues that "urban contexts ... provided the loci for mystery and terror"[4]: the city presented a new host of threats and anxieties for the Gothic writer to utilize and explore. So while the eighteenth-century Gothic was pre-occupied with dangerous elements within the realm of the supernatural, the Gothic shifted in the late nineteenth century to a fixation with the potential threats present in the advancements of science. The figure of the ghost and the demon (clearly identifiable as non-human) underwent a transformation — in the nineteenth century we see the figure of the vampire, who is able to cast itself as beguilingly human or frighteningly monstrous. Representing the *fin-de-siècle*[5] pre-occupation with the beast which exists *within* the human body, the body in the nineteenth-century Gothic becomes a site of uncanny destabilization. Due to the emergent figure of the New Woman it is the female body in particular that undergoes this scrutiny and literary exploration. As Kelly Hurley articulates it, the late nineteenth century Gothic "identifies women as entities defined by and entrapped within their bodies, in contrast to the man, who is governed by rationality and [is] capable of transcending the fact of his embodiment."[6] Botting argues that a contemporary Gothic is "an indeterminate zone in which the differences between fantasy and actuality [are] no longer secure."[7] This, then, is the Cardiff of *Torchwood*: a modern Gothic text.

Gwen and Captain Jack (along with the Torchwood team) are Cardiff's respective modern Gothic heroine and hero; fighting together to make sure the malignant and chaotic forces besetting the city are kept at bay. Yet there is a deeper struggle and a darker battle being fought. Gwen is a 21st century science-fiction Gothic heroine; though she is strong of will and body like her forerunner Ellen Ripley of Scott's *Alien*, she is visibly straining against confines laid down for her by the Gothic genre. With its heavy emphasis on Gothic aesthetics *Torchwood* presents Gwen as a half-Ripley; all of her strength is there certainly yet it is hampered by her reliance on the male characters of Rhys, Owen and Captain Jack. Her darker strength is located firmly in the construction of her doppelgänger Suzie Costello whom she must fight against, instead of alongside.

The excessive and gregarious nature of her leader however remains largely liberated from this confine. Captain Jack bestrides everything, from chronological placement (That is, his ability to have existed seemingly throughout time, inhabiting the past, present and future) to sexual orientation; his nature is multiform and multi-sexed. He appears to embody both the heroic defender of the planet and, uncannily, the threat posed to it. By refusing the rigorous categorization which is placed on Gwen he manages to escape her fate of a split identity. At least, this is the case for the majority of the first season. Though he cannot be ascribed a double in the same way that Gwen is, he does encounter beings which mirror his own identity in a number of key aspects. The fairies presented in "Small Worlds" are, like Captain Jack, both beautiful and threatening, unquantifiable and endlessly mutable, as well as eternal. They hold up an uncanny mirror to Captain Jack's identity, rendering him unsure and afraid. This is evidenced particularly in his first encounter with them presented to us in flash backs during "Small Worlds." A mysterious unseen force attacks a troop of soldiers aboard a freight train leaving only a disturbed and frightened looking Captain Jack behind.

"Something out of the corner of the eye"

Sigmund Freud described the uncanny as a sentiment which "belongs to the realm of the frightening"[8]; a peculiar breed of dread that arises when one encounters something familiar made strange or something strange made familiar. Freud describes these instances thus: "an uncanny effect often arises when the boundary between fantasy and reality is blurred ... when a symbol takes on the full function and significance of what it symbolizes."[9] Fiction then provides a fertile playground in which the uncanny is able to manifest itself; seemingly mundane environments based in reality, such as the city of Cardiff, can be fictionalized to include numerous uncanny elements. The dead are resurrected; men in hideous masks are not men at all; aliens walk amongst humans and fairy tales are more real and deadly than one might believe. The uncanny allows for a destabilization of what is deemed normal, acceptable and mundane; the boundaries between good and evil, male and female, heterosexual and homosexual, past and future and human and extraterrestrial are all rendered uncertain and subject to change. *Torchwood* presents a world where Gothic notions of the uncanny occur on a daily basis; nothing is fixed or can be maintained as the truth. This unstable environment, then, allows the aforementioned binaries to be opened up and subjected to interrogation; someone who is initially identified as heterosexual, does not mind sleeping with someone of their own gender, a human is actually an alien in disguise and so on. Each episode of *Torchwood* deals with a situation that inhabits the frightening realm mentioned by Freud because each episode calls into the question our notions of what is normal, acceptable and mundane.

In the premiere episode "Everything Changes," Gwen witnesses the Torchwood team resurrecting a dead body, an event that defies and upsets her notions of what is normal, her encounter with the uncanny is presented later, when she meets her first Weevil. As the encounter occurs almost directly after Gwen experiences a concussion in her line of work as a police officer, the situation is rendered as doubly uncanny as she is unable to rely on her rationality. Approaching what she assumes to be a man wearing an elaborate and "very good" theatrical mask, Gwen's lack of fear in confronting the Weevil indicates her initial thoughts towards it. She sees a man in a mask because in her mind *that* is all it could possibly be. The Weevil's attack on a hospital caretaker signifies a violent example of something uncanny, existing hitherto only "in the depths of the unconscious" attaining a grim reality or actualization of what it represents; thus the mask is not a mask, and what Gwen thinks to be human is nothing of the sort.[10] The Weevils' anthropomorphic appearance underscores the destabilizing effect they have on the Torchwood team's thoughts about what it means to be human. They are clearly monstrous yet retain a vestige of something vaguely human that becomes visible once a person looks in their eyes. According to Punter and Byron the monster, through "difference, whether in appearance or behavior [...] functions to define and construct the politics of the 'normal.'"[11] The Weevils therefore reinforce a prescribed idea of what is the correct way to be human by way of illustrating what is deemed monstrous or Other. *Torchwood* makes constant reference to the idea that looking into the eyes of the Weevil aids in the acceptance of the idea that life exists on other worlds. That is, confronting something that is essentially monstrous manages to instill a sense of normality while at the same time calling it into question.

The Weevils present a visceral example of the uncanny in *Torchwood*; the menacing nature of their appearance is reliant on a feral physicality, one which is heavily gendered as masculine. Their bodies are strictly confined to the brute nature ascribed to the monstrous masculine; they are bodies that are purely physical, that appear to share movements and postures commonly associated with primates. They appear to be unable to transcend this categorization, possessing no language or sophisticated mode of communication. The hybrid shape-shifting bodies presented in the fairies of episode "Small Worlds" on the other hand, manage to achieve this transcendence. Unbound by the laws of the physical world, they can appear as ethereal slyph-like constructs or monstrous wraiths. Their origins are, like those of the Weevils, shrouded in obscurity. Described by Captain Jack as "a glimpse, something out of the corner of the eye, a touch of myth, reality, the spirit world all jumbled together" they pose a seemingly insurmountable threat to the Torchwood team. Their uncanny powers are underscored by the reaction of Captain Jack when confronted with them. These creatures perturb Captain Jack and in viewing them through the lens of Freud's uncanny it is easier to understand why. Their hybrid and supposedly immortal bodies form a mirror of sorts to Captain Jack's own; both cannot die and both refuse categorization in fashions not dissimilar from one another. Jack's undefined sexual orientation and ambiguous moral decisions are comparable to the intentions of the fairies; they are simultaneously ascribed as both benevolent and belligerent. This mutable status is clearly uncanny as it possesses no fixed identity; in being able to choose an appearance that matches their intentions, which are eternally shrouded in mystery, they evade, as Captain Jack has done, the strict categorization of either good or evil.

A Persecuted Femininity

Gwen's relentless curiosity is just one factor that indicates her status as a twenty-first century science-fiction Gothic heroine. "Everything Changes" borrows substantially from the plot of a hard-boiled detective narrative and follows Gwen's attempts to discover the mysterious nature of Torchwood. Witnessing the resurrection of a murder victim is clearly something she should *not* be privy to; yet instead of dismissing what she has seen as imaginary she chooses to pursue her line of enquiry. Despite assertions from her police force work colleagues that she "isn't well" she continues her investigations and manages to gain access to the Hub. Though she has inherited this curiosity from her Gothic foremothers (such as Jane Austen's Catherine Morland and Bram Stoker's Mina Harker), she exhibits a steely opposition to the enigmatic and dangerous Captain Jack that is more redolent of *Alien* science-fiction heroine Ellen Ripley. Botting cites Ripley as different "from earlier figures whose faintings and flight [signaled] the powerlessness of persecuted femininity."[12] Gwen falls into the same category; that of a female character who is portrayed as physically, mentally and emotionally strong. Even when she falls victim to Captain Jack's rape of her memories she is intelligent enough to trip the amnesia and snatch them back, remembering all she has seen of Torchwood. This illustrates her reluctance to accept the male authority of Captain Jack; yet it is a reluctance that will gradually be seen to diminish as the first season progresses. For Gwen, like all characters in *Torchwood*, falls prey to Captain Jack's charms. Though her questioning of his methods continues, it notably diminishes in its intensity; her anger at Captain Jack's varying ambiguous moral decisions gradually gives way to affection and eventually love. Gwen has fallen into the trap like many other Gothic heroines before her; she has fallen under the spell of Captain Jack's Byronic patriarch.

Gwen also stands as the series' primary example of a character who possesses a Gothic doppelgänger. The double's presence in Gothic literature predates Freud's uncanny yet falls neatly into his categorization of what conjures the sentiments associated with encountering one's double. Suzie Costello is presented as Jack's second-in-command, she is his "Gwen before Gwen" (*Torchwood Declassified*). Indeed, Gwen's position working for Torchwood only becomes available when Suzi commits suicide. The act of replacement is one that appears again and again in discussions appertaining to doppelgangers; the two parties in question must constantly vie with one another for their own survival. Yet killing one's doppelgänger is unthinkable to both parties for though "one may want one's double dead ... the death of the double will also be the death of oneself."[13] Though Suzie dies in Episode One, her presence is felt throughout the season in the form of her replacement: Gwen. The resurrection of Suzie in "They Keep Killing Suzie" signals the repetition of this process of replacement by one's double. As Gwen's body is slowly subjected to the same wound suffered by Suzie the similarities between the two women could not be more apparent. It is Gwen who suggests the use of the resurrection glove to bring Suzie back to life; she is the one who appears to have the greatest success in using the glove and she also exhibits an addictive impulse to utilize it. By deliberately pairing these two female characters bodies as not able to co-exist with one another, *Torchwood* appears to be fostering a narrative environment whereby Gwen must constantly be placed in competition, not merely with other female characters but with *herself*.

Suzie's attempt to replace Gwen fails ultimately because Gwen is able to anchor herself in a mundane environment outside of Torchwood. While Suzie's psychological state deteriorates due to her work at Torchwood, Gwen's remains intact due to her relationship with boyfriend Rhys. I would argue that the importance placed on Gwen's reliance upon Rhys for psychological stability undermines the stronger aspects of her character. She is at once anchored and hindered by Rhys in that he allows her to retain a sense of what life was like before the complications of working for Torchwood. She is described as "feisty ... bold ... exciting [and] sexy" (*Torchwood: Declassified*) by the actress who portrays her and while this certainly holds true, it would appear that these qualities only exist due to her relationships with male characters. Though her love for Rhys spurs her to fearless acts of bravery, she only appears to act this way in response to actions from other male characters. Although she is initially repelled by the obnoxious mannerisms of Owen her dislike belies a simmering sexual tension which is finally realized in Episode Six. Gwen switches her romantic allegiance to Owen in order to possess a companion with whom she can share her fantastic experiences. For all her independence, it would seem that Gwen only possesses them when she is seen to be protecting or protesting against a corresponding masculine personality. This is why Gwen is not permitted to exist alongside Suzie; by situating Gwen's vibrant and tenacious approach to life as purely a reaction to the male characters around her, an equality between the two women is denied. Gwen must constantly be in competition with Suzie, that is *herself*, if she is to be regarded as worthy of working alongside Captain Jack.

Bearing Horrible Knowledge

Refusing hetero-normative sexual classification is one of many character traits which mark Captain Jack as a twenty-first-century Gothic science fiction hero. His mysterious origins, questionable actions and immortal status all serve to inscribe him with the power to transcend the confines of the Gothic that holds influence over Gwen. Where Gwen must be seen to be acting alongside or *because of* the male characters around her, Jack frequently acts alone; in this respect he acts the role attributed to other wanderers from earlier Gothic texts. Like Coleridge's Mariner or Shelley's Frankenstein, Jack fills Botting's notion of this figure in Gothic literature as a character who must "roam the borders of social worlds ... [the] bearer of ... horrible knowledge."[14] Indeed Jack is arguably as comparatively alien to the rest of his team as the otherworldly technology and creatures they encounter; with mention of his unknown origins made frequently throughout the first season. A fact which can undoubtedly be read as uncanny. As leader of a team of people who must investigate anything that might pose an extraterrestrial threat, yet simultaneously embodying that threat; it is difficult to ascertain where his loyalties lie at any one time. Much of the speculation surrounding him is focused on his sexual orientation; the team discuss their leader and arrive at varying conclusions. Owen assumes he is gay, Gwen thinks he is straight and Toshiko, in "Day One," appears to provide the best suggestion in that "he'll shag anything as long as it's gorgeous enough." Thus Jack can *and does* attach himself to any character of either gender; this indeterminate yet distinctly omni-sexual queer masculinity permits him certain freedoms which are denied to the characters around him. He flirts with seemingly every life-form he encounters whether it be female, male, alien or human; this being illustrative of transcendent ability to shake off heteronormative stereotypes. The fact that he is also immortal lends him yet another advantage.

Gwen learns Jack cannot die in the first episode of season one, as does her double, Suzie. It is significant that these two women, who will vie with one another for survival later on in the season, are marked from the outset through their shared experience of witnessing Jack's resurrection. In exposing his immortality to them, Jack is permitting them a level of intimacy not afforded to the rest of the team but this privileged knowledge is dangerous. For Jack's transcendence of the heteronormative confines of sexuality, choosing to self-identify as an omni-sexual queer masculinity, coupled with his immortality inscribe him with traits usually associated with the figure of the vampire. Another dangerous character who exists on the peripheries of society, the vampire could also be referred to as queer in that it holds "the open mesh of possibilities" as articulated by Sedgwick, before it.[15] Captain Jack, like the vampire, plays on his mutable status as both predatory and beguiling in order to get what he wants. In coding him as an ostensibly queer character *Torchwood* grants him the opportunity to disregard the confines prescribed to Gwen. The vampire is most successfully exemplified by Stoker's *Dracula*. Like the Count, Jack is a man out of his time; although clad in 1940s military period clothing, suggestive of his belonging to a bygone era he is also clearly shown as possessing links to the future, further problematizing his origins. The Count disturbs those around him through his ambivalent origination from an exotic yet barbaric past inherent in the novel's description of the Transylvanian wilderness. Yet Jack's refusal to be categorized as exclusively from the future *or* the past marks him as even more uncannily disturbing; and also, like the Count, more attractive. Throughout *Torchwood* much is made of how good looking, flirtatious and seductive Jack is and his abnormal immortality and unknown origins, though potentially disturbing, are overlooked.

The more ambivalent and somewhat dangerous aspects of his character are masked by a veneer of kitsch one-liners and occasional camp mannerisms. While not exclusively traits attributed to Jack (as all members of the team are at one point responsible for undermining the seriousness of a disturbing situation with a joke) he is a nexus point from which a lot of the show's humor originates. Royle states that the uncanny, though often terrifying, is "never far from something comic," an argument which is particularly applicable to *Torchwood*.[16] The myriad instances of potentially disturbing occurrences undercut moments afterwards with comedy are all examples of the show's preoccupation of this aspect of the uncanny. That Jack is often the initiator of these moments is significant as it conveniently distracts from the fact that he is also one if not *the* most disturbing character in the show. His cavalier approach to leading the Torchwood team is problematized by the occasional moments of abject seriousness he displays. An example of this is his behavior and reaction to the malevolent fairies of "Small Worlds." For the first time in the series, this episode presents Jack as genuinely frightened and largely devoid of his trademark camp one-liners. Quite simply, he has met his match. While able to transcend the confines of sexual orientation classification and chronological categorization, when faced with the similarly unquantifiable and unpredictable fairies Jack momentarily loses his power. The fairies represent for Jack what Suzie represents for Gwen; namely a recognizable foe who uncannily shares many, if not all, of the traits inherent in the self. His mutability is *their* mutability in representing his equal, they are just as ambivalent and dangerous as he can be and as a consequence, he cannot defeat them.

Conclusion

The confines of the Gothic then affect Captain Jack as well as Gwen but in differing ways. While Gwen must constantly be seen to be struggling against herself by competing with the woman she replaced, continually relying on the male figures of Captain Jack and Rhys to anchor in either the world of the fantastic or the mundane respectively: Captain Jack rejects such strict categorization. In creating a character as strong as Gwen, who must exist in the mutable and multiform shadow of Captain Jack, *Torchwood* places on her the Gothic confines which a 21st century science fiction heroine (Ellen Ripley, for example) would usually avoid. Her purity and virtue are so great that the darker side of her nature must take up residence in another body, namely the body of her doppelgänger Suzie. In embodying a split identity she must then come to rely on reacting against (either protecting or protesting) male characters around her, in order to exhibit the stronger aspects of her character.

Captain Jack, on the other hand, escapes such confinement. As he is ascribed a masculine identity, the Gothic offers him a more liberated pathway than Gwen. This identity is strengthened further by Captain Jack's refusal to adhere to heteronormative categorizations of sexual orientation, or chronological origin. As he is from the past and the future, he is able to be simultaneously everywhere and nowhere. The uncanny ability to appear unfixed and constantly mutable is one he does not share with any other character in the series; allowing for him to lead the Torchwood team fearlessly against whatever they may come up against. His fearlessness is not constant, however, as has been evidenced in his reactions against the uncanny Gothic mirrors posed to him by the similarly multiform and ambiguous fairies. Illustrating that although Captain Jack may carry the brightest torch against the confines of the Gothic he is not free from them entirely; there will always be something out of the corner of his eye, waiting.

Notes

1. Fred Botting, *Gothic: The New Critical Idiom* (London: Routledge, 2002), 1.
2. Enlightenment discourses refers to those tenets held sacred by rationalists in the 18th century onwards, namely those of reason, common sense, investigation via scientific method and natural law.
3. David Punter and Glennis Byron, *The Gothic* (Oxford: Blackwell, 2004), 7.
4. Fred Botting, *Gothic*, 123.
5. Refers to the end of the 19th century. A period when scientific advancements exacerbated fears of what the coming century would bring with it.
6. Kelly Hurley, *The Gothic Body: Sexuality, Materialism and Degeneration at the Fin de siècle* (Cambridge: Cambridge University Press, 1996),119.
7. Fred Botting, *Gothic*, 12.
8. Sigmund Freud, *The Uncanny* (London: Penguin Books, 2003), 123.
9. *Ibid.*, 150.
10. David Punter and Glennis Byron, *The Gothic* (Oxford: Blackwell, 2004), 285.
11. *Ibid.*, 263.
12. Fred Botting, *Gothic*, 165.
13. Nicholas Royle, *The Uncanny* (Manchester: Manchester University Press), 190.
14. Fred Botting, *Gothic*, 98
15. Eve Kosofsky Sedgwick. *Epistemology of the Closet* (Berkeley: University of California Press, 2008), 8.
16. Nicholas Royle, *The Uncanny*, 2.

Ten

The Alien Woman: Othering and the Oriental

Carrie Dunn

The idea of The Other stems from philosopher and critic G.W.F. Hegel. He argued in *The Phenomenology of Spirit* that the existence of The Other makes you aware of yourself— knowing that there is an Other out there makes you feel alienated from it and want to resolve that separateness. This idea has unsurprisingly been adopted by feminist critics, who use it as symbolic of man's relationship with woman — indeed, Simone de Beauvoir, who did the most to appropriate this concept, uses the quote of "each consciousness pursues the death of the other" in the preface to her novel *She Came To Stay*; and equally unsurprisingly her long-term partner and collaborator Sartre also uses it.[1]

The feminist argument is that the sex and gender system operates by interpreting difference between genders as the difference between the Self and the Other. De Beauvoir explains that man is the subject and woman is the Other; this is not just because it is what men would like to believe, but it is the psychic structure of gender. Femininity is learnt as a way of constructing the self as an object.[2] This binary division isn't simply an observation of material differences; it regulates behavior.[3] Male is the default. The difference presented by the female, the Other gender, disrupts the status quo, and if the threat of the Other is not subdued, it leads to confusion and anger for males. As Stanley and Wise explain, "Women are bound to be experienced as threatening, are bound to be reacted to with frequent violence and even more frequent scorn, puzzlement and dismissal. Our very existence suggests that reality isn't as it is said to be."[4] Where two sexes co-exist in an unequal power dynamic, the female is coded as Other, as dangerous, as confusing, as abject, as threatening, and the male cannot help but bring this to her attention over and over again by reiterating her disturbing difference.

In the world of *Torchwood*, one might expect "human" to be the default and "alien" to be the Other (that is, literal "alien," as in a life form from another planet). However, the difference of the female still makes its presence felt. At Torchwood Three, three women (Gwen, Toshiko and Suzie) are members of the Torchwood team; Ianto has a girlfriend, Lisa; Owen had a fiancée, Katie. Alien life-forms are frequently gendered as female — the Weevil in the hub basement is called "Janet"; Carys seeks life energy through orgasm ("Day One"); Mary manipulates and murders to get her transporter back ("Greeks Bearing Gifts"), to name but a few. Women are continually presented as physically Other and sexually rapacious, or invaded by the Other (usually an alien or alien technology), making them abject and disturbing to the "normal," "healthy" male onlooker.

Here I will examine three notable case studies of exceptionally Othered women in Torchwood — Lisa, the cyberwoman; Martha, whose DNA has been altered; and Gwen, who is impregnated by a shapeshifter. Though all three are Other to begin with by virtue of their femaleness, their physical difference is augmented by invasion, both by alien and by human males.

In "Cyberwoman," we learn that Ianto has been hiding his girlfriend Lisa in the basement, and no wonder, because she's part human, part cyberwoman. She's still female and highly sexualized in her appearance, even with her cybernetic body, with her midriff exposed and her breasts and genitalia covered in a metal bikini. Significantly, this Othered female is also black, making her difference doubly obvious in comparison to the all-white Torchwood men.

Ianto invites a scientist, Dr. Tanisaki, to inspect her. (Dr. Tanisaki's very unusual specialist knowledge of cybermen combined with his apparent Japanese heritage makes him somewhat Other as well, though as his role in this episode is rather truncated there isn't a great deal of evidence to support this argument.) Ianto claims to have done the best he could to keep her alive, by wiring her up to a plethora of machines and feeds. As Lisa lies unconscious, the scientist begins to assess her, and expresses his delight in working with "anything like this." Ianto corrects him — "Anyone." He explains: "They started upgrading whole bodies instead of transplanting brains, using Earth technology. Lisa was halfway through the process when the machinery shut down."

The scientist is not interested in Ianto's experience of pulling Lisa out of the wreckage, because this is no longer a human love story; it is deviant. Some parts of Lisa are augmented, some are still human, but that is irrelevant because now she is no longer entirely human she is abject and Other. He feels free to touch the "bare flesh" by which he is enthralled, and Ianto does not stop him, because the body of the Other is sexed and sexualized and is open to all. Though it is she who has the knowledge to instruct Ianto on how to operate the cybernetic unit, Dr. Tanisaki tells Ianto that he wants to ask her some questions. When the scientist talks to Lisa, he refers to "your friend, Mr. Jones." The human love affair, which he evidently knows about, is not acknowledged.

Dr. Tanisaki operates on her and frees her from relying on the machines to breathe. Her independent respiration makes her "alive," according to her and Ianto. It is at this point, after she and Ianto have established that she is "alive" and fully human again, that she begins to attack, converting her victims and in the process Othering them too, promising to make them strong. Dr. Tanisaki is unsuccessfully Othered, though; he is killed rather than made into a cyberman (and again, if he was Othered to begin with because of his Japanese heritage combined with his non–Torchwood outsider status, perhaps it is no wonder that this death is categorized as unimportant by the narrative and is then glossed over). When Lisa seeks to convert Gwen, Jack stops her, and when he realizes she is female, his shock and disgust at her body's abjectness and her non-feminine behavior is made explicit: "You're a woman!" Jack goes on to refer to her as "a thing," and Ianto responds angrily, telling them, "She's my girlfriend!" Jack tells him there is no cure—"Those who are converted stay that way." There is no escape from Otherness. Ianto tries to convince Jack otherwise: "The conversion was never completed!" Jack will not listen: "There is no turning back for her now." Ianto's expressions of love for her are irrelevant.

When Lisa surveys herself, she recognizes that she is abject. "I am disgusting ... I am wrong." Prior to her death she is left to be consumed by a pterodactyl, but is rescued by Ianto's need to consume pizza—she puts her brain into the pizza delivery girl's body, leaving a trail of blood around the building. Her blood-spattered cybernized body remains on the floor, while the pizza delivery girl's head wound is loosely stitched, with blood trickling from the sutures. The abjectness and the Otherness must both be stopped, and the Torchwood team combine to shoot her en masse. She is invaded by their bullets, and thus her threat is curtailed.

Though Martha is not a permanent member of the Torchwood team, she joins them for three episodes in the second season. Immediately, her femaleness and her Otherness begin to be marked out (and again the fact that she is a black woman is significant in her construction as Other). In the season two episode "Reset" she is announced by Ianto as a "VIP visitor," and though Jack doesn't accord her the title of "Doctor" (and instead calls her "Miss," in a rather old-fashioned, patronizing way), he welcomes her into the Torchwood base. When Jack discovers that Martha is now theoretically his superior, he makes a joke out of it, calling her "Ma'am," though he obviously recognizes her abilities, hence allowing her to take over a post-mortem that Owen had started, and declaring that everyone owes her a debt for saving the world. Indeed, throughout the episode, Jack lauds her brilliance and bravery. These qualities in a woman are clearly so unusual that they need to be remarked upon on a regular basis lest anyone forget that she is special.

The team find out that there are a series of attacks, where victims are attacked with hypodermic needles, injected with ammonium hydroxide, and have their medical records wiped. Their investigation leads to the Pharm, a medical research center that uses people with long-term incurable medical conditions for experiments, inserting alien "mayfly" larvae into their bodies to incubate.

Jack agrees to send Martha in undercover as a volunteer, Samantha, and the team kit her up for her industrial espionage, beginning with contact lenses. Martha objects that she doesn't need them, but once she puts them in, she cries, "Oh, I'm a camera!" The lenses enable the team to see what she is seeing—but they have also turned her into a host unit for alien technology.

Inside the medical research center, Martha has blood samples taken from her, and she meets Professor Aaron Copley, the institute director. She lies that she has previously had hepatitis, and this convinces him to enroll her on the clinical trial program. She is allocated quarters, but chooses to explore the compound instead, at which point a fully grown mayfly breaks out. In the ensuing chaos, Martha loses her contact lenses, is drugged, and tied to a couch in one of the labs. "We've analysed your test results," says Copley. "You really are something special."

We learn that Martha's lymphocytes are "quite extraordinary," and Copley's assistant tells her, "Your lymphocytes and God knows what other cells have mutated." Though they have seen such cases in alien life forms before, they have never seen it in humans. "We've dealt with aliens before, but we have never come across something as exotic as you—a human being who's travelled in time and space," says Copley. Though Martha's experiences may indeed be extraordinary, the choice of the word "exotic" is significant—the black woman is out of the ordinary, exciting, foreign.

As Copley experiments on Martha, Torchwood break into the compound to rescue her, and the professor informs Jack and Owen that she is the only trial subject ever to survive the larval stage. We see the mayfly moving in Martha's abdomen, and Owen uses the alien "singularity scalpel" to kill it and save her. Contrary to appearances, Martha isn't completely human. She isn't like other women, because of her brilliance and bravery. Aliens don't scare her; only an alien invasion of her body can endanger her, and only alien technology can keep her safe and then rescue her. The pattern repeats itself in the following episode when Martha is aged by nearly 60 years as Death attacks her through the resurrection glove.

As the human heart of the Torchwood team, it might not be expected that Gwen is Othered at all, but in "Something Borrowed" she is attacked by a shape-shifter prior to her bachelorette night. Waking up on her wedding morning, she is full-term pregnant, having been inseminated through the bite of the alien. Usually the pregnant woman is caught in a dichotomy: she is at once highly sexualized, as she is displaying evidence of her sexual activity, and also sexually unavailable, as she has been claimed and impregnated by one man already, and is now no longer a "woman" but a "mother," preparing to give birth to the sentient being she is carrying inside her. Either way, she is marked as Other. Gwen is doubly Other now because she has been appropriated by aliens to host their offspring.

It is the mother-shape-shifter who goes on a rampage to reclaim her child, invading Gwen and Rhys's wedding, seducing and killing selected guests — and again this is Othered, non-feminine behavior. She is in a place that she has not been invited to be in, she is highly sexualized, she is violent and murderous, and when she is wounded, her blood is black and abject — even more so than red blood would be. Despite this, her motive is her maternal instinct, and she uses that knowledge throughout her quest, taking Gwen's mother hostage in an effort to blackmail Gwen and the team, and telling her, "The bond between mother and child is a wonderful thing." Owen concludes, "Some mother instinct or something is making that cow unstoppable."

Owen's plan to extract the fetus from Gwen centers on the use of the singularity scalpel — again, just as he did with Martha, using alien technology to save her from the alien invasion. In the end, responsibility for unOthering her lies with her new husband Rhys, who uses the scalpel to rid her of the unwanted alien fetus and return her to her "normal" state. (Bearing in mind Gwen's desire to have her wedding and remain pregnant until after the ceremony, her demands to abort the fetus as soon as possible, and her reliance on the men around her — Jack, Owen and Rhys — to take action, there is certainly analysis to be done here on the issue of a woman's right to control her own reproduction.)

Tosh is ostensibly the most unOthered major female character in the show. Her lack of romantic relationship and her love of mathematics may be mocked on occasion, as at the end of "Adam," where she reminisces over her unhappy younger years, but she is never shown as not-fully-human. Ianto may call her "warped on the inside" when she formulates her plan to use the corpse of a hitman to get into his employers' headquarters, but he does not really mean that she is deranged — it is another acknowledgement of her ingenuity ("Reset").

This lack of obvious Othering may well be because as a woman of Japanese heritage, she is already Othered. Tosh fits into Edward Said's category of "Oriental"— she is a cipher of exotic appearance, constructed by Western culture. Said theorizes that "Orientalism" is a Western way of coming to terms with "the Orient" that is based on the perception of those countries as "special" and "different," and that is certainly how Tosh is presented.[5]

Her Japanese heritage is referred to as her distinguishing feature on several occasions — for example, by Mr. Parker, who wishes that "the lovely Japanese girl" had been sent to see him rather than Owen, and also comments on her legs ("A Day in the Death"); and by Rhys's mother, who calls her "that Japanese girl" ("Something Borrowed"). As a technology expert, she is a cliché of the Orient — studious, hardworking, scientific. There is no need for any further Othering — she is already an outsider, and she doesn't need to be invaded by aliens because as a woman of the Orient her body is already colonized. As a foreigner, Kristevan theory would argue that she is disturbing and abject simply by her presence. "A nation-state constitutes its own boundaries by excluding what is Other. But insofar as the other (someone who constitutes/threatens identity) resides within the nation-state, the foreign object becomes the foreign abject. The foreigner must be abjected, if not physically, then psychically."[6] In "Fragments" we see that she has been appropriated by Jack — he has reclaimed her from jail, demanded her loyalty, and holds total authority over her, and it is a demonstration of Said's words: Orientalism is "a Western style for dominating, restructuring, and having authority over the Orient."[7]

Seeing as the women of Torchwood are so obviously Othered, it is worth assessing whether or not men get equal treatment. Certainly on a cursory assessment it seems that men can indeed be made not-human, but on closer examination it is not so much an experience of alienation, but an upgrade of their humanity to become super-human.

During "Combat," Owen is shown to have no fear of death, putting himself in a cage with an enraged Weevil and happy to face death. The closing shots show that he also has some kind of power over the Weevils; in the hub, visiting the two captives, he responds to their growling by baring his teeth and hissing at them, scaring them so much that they retreat and cower.

His Weevil tendencies remain subdued until the middle of the second season, when he is shot dead by Copley at the end of "Reset." Jack chooses to use a resurrection glove in "Dead Man Walking" to bring Owen back, believing that it will work for a couple of minutes. Owen is shocked, frightened and angry when he learns that he died and he's been brought back for what he sees as pointless, insignificant chatter. After the two minutes are up, the team hear him flatline again, but then he sits up. He examines himself and finds he has no pulse. Gwen realizes that Susie survived when she drained energy from her; but it seems that Owen is not draining energy from Jack. Martha's examination concludes that energy is emanating through his body and changing his chemical composition. In other words, he's neither alive nor dead, human nor alien. When he goes into Cardiff, he visits a bar, and after a woman makes a pass at him, he realizes that because of his lack of blood flow he's unable to get an erection — and in a world as highly sexualized as Torchwood's, and Owen's in particular, a lack of capacity to have sex inevitably makes him Other.

Yet we see time and again that Owen's Otherness proves useful to the team. Being part-Weevil, he subdues the gang of creatures looking to attack Jack for stealing the resurrection glove, and demonstrates his ability again back at the base — "I'm king of the Weevils. Or the Weevil Messiah. Either way, it ain't good" ("Dead Man Walking"). Later, he fights and defeats the shadowy, skeletal figure of Death, concluding that he has nothing left to lose — "What else can you do to the dead?" He enters Mr. Parker's home because his lack of life signs mean he can sneak in undetected ("A Day in the Death"). His eventual destruction ("Exit Wounds") comes when he is the only person who can run through Cardiff to the central server building and thus save the city and remain unmolested by Weevils.

Jack's apparent immortality is never a disadvantage for Torchwood. Though he too has many time-traveling exploits to speak of, no changes in his DNA are ever picked up, nor is he subjected to any kind of experimentation, unlike Martha. When attackers attempt to kill Jack, he comes back to life — and according to the captioning this has happened 1,392 times before the penultimate episode of season two ("Fragments"). We have already seen him die and come back to life on several occasions, and this episode shows us that his immortality brought him to the notice of Torchwood in the 19th century. At other points, Captain John pushes Jack off a building and severs his spine ("Kiss Kiss, Bang Bang") and murders him with two machine guns and he is still resurrected ("Exit Wounds").

In a world where nothing is what it might initially seem, surprise is inevitable. Torchwood's headquarters appear on the surface to be a sculpture, but underneath it is a buzzing hub of secret, covert operations. Similarly, *Torchwood* appears on the surface to be a very 21st-century sci-fi series — indeed, Jack's voiceover reminds us of its modernity at the start of every episode — but underneath its sexual politics remain very conservative. Where men are the norm, women are Other; where men's desire is the norm, women's sexuality is unfettered and dangerous; where men can be enhanced, women are endangered.

Notes

1. Jean-Paul Sartre, translated by David Pellauer, *Notebooks for an Ethics* (Chicago: University Press, 1992), 428.
2. Joseph A. Boone and Michael Cadden, *Engendering Men: The Question of Male Feminist Criticism* (London: Routledge, 1990), 191.
3. Judith Butler, *Bodies That Matter* (London: Routledge, 1993). 1.
4. Liz Stanley and Sue Wise, *Breaking Out Again: Feminist Ontology and Epistemology* (London: Routledge, 1993), 146.
5. Edward Said, *Orientalism* (London: Routledge and Kegan Paul, 1978), 1.
6. Natalie McAfee, "Abject Strangers: Toward an Ethics of Respect," in Kelly Oliver, ed., *Ethics, Politics and Difference in Julia Kristeva's Writing* (London: Routledge, 1993), 124.
7. Edward Said, *Orientalism*, 3.

Eleven

Outside the Heroic Paradigm
Tom Powers

"He who is too busy doing good finds no time to be good."[1]

"Don't try to be a great man — just be a man — and let history make its own judgments."[2]

According to the online news site *Digital Spy*, when Russell T. Davies was developing the idea of *Torchwood*, he wanted to create a post-watershed BBC science-fiction series that could serve as a British cousin to such American genre television shows as *Buffy the Vampire Slayer* (20th Century–Fox Television, 1997–2003) and *Angel* (20th Century–Fox Television, 1999–2004).[3] Both series, indeed, are successful in that they present realistic, flawed characters, initially antiheroes, who serve as viewer surrogates as we witness their struggles to overcome personal flaws and redeem themselves as true heroes. British genre TV is likewise replete with examples of imperfect heroes. To cite several notable iterations, we can look at Arthur Dent in the six-part *Hitchhiker's Guide to the Galaxy* (BBC, 1981). After the Earth is destroyed by the Vogans to make way for an interplanetary highway, the everyman Dent is forced to embark on a personal journey to discover the mysteries of creation and his place in the greater schema. On a similar trajectory is the underachieving Dave Lister in *Red Dwarf* (BBC, 1988–2009), as he associates with a motley crew, which includes a hologram of his dead bunkmate and a humanoid cat, as he tries to find Earth six million years in the future. Perhaps the best iteration of the damaged hero, however, is found in the sociopathic Kerr Avon of *Blake's 7* (BBC, 1978–1981), as he repeatedly struggles between the extremes of being loyal to his quest to defeat the fascist Federation and to a person equally dear to his heart — himself.

To place his unique spin on this well-tested antiheroic formula with *Torchwood*, Davies ups the ante on the sexual politics and offers us male characters who are not instantly likeable in the form of Captain Jack Harkness, Dr. Owen Harper, Ianto Jones, Rhys Williams and Captain John.

Unlike modern *Doctor Who*, from which it is anagrammatically and spiritually derived, *Torchwood* thus repeatedly promotes the theme that its heroically reluctant male leads must pass through an extended filtering process in the viewers' eyes before they can be perceived as selfless protagonists. This chapter, then, will explore how *Torchwood* echoes and refines the tropes of the antihero.[4]

In addition to acknowledging classic British sci-fi TV antiheroes, we can look at the example of the Marvel Comics antihero Wolverine in order to better understand the Torchwood team. In his initial depiction as a member of the new team of X-Men introduced in *Giant-Size X-Men #1*,[5] Wolverine is a mysterious mutant who was formerly known as Weapon X when he worked for the Canadian government. Occasionally reverting to his feral, berserker mode when under extreme attack, Wolverine is not against maiming and killing his enemies. To rationalize his existence, Wolverine famously states in the first issue of his original limited series, "I'm the best at what I do, but what I do best isn't very nice."[6] In a similar fashion, Jack, at the coda to "Sleeper," remarks, "We keep on doing what we do."

What Torchwood must do is defend the Earth from the dangers of the Rift, even if it requires taking extreme measures against alien threats. They also procure alien technology either through salvaging operations or taking it from their bested otherworldly opponents. Whether this is fair game is probably best left to the domain of an intergalactic court to decide, but we can agree that their actions are aggressive and militant at the very least.[7] Allusions to Black Ops groups, CIA, MI5 and sundry other secret military operations can also be applied at this moment. Yet, if members of these espionage organizations were questioned for their behavior, they, like the members of Torchwood, would defend their deeds as a necessary evil for the greater good of their respective nations.

The Immortal Captain Jack: He Who Has Both Won and Lost

But what type of man is this Captain Jack who has assumed leadership of such an extreme, cavalier scientific, ersatz military organization? Regarding Jack's true nature, we must examine the history of the man himself until he assumes leadership of the twenty-first century version of Torchwood. If we start with his name, Captain Jack Harkness, we have a man whose title evokes images of a heroic military officer. Unfortunately, the name is borrowed from a dead man, and the Jack we know, whatever his true forename, is a character with a shady past. Jack does reveal in the *Doctor Who* episode

"The Empty Child"[8] that he is a former member of the Time Agency, which operates from the fifty-first century. Whether this agency is at its core bureaucratic (i.e., hopelessly inefficient) or simply corrupt is fertile ground for future episodic, or media spin-off, exposition. What we can surmise, however, is that this Time Agency is unable to police their former members since both Jack and Captain John roam freely through the time stream. Notwithstanding the true nature of this organization, we know that Jack left its ranks to pursue his own selfish objectives — an act that is definitely not heroic.

Perhaps then it is only appropriate that the rebellious Ninth Doctor is the one who sets a higher heroic standard for Jack. After all, this is the same Doctor who has become a better Time Lord as a result of the humanizing influences of his numerous companions over the years, so is fitting that he passes this lesson onto Jack.[9] In season one of the revitalized *Doctor Who*, we watch Captain Jack's successful metamorphosis from charming rogue Time Agent to selfless hero in his five-episode character arc that spans "The Empty Child" to "The Parting of the Ways."[10] The most telling line of this dramatic transformation occurs when Jack, about to embark on defending the Game Station from the attacking Daleks, tells the Doctor, "Wish I'd never met you, Doctor. I was much better off as a coward."[11]

Jack's subsequent death via Dalek extermination closes the book on this chapter of his life, and a more complicated one begins once the time-vortex-charged Rose Tyler resurrects him and inadvertently grants him eternal life. The next time we see Jack, in the beginning of "Everything Changes," his Torchwood team is investigating a series of stabbings. With the use of the Resurrection Gauntlet, they are able to temporarily resuscitate John Tucker, the newest deceased victim. However, while Toshiko, Owen and Suzie are trying to gather information leading to the identity of John's killer, Jack takes the last thirty seconds of the man's extended life to ask him, "Tell me: what was it like when you died? What did you see?" Obviously, Jack is not exactly being objective in this situation, and his line of questioning is entirely subjective and thereby selfish. The rest of the team clearly respects him, but his flawed behavior categorically posits him once more as an antihero. At the same time, as the episode progresses, he more or less seems like his former upbeat self, particularly when Gwen remarks, "I'm getting tired of following you," and he cockily retorts, "No you're not, and you never will."

The rest of the series, however, charts Jack's descent into personal despair and confusion. Immortality for Jack then, to borrow from the mouth of the great, wise Time Lord Rassilon in the *Doctor Who* story "The Five Doctors," is an example of "He who wins shall lose,"[12] meaning Jack has achieved what many a mortal and megalomaniac desire — eternal life — but he is not the least satisfied with his fate. In fact, it is quite telling when Jack confesses to Gwen at the conclusion of "Cyberwoman" that he was excited to believe he was in danger of not resurrecting while the cybernetic Lisa Hallett was electrocuting him to the extent that he briefly felt that he was "so alive." In other words, Jack is more or less admitting he has a death wish, which is not the healthiest trait for a leader to possess, most especially one who is responsible for the lives of his teammates. By extension, Jack is also the protector of Cardiff, and the entire Earth itself, depending on the severity of the alien-threat-of-the-week.

At the same time, Jack achieves Torchwood's objective of protecting the Earth, with his immortality helping him to defeat the demon Abaddon in the season one finale "End of Days." He even finds closure of a sort when he learns the truth of his immortal existence during his adventures with the Tenth Doctor in the Master-trilogy episode arc of *Doctor Who* series three.[13] But, once more, another chapter in the novel that is his journey to becoming a complete hero awaits Jack. Despite his success at reestablishing himself as the Torchwood team leader after regaining his estranged teammates' trust in "Kiss Kiss, Bang Bang," Jack struggles with a long-dormant inner demon in season two — the guilt he feels over being instrumental in losing his brother Gray to the mysterious sadistic aliens who attacked the Boeshane Peninsula during their childhood.

Before we return to Jack's ongoing quest for self-harmony, however, we should take the opportunity to look at how he affects the people around him.

The Antiheroic Value of Ex-Wives, Eye-Candy and Future Husbands

Exploding onto the Cardiff scene in Torchwood season two as a psychotic, yet sexy, killer, Captain John Hart, played *by Buffy the Vampire Slayer* and *Angel* alum James Marsters, heralds the more upbeat, action-oriented vibe of the show's sophomore season.[14] John, while ostensibly villainous, is a substantially complex character, which allows him to skirt the edges of being categorized as an antihero. In his very first scene, he rescues a man being attacked by another on a rooftop. However, in the midst of this heroic act, he takes glee in hurling the attacker off the building to his death. At this moment, we may believe John to be a vigilante-type antihero spun from the same cloth as *Dirty Harry* and *The Punisher*. We soon learn, nonetheless, that John's decision to travel to the past is twofold: to retrieve three valuable canisters with Torchwood's unwitting assistance and to attempt to win Jack back as his partner-in-crime and lover. To further complicate matters, John and Jack's past relationship is revealed to be substantially more personal when

John reminds the omnisexual Jack they were once virtually married, with John playing the role of "wife," while they were trapped together in a two-week time loop that amounted to five years' time. John, thus, already a vigilante and rogue, also assumes the mantle of the bitter spouse who wants some sort of revenge against his former "husband."

After successfully "killing" Jack as a means of his vengeance and incapacitating Gwen, Owen, and Toshiko while they are looking for the three canisters, John gives Ianto the chance to go rescue his suffering teammates. Ianto, despite the fact that John is holding him at gunpoint, angrily rails at his tormentor, "Why are you doing this?" to which John poetically replies, "What a cosmic joke, Eye-Candy, an accident of chemicals and evolution, the jokes, the sex, just to cover the fact that nothing means anything, and the only consolation is money!" John obviously is a nihilist, but, underneath this faithless exterior, he betrays the fact that he has hope in others, particularly in Ianto, to be heroic and successfully "save the day." Even more remarkable is the fact that John easily could have killed the entire Torchwood team and run off with the canisters, yet he chose not to do so, proving that a vestige of a compassionate human being dwells within him. For John, then, this flicker of human decency is his personal "character flaw" that precludes him from being a complete villain and consequently places him on the periphery of the ranks of the antihero.

Captain John may be a psychotic killer in "Kiss Kiss, Bang Bang," but his right to redemption is not without precedent in the sci-fi genre. If we were to write him off as irredeemable, then we may as well never give Han Solo a chance to become a General in the Rebellion. After all, the selfish, money-motivated smuggler does shoot the bounty hunter Greedo in cold blood in the original version of *Star Wars: A New Hope*. We can also cite the example of the first Doctor who is ready to bash in an unconscious caveman's brains in "An Unearthly Child"[15] before his companion Ian Chesterton stops him. Where would the universe be without *Doctor Who*, or by extension, *Torchwood*, if the viewing audience of 1963 did not give the antihero First Doctor the chance to prove he can grow into a true hero? John, in spite of his murderous past, delivers on his character's potential to redeem himself in "Exit Wounds" as we behold a man who puts his romantic grievances against his former lover aside to assist Jack in overcoming the troubled, homicidal Gray.

As for Ianto, he essentially serves as the Torchwood team's butler in season one. Simultaneously, he is fiercely loyal to his teammates, dependable and a good muscle in a fight. The only time he jeopardizes this stable relationship with Torchwood is in "Cyberwoman," when he endangers everyone trapped inside the Hub due to his almost deranged effort to find a way to undo the partial cybernization of his girlfriend, Lisa Hallett. After the team rightfully criticizes Ianto for this decision, he retorts, "Like you care; I clean up your shit no questions asked — just the way you like it!" Ianto definitely points out the truth that he serves as the team's emotional and physical janitor, but he is also admitting that he is aware of his station within the Torchwood ranks and chooses to stay with them.

Nevertheless, since this memorable episode depicts Ianto in an antiheroic light, it is almost as if his subsequent actions on the show serve as a means of atonement for the deaths Lisa causes. Even Jack often relegates him to the role of convenient lover, so it is only during the times when Ianto puts his life on the line during field missions in season two do we suspect he has the potential to become a bona-fide hero.

While Ianto's characterization remains rather static after "Cyberwoman," the evolution of another loyal male character, Rhys, is more fascinating. Gwen's boyfriend Rhys, initially a peripheral character in that he firmly grounds Gwen in a domestic setting distinct from the fantastic world of Torchwood, is barely likeable. After all, Gwen is an eminently likeable character on account of her being sweet, brave, and ever supportive of her teammates. Case in point: when we witness Rhys interrupting the dramatic tension of the narrative in "Cyberwoman," with his mundane drunken phone call to Gwen as she's threatened by the cybernized Lisa, we are frustrated that his petty need for her to tape one of his favorite shows is endangering our beloved heroine. The fact that in our own lives we are trying our best not to miss any new episode of *Torchwood* is not likely to be crossing our minds at the moment. No, we want Gwen out of danger, and we certainly do not wish to hear Rhys' inebriated whining, even if it were to occur at a slower link in the chain of the episode's narrative.

Ultimately, it is a pleasant surprise to us when Rhys evolves into a proactive Everyman hero over the course of season two. The episode, then, that most dramatically depicts Rhys' metamorphosis into a hero truly worthy of being Gwen's husband is "Meat," which propels him to the narrative forefront. In the episode, Rhys takes the initiative to investigate why Harris and Harris, a meat-packing plant to whom his business, Harwood's Haulage, supplies lorries is being investigated by the police (in actuality, Torchwood). He even goes as far as to convince the Harris and Harris managers that he wants in on the shady deal so he can help Torchwood infiltrate the operation. Literally taking a bullet meant for Gwen during the episode's climatic battle scene in the meat-packing plant, Rhys completes the circuit of convincing us he is worthy of her. Therefore it is fitting that Gwen defends her decision not to administer an amnesia pill to her fiancée when she screams at her teammates: "What he did today was so brave, braver than any of us because we signed up for this, but he didn't! He did it because he loves me! I won't take that away from him! I won't! And if that means I have to quit, or you ret-con me — fine. Fine!" Certainly, Gwen, to the point where she is ready to resign from Torchwood, shows her teammates that, as much as they repeatedly put their lives on the line, they all are bound by their shared common oath to their jobs, while, Rhys, a simple trucking manager, rises to the occasion of being heroic without being obligated to anyone or anything except for his own conscience — the true hallmark of a hero.

The True Heroes or Torchwood?

Torchwood fans can probably agree that Gwen Cooper and Toshiko Sato, for the most part, are strong characters who are presented in a positive light by both the show's writers and the actors themselves.[16] When Gwen officially joins the Torchwood team in "Day One," she instantly humanizes the team by making them see the alien-possessed Carys Fletcher as a person with a life of her own, not as a threat to humanity that must be eliminated. Toshiko, in turn, empowered from the sense of feminine solidarity her teammate grants her to honestly express herself to her headstrong male teammates, comes into her own in a telling scene in "Combat." After she and Jack release a captive Weevil and watch the men whom they have been following attack and abduct the creature, the shaken Toshiko asks Jack, "Just so I know where we stand: we would never deliberately put a human being through that, but Weevils are fair game? Is that right?" Jack's subsequent sad reply of "We need to follow them" barely covers his dubious decision to endanger the Weevil. From this scene, moreover, we can qualify the fundamental difference between Toshiko and Jack. Whereas Toshiko would never directly endanger a life, no matter what its savage state, Jack would, in order to serve the greater good. We could, of course, attribute this division according to gender lines, saying that the masculine Jack is pragmatically aggressive in order to solve a case while the feminine Toshiko is compassionately protective of all life, but the simple answer is that Jack's moral code obviously does not subscribe to a traditional heroes' handbook for such values.

At the same time as Gwen and Toshiko are nearly ready-made heroic, they are also both quite vulnerable when it comes to romance. Since their male comrades are likewise subject to the follies of Cupid's arrow, we cannot create a gendered division of this subject, but we say that if anything is prone to make these women act in an antiheroic manner, it is love. On this romantic note, we can look at the possibility in the first season that Gwen will somehow end up with Jack. When she later sleeps with Owen at the conclusion of "Countrycide," we are thrown a romantic curveball in the form of this unexpected ménage á trios in which she has immersed herself. Shocked and confused, we are probably hoping that she comes to her senses and commits herself to Rhys, who is the lesser of two evils if she must decide on a mate. This discussion may seem to be degenerating into gossipy speculation, but we must also remember that one of the core storytelling threads of *Torchwood* is soap opera. Gwen is still unmarried at this time, and so we can still hold out hope that she will end up with someone who understands her personal and professional needs.

We must also recognize that Toshiko is herself prone to acts of misjudgment, especially when she allows her relationship with an alien posing as a human called Mary in "Greeks Bearing Gifts" to make her question her loyalty to her teammates. Through the pendant that Mary lends her, Toshiko is able to hear her teammates' innermost thoughts, including ones that reveal Gwen and Owen are having an affair. Even knowing these facts, she is honorable enough to not judge them. While she ultimately remains true to the Torchwood team, she is constantly weakened by her love for Owen as he repeatedly rejects her and sleeps with other women. By the time he finally reciprocates her feelings, he is ironically dead, by all clinical terms, and so unable to consummate their budding relationship on a physical level. Despite all of these setbacks, it is Toshiko's unwavering loyalty to Owen, most strikingly shown when she places her own dying agony aside to console him when he hovers on the edge of his final death in "Exit Wounds" that undoubtedly defines her as a fallen hero.

The Heroic Journey of Repeated Deaths

By far, the most significant example of a Torchwood member bettering him or herself is Owen. When we are first exposed to this irascible doctor in "Everything Changes," we see that he is an immoral man who is guilty of date rape—the "roofies" in his case being the alien pheromone spray he has lifted from the Torchwood alien artifact storage area. In this sequence played for comedic effect in the episode, Owen sprays the pheromone on his face to make himself sexually irresistible to a woman who is clearly not interested in him, and, shortly thereafter, to her pugnacious boyfriend. One can argue that the couple, with their inhibitions drastically lowered, went on to experience a night of sexual experimentation and bliss. The somber fact remains, nonetheless, that the couple entered into a sexual tryst that they otherwise would have avoided if not for the overpowering effects of the pheromone. Consequently, Owen is undeniably guilty of rape, especially when one considers that he is a doctor bound by the Hippocratic Oath. These moral grey areas are easily written off by us as one of Owen's many character flaws that he is not alone in possessing at the beginning of the show. As for us, caught up in the many other tendrils of the show's narrative, including the plot-of-the-week, character development, soap opera elements, and *Torchwood*'s season one mythology arc that is Jack's quest to understand himself, we can easily dismiss Jack and his teammates' intermittently dubious actions.[17]

Later in season one, Owen claims that he is upset after his newest lover, Diane Holmes, decides to leave him in order to explore the space-time rift in "Out of Time," but the truth is that she was a temporary romantic interest who could barely divert him from his deeper-rooted pain and rage. Consequently, after Owen enters into a cage fight with a Weevil in "Combat" and admits that the dangerous match made him feel a sense of peace for a few seconds, we begin to question his love of self. In a latter episode, "Fragments," a flashback scene depicts Owen physically attacking Jack in a graveyard where Owen's fiancée Katie has been buried. Although it is understandable that Owen is lashing out at Jack since he somewhat believes Jack could have saved Katie from being killed by a parasitic alien tumor harboring in her head, his choice of violence as his means of expression is not a healthy alternative. Then again, if we go back to Owen's childhood, we learn that his mother was verbally, and potentially physically, abusive to him in "Adam."

What really makes viewers regard Owen in a sympathetic light, however, is his death at the end of "Reset." Upon his reanimation via the second Resurrection Gauntlet into a state of living death, Owen truly becomes a sympathetic character. A telling episode of this transformation is "A Day in the Death," in which Owen peacefully sits on a rooftop with a suicidal woman, Maggie, and gradually talks her out of jumping off the building. Death, without a doubt, has given the cynical Owen a fuller appreciation of life. Coupled with Jack, who is practically an expert when it comes to one being resurrected, Owen hence serves as a self-help blueprint for how all of us can better appreciate our lives.

To aid us in this understanding, we can refer to Joseph Campbell, who, in his magnum opus *The Hero with a Thousand Faces*, offers a brilliant formula for a hero's rite of passage: "separation — initiation — return."[18] With this formula in mind, we can then illuminate Jack and Owen's struggles with death and life. "A hero ventures forth from the world of common day," Campbell writes, "into a region of supernatural wonder: fabulous forces are there encountered and a decisive victory is won: the hero comes back from this mysterious adventure with the power to bestow boons on his fellow man."

Aside from the creepy, evil and downright bizarre threats Jack and Owen have fought during their time with Torchwood, the most challenging adversity they fight is death itself. For Jack, dying is a pain to which he is continually subjected. As for Owen, death is more final in that his body cannot feel any sensory input, meaning he cannot enjoy food, sleep or the comfort of another's touch. Although these brave men prove they can continue living after their initial deaths, their resolve is truly tested in the season two finale "Exit Wounds," where they respectively complete the journey of "separation — initiation — return."

At the beginning of "Exit Wounds," Jack is dealing with the return of his brother Gray, who is obsessed with revenging himself upon Jack since he blames his older brother for abandoning him to vicious aliens years earlier. Later in the episode, when Gray, via Captain John, transports Jack to 27AD Cardiff and buries him in the ground, Jack does not resist. In fact, he accepts his fate and endures the agony of continuous death and resurrection until the Torchwood team of 1901 finds him and places him in cryogenic storage in the Hub's morgue so he can revive in the twenty-first century. Upon discovering his brother-nemesis alive inside the Hub in that time zone, Gray is shocked to hear Jack forgive him, obviously believing that the only one who wields the power of absolution is him. Jack, then, completes his rite of passage that began with his "separation" from the rest of humanity, which occurred when he became immortal, continued with his "initiation," which is how he dealt with the agony that is repeated death in the Cardiff earth for nearly two millennia, and concluded with his "return," which is the message of absolution he offers Gray. On a greater, communal scale, Jack delivers the message to us, the television audience, that forgiveness is a virtue we all can embrace.

Returning to Owen, who, unlike Jack, is not too experienced with dying, which is his "separation," and living, which is "his return," we find a man who exposes his antiheroic traits as he faces his fate of final dissolution after he has been trapped in a nuclear failsafe lockdown in the Turnmill Nuclear Power Station's control room. Instead of reacting with dignity to Toshiko's grim prognosis of his situation regarding the radioactive waste that will vent into his area, Owen rails, "Not like this! I'm not doing it! Get me out of here, Tosh! Get me out of here! I died once! I'm not doing it again!" Gradually, under Toshiko's calming influence, he recovers his composure, soon gently reassuring her, "It's all right. Really, Tosh — it's all right."

As Owen achieves his "return" by accepting his looming decomposition-by-radiation death, he finally shines as an absolute hero, not because he is perfect, but since he is like all of us, as we strive to be strong in the face of our inevitable deaths. *Torchwood*, then, a show ostensibly about a team of flawed heroes repeatedly saving Cardiff from a myriad of alien threats, reveals itself to be a televised guide for improving ourselves, regardless of whether or not we classify ourselves as heroes, villains, or antiheroes.

Notes

1. See Rabindranath Tagore, *Stray Birds* (New York: Macmillan, 1916).
2. Attributed to Zefram Cochrane by Commander William Riker, *Star Trek: First Contact* (Paramount, 1998).
3. Ben Rawson-Jones, "Davies: 'Buffy,' 'Angel' inspired 'Torchwood,'" *Digital Spy*, October 17, 2006. http://www.digitalspy.com/cult/a38295/davies-buffy-angel-inspired-torchwood.html
4. I have elected to supply contemporary, pop-culture examples of the antihero instead of such literary figures as Falstaff, Ebenezer Scrooge and Scarlett O'Hara since *Torchwood* is a television show whose ethos, I'd argue, stems from the various contemporary pop culture media of the later twentieth and early twenty-first centuries — genre television, cinema, and comic books.
5. Chris Claremont and Frank Miller, "I'm Wolverine," *Wolverine*, issue 1 (New York: Marvel Comics, September 1982).
6. *Ibid.*
7. Since Torchwood is, according to Jack in "Everything Changes," "separate from the government, outside the police [and] beyond the United Nations," they can be pegged as unstoppable vigilantes. In terms of the manner in which they can indefinitely detain prisoners, apply questionable interrogation techniques, cover up extraordinary murders and instantly wipe memories, uncomfortable comparisons to the President George W. Bush-era United States' Guantanamo Bay Detention Camp, with its indefinite imprisonment of detainees and nefarious torture techniques are mostly unavoidable.
8. "The Empty Child," *Doctor Who* (BBC, 2005, UK).
9. We can also examine the Ninth Doctor's sartorial tastes: his choice to wear a tee-shirt and leather jacket eschews his previous eight incarnations' penchant for ties (or at least a button-down shirt as seen in the case of the Fifth Doctor's cricketer garb) situates him as the perfect rebel-with-a-cause with whom the morally confused Jack can identify.
10. See "The Empty Child," "The Doctor Dances," "Boom Town," "Bad Wolf," and "The Parting of the Ways," *Doctor Who* (BBC, 2005, UK).
11. "The Parting of the Ways," *Doctor Who* (BBC, 2005, UK).
12. "The Five Doctors," *Doctor Who* (BBC, 1983, UK).
13. See "Utopia," "The Sound of Drums," and "Last of the Time Lords," *Doctor Who* (BBC, 2007, UK).
14. A comparison to *Angel* is necessary since James Marsters joined that show in its fourth season in an attempt to boost the show's ratings by adding sex appeal and dramatic tension to the cast. We can also draw parallels between the characters of Captain Jack and Angelus in that both brooding, tortured figures have lived for over a century. Simultaneously, they are flawed leaders of teammates who need the group solidarity their respective groups (Torchwood and Angel Investigations) offer in order for them to experience a sense of belonging.
15. "An Unearthly Child," *Doctor Who* (BBC, 1963, UK).
16. Gwen and Toshiko are practically shining heroic paragons when compared to past female members of the Torchwood organization. For instance, "Everything Changes" and "They Keep Killing Suzie" present us with the manipulative scientist Suzie Costello, who will sacrifice anyone to harness the power of the Resurrection Gauntlet. We can also delve into the London Torchwood Branch and look at its Director, Yvonne Hartman, whose obsession with controlling the Void in the *Doctor Who* episode "Army of Ghosts" leads to the destruction of not only herself but her Torchwood as well. The only fact redeeming her, however, is her deter-

mination to retain control over her Cyber-steel encased brain while she defends the Torchwood Institute against a group of attacking Cybermen. If we go back one century to the Victorian era, we can likewise examine Emily Holroyd and Alice Guppy, who recruit the time-displaced Jack as a freelance Torchwood agent by duress in "Fragments." While their hinted same-sex relationship prefigures the future pairing of Jack and Ianto, their innate cruel nature, evinced when Guppy shoots an unarmed Blowfish prisoner as a means of "protecting" the British Empire, is a trait Jack will never share.

17. The other mythology arc is stated in Captain Jack's opening narration of every episode: "The twenty-first century is when everything changes," a phrase obviously echoed in the first episode's title "Everything Changes" and developed over the course of the series as the Torchwood team face increasingly challenging and complex alien threats.

18. Joseph Campbell, *The Hero with A Thousand Faces* (Princeton: Princeton University Press, 1968).

Part III

Sexuality and *Torchwood*

TWELVE

"Love the coat":
Bisexuality, the Female Gaze
and the Romance of Sexual Politics

CHRISTOPHER PULLEN

Torchwood is a series adaptation of *Doctor Who* (BBC, 2005-present, UK), a long-term mainstream all-ages television science fiction series which Russell T. Davies led to renewed popularity, in the early part of the twenty-first century.[1] The invention of the bisexual character[2] of Captain Jack Harkness within *Doctor Who* in a supporting role, who would become lead protagonist within the more adult-oriented *Torchwood*, is evocative of Davies' support for sexual diversity. Also notable within this is the sexual identity of Davies as writer and John Barrowman as actor (who plays Harkness in *Torchwood*), both of whom identify as gay, and openly publicize this.[3]

This alliance stimulates homosexual discourse, extending Davies' influential work within this area as the writer of the groundbreaking television drama *Queer as Folk* (Channel 4, 1999, UK). Despite this, the representation of bisexual Captain Jack Harkness within *Torchwood* may be contentious. As Jonathan David White tells us, "Male bisexuality is a dangerous eruption of homosexuality within the heterosexual matrix."[4] Russell T. Davies' construction (and John Barrowman's performance) of bisexual Captain Jack Harkness transgresses sexual identity ideals, and the presentation of a supernatural bisexual character who is unable to die offers scope for foundation, and permanence. Despite this, I would argue that the "dangerous eruption" of Jack Harkness reveals strategies of compliance to heteronormativity, in the character's construction. While *Torchwood* suggests ambivalence in its narrative construction centered on bisexuality, it prioritizes a female gaze (discussed later) in its deliberation on homosexual lives. This female-oriented approach is not extraordinary for Russell T. Davies, as his high-profile mainstream television drama series *Bob and Rose* (ITV, 2001,

UK) set a precedent in this. In *Bob and Rose* Davies foregrounded the representation of a female heterosexual character who would stimulate a (previously exclusively) homosexual man to fall in love with her, and reject a prior "queer" life. Consequently Russell T. Davies' approach is provocative, and *Torchwood* is no exception to this in the representation of bisexuality.

Evidence of such provocation may be seen in a pivotal episode of *Torchwood* from season two entitled "Fragments," where we discover how all the members of the supporting team for Jack Harkness were recruited (to help solve alien crimes or extraterrestrial issues). Here we are presented with an overt sexual tension between masculine hero Captain Jack and recruited subordinate male love interest Ianto Jones. This is evident in the line "By the way ... love the coat," which alludes to Ianto's assessment of Jacks "masculine" apparel (an army trench suit). However, while this vivifies homosexual tension suggesting possibility, at the same time it represses homosexual identity and is symptomatic of denial. It reveals covert imaginings and readings, as offering more substance than verbal affirmation or overt physical display. While the series undoubtedly offers hyperreal and often gratuitous intimate display connoting Harkness as sexualized and bisexual, it is the resistance of an affirmed homosexual identity, and the allusion to a "hidden story" which offers substance. In this way not that dissimilar to the historical representation of gay men on stage which had been denied though legislation in the UK (such as the imposition of the Lord Chamberlains Act, imposed between 1737 and 1968),[5] covert, underhand and subliminal readings are necessary for "queer audiences" in order to excavate not only the author's imagined subversive intent, but also the greatest satisfaction.

Consequently this essay explores the representation of bisexuality within *Torchwood*, as both pleasurable and problematic. It is pleasurable, as it vividly represents male to male intimacy and same sex desire; it is problematic as it does this by employing a preferred bisexual representation as a substitute for homosexual identity. This is contentious for both, in the examination of homosexual and bisexual representations. Furthermore, "female-oriented" heterosexual worlds are foregrounded here, subverting male homosexual desire.

I would argue that the emergence of Captain Jack Harkness is contiguous with the representation of gay man and the "fag hag,"[6] and that heterosexual narratives are primary. This may be evident in considering the relationship between the gay man and the straight woman, which has become an iconic substance of mainstream media. This representation is subtly deployed, but is deeply resonant within *Torchwood*. This configuration was endlessly played out within *Will & Grace* (NBC, 1998–2006, U.S.), evident between the central characters, which may be considered as unfulfilled heterosexual icons of partnership, as much as representing alliances between sexualities.[7] Although the creators of *Will & Grace* (David Kohan and Max Mutchnick) express a political ideology[8] in representing a gay man as co-lead character with a straight girl, the narrative is largely heterocentric.[9]

The coupling of the female heterosexual and the homosexual male builds upon a tradition which emerged in American television, and may be considered as founded within NBC's *Love, Sydney* (1981–83, U.S.). However, imagined homosexual "lifestyles" are obscured by female heterosexual production, and dominant social needs. As Steven Capsuto tells us in *Love, Sydney*, "Gay Sydney finds new meaning to life after he invites a vivacious sexually active nineteen-year-old, Laurie, into his home; together, they lovingly raise the bastard baby she conceived during an affair with a married man."[10] In this sense predating *Will & Grace* by some nineteen years, the gay man is offered a textual home, in order to support the needs of productive heterosexuality. This prioritizes female heterosexual desire and dominant social responsibilities, rejecting imagined homosexual lives.[11] Within *Torchwood*, the character of Gwen Cooper represents the heterosexual female archetype offering potential for dominance, at the same time contributing to the "gay guy" and "fag hag" coupling continuum. While Jack displays a sexual interest in Gwen (and females generally), the overarching narrative predominance is the investigation of Jack's homosexual encounters, as viewed through a heterosexual female-oriented gaze.

Therefore this essay considers not only the tension between bisexuality and homosexuality, equally it explores "unfulfilled" female desire, evident within a bias towards a heterosexual frame. I would also argue that this extends notions of female-oriented spectatorship evident within melodrama and soap opera, as discussed by Charlotte Brunsdon and Christine Geraghty,[12] and that female audience identification and unresolved heterosexual desire for the male homosexual body is a contingent mode of narrative expression supporting heteronormativity. Additionally such female-oriented framing essentially stimulates the romance of desire, more than focuses on the action of sexuality. This may reveal new scope in examining sexual diversity, despite allusions to the compression of homosexual identity within the heterosexual frame.

In order to explore this within *Torchwood*, it will be necessary to focus on the construction of Gwen Cooper's character in relation to Jack Harkness, established within the first season premiere episode. Later vivid representations of homosexuality will be explored, largely focusing on the relationship between Captain Jack Harkness and Ianto Jones throughout the series and Captain Jack with Captain John (as past lovers) from the second season. In addition the context of childhood and family history are evident here, in the iconography of domesticity. However, before embarking on this, it will be first necessary to consider the representation of gay identity and bisexuality within the media. This reveals the problematic construction of diverse sexuality, within mainstream arenas of American and British television.

Gay Identity, Bisexuality and the Media

In the 1976 fall edition of *Television Quarterly*, Newton E. Deiter, considering the potential of non-heterosexual identity within contemporary media, tells us (in an aptly titled and succinctly formed three-page article "The Last Minority: Television and Gay People"):

> It is anticipated that in the next two years, one of the networks will present a series built around gay characters.... It should be noted, however, that all is not sweet harmony; problems still exist. In 1974, executive producer David Gerber presented "Flowers of Evil" on the Police Woman series. This program, which presented Lesbians as psychopathic killers, exacerbated an already unpleasant situation.[13]

Deiter's prophesy proved to be overly optimistic, in that it would not be until the advent of *Will & Grace* (NBC) some twenty-four years later (in 1998) that a network television channel would build a series around gay characters.[14] Despite such an "advance," it is likely that Deiter could have anticipated the eventual problem of *Will & Grace*, in its reliance on a heterocentric discourse, in his protestation at the crime series *Police Woman* (Columbia Pictures Television, 1974–78, U.S.) and the 1974 episode "Flowers of Evil." Steven Capsuto describes this episode:

> "Flowers of Evil" deals with three deadly lesbians — Mame, Gladys and Janet — who run a nursing home.... The murderous trio starves and drugs the elderly residents, steals their money, then kills them. [The episode] eventually provoked more persistent gay protests than any TV show before or since.[15]

While this representation would stimulate the further employment of gay consultants to comment on American network television production, this episode represents the problematic paradigm of gay representation within mainstream media. An historical and recurring theme of homosexual representation on television would be the "disavowal" of diverse sexuality. As Stuart Hall discusses, disavowal involves an intense interest in "other" identities, but also there is a profound rejection of them.[16]

Central within the disavowal and rejection of homosexuality is the need to distance the mainstream or normative (general) audience from the "other," despite their textual engagement and general intrigue for sexual diversity. Such strategies had historically occurred within theatre drama and Hollywood film.[17] Not only does Vito Russo record the instance and impact of the feminized male "sissy" as a prime stock character and reductive representational device in Hollywood (not that dissimilar to the stereotyping of black identity at the time in characters such as "Stepin Fetchit"),[18] but also the closure of the narrative usually involved the removal or punishment of the "other" character. As Alan Sinfield tells us "the outlaw intruder who threatens the security of the characters, and by inference, the audience"[19] must be removed before the close of the play or film, to restore equilibrium, and the normative and "safe" world. In this way as evidenced in *Police Woman* "Flowers of Evil," other characters, such as masculinized and murderous lesbians, are employed as narrative devices which are intensely engaging, but also are pleasurable to dispense with.

Within mainstream television, historically there has been a plenitude of "disposable" gay and lesbian characters contextualizing the general idea of commodity and disposal.[20] Furthermore the significance of bisexual identity presents not only an integral part of this, but also ambivalence in the connection between homosexual and heterosexual worlds. The bisexual character of Captain Jack Harkness within *Torchwood* extends a tradition in media dramatic representation which may be considered as problematic.

As Brett Beemyn and Erich Steinman tell us, "Since the late twentieth century, bisexuality has seemed to be both everywhere and nowhere in popular culture."[21] It is possible to argue that early representations of androgynous bisexual men have proliferated within our popular music culture, particularly achieving attention within the glam rock movement in the 1970s in the United Kingdom.[22] This is evident in the tabloid representations of popular musicians, such as David Bowie, who claimed he was bisexual and had engaged in a sexual relationship with pop star peer Marc Bolan, and Elton John, who also attested that he was bisexual (until he announced his homosexuality later in his career). Furthermore, bisexuality within the glam rock movement was seen as a progressive sexual political stance, inherited from the sexual revolution of the 1960s.[23]

Todd Haynes's pastiche film on the glam rock movement *Velvet Goldmine* (1998, U.S.) pays homage to the potential of bisexuality as a popular culture movement which may be political.[24] In an early "establishing" part of the film we are presented not only with the fantasy idea of Oscar Wilde as a mythical and supernatural force in expressing a continuum of sexual diversity, but also we are offered a reconstructed "vox pop" from the 1970s. In a performative sequence in the manner of a television news extract examining the glam rock movement, we see lead character pop star Brian Slade wandering down a street dressed in feminized clothing hugging and kissing a young male passerby who is dressed in a sailor suit. This is followed with a voice over and an interview with a young man (with long hair, and arm casually stretched over the shoulder of young girl).

> VOICE OVER: Thanks to Slade, today's youngsters are singing a whole new tune.
> INTERVIEWER: So you are saying that you are bisexual?
> YOUNG MAN: Yeah! I like boys, I like girls. They are all great. There is no difference, is there?
> [Pause, engaging and provocative expression exhibited by the young man towards the interviewer]
> YOUNG MAN: [with dissent] ... Mr. BBC!

Haynes's film expresses the popular culture representation of bisexuality in the 1970s, which through the glam rock movement offered a challenge to dominant heterosexuality. This revealed the bisexual character as political, and to a degree androgenized in the limiting of masculine oppressive identity, in the textual expressions offered. However, such a short lived popular music culture movement could not be considered to have eclipsed the dominant representation of sexual diversity within film and television at that time. Mainstream narratives may have recorded an increasing interest in homosexuality (as discussed by Russo and Capsuto), but in these instances generally such characters remained other and problematic, rather than sensual and political.

Furthermore the advent of AIDS in the early 1980s engendered bisexuals to be further distanced from the norm. Bisexual men, in their likely contact with homosexual men, "supposedly pos[ed] a hidden threat to heterosexual women,"[25] in the possible transmission of HIV and AIDS. This translated into an increased fear, and further demonization of the bisexual man. Jonathan David White reports:

> According to Hollywood [representations in the late twentieth century, the United States was] in the throes of a bisexual crime wave.... [T]he cinematic killing spree may help to explain the peculiar visibility of bisexual men in popular culture in the mid-and late 1980s, and the subsequent near-total disappearance of the figure of the bi man, to be replaced by the equally stereotyped and ideologized bi woman.[26]

Within this analogy White reports that the advent of AIDS stimulated the demonization of bisexual men as agents of nemeses, to be replaced later by bisexual women who would offer the same threat to society, but would be commodified as glamorous representations of this device. Films such as *Basic Instinct* (Paul Verhoeven, 1992, U.S.) and *Showgirls* (Paul Verhoeven,

1995, U.S.) capitalized on these ideals, notably with the former showcasing Sharon Stone in the role of Catherine Tremayne as a central sexual object of desire who must be punished for her bisexuality (in the death of her female lover), but remains unaccountable for a murder that she has committed. In the analogy to AIDS, she is signaled as bisexual and causes death, yet her crimes are undetected, and she remains a threat. This is ironically represented at the close of the film where she has just had sex with her male heterosexual lover (played by Michael Douglas), and we see an ice pick under the bed (the supposed murder weapon from the earlier central crime). This might be considered in Kylo-Patrick R. Hart's terms as an "AIDS metaphor" film,[27] where cinema would make allusions to the disease, but there would be no express representation.[28]

Within television drama, however, due to the domestic and educational nature of the medium which might evoke the ethos of public service,[29] bisexuality was more directly connected to AIDS, potentially alluding to the issue of health warnings.[30] Evidence of this may be seen in the UK single television dramas *Intimate Contact* (Central Television, 1987) and *Sweet as You Are* (BBC2, 1988).[31] Here married men are represented as contracting AIDS though homosexual relationships and this foregrounds a threat to his wife and family. In these instances, I would argue that bisexual identity is contextualized through the narratives of dominant female heterosexual identity, in order to represent the threat to society.

Furthermore, diverse generic influences may be relevant within this construction. While the dramas *Intimate Contact* and *Sweet as You Are* offer resonance with the generic expectations of single drama, in their offering of complete and contained narratives, the textual address stimulates an ongoing popular culture narrative address which may be feminized.

Soap Opera and Female Identification

This address may be considered as revealing oppositions between mass and high culture. Christine Gledhill extends this idea.

Soap Opera	**Single Drama**
Mass Culture/Entertainment	**High Culture/Art**
Popular genre conventions	Realism
Glamour	Severity
Expressive performance	Underplaying/understatement
Talk about feelings	Taciturnity, decisive action
Private domesticity	The public world
Femininity	**Masculinity**[32]

An emerging female address concerned with issues of masculinity might reveal such oppositions in diverse generic forms. Although I am arguing that the AIDS single dramas (discussed above) reveal the problem of bisexual male partners, equally this context applies to any male/female opposition, where there is engagement or distance. In the case of *Torchwood*, I am arguing that this concerns the distance of possible male "partners," who are signaled as homosexual and deny sexual engagement. Furthermore the oppositions above reveal issues of female expressive identification, not only as displaying the traits of intimacy, domesticity and accord with popular and mass cultural modes, but also that this reveals a sense group membership, relative to female audiences.

As Christine Geraghty tells us, considering soap operas and potential female domestic audience identifications, "Enjoyment will be affected by the way in which the woman viewer is herself positioned within the home as mother/wife/daughter."[33] Furthermore:

> Consistent recognition is given is given to the emotional situations which women are deemed to share. At its most obvious, this sense of common feeling marks major events such as birth, marriage, the death of a child or the development of a romance.... This sense of common feeling is more rueful than celebratory, rooted in a shared perception that men can never live up to the demands women make of them.[34]

Consequently female audience identifications within soap operas (and I am arguing wider genres, potentially including science fiction) relies on a gender-oriented sense of group membership, not only in oppositional relationships to men, but in framing shared perceptions. These framed perceptions might focus on the potential of romance. In the case of *Torchwood* and female engagements with male homosexual/bisexual men, this might be constituted as unrequited love. In this sense *Torchwood* offers the potential of romance, but in its inability to offer commitment between imagined partners, it is romanticized more than sexualized.

Such framing of romance relies on a female-oriented address, and the stimulation of intimate gendered discourse. Evidence of this may be found not only in the program itself, but also in the fan oriented publications. For example, the second issue of the *Torchwood Magazine*[35] prioritizes on its cover images of lead female character Gwen Cooper (played by Eve Myles) accompanied by the female assistant Martha Jones (played by Freema Ageyman) from *Doctor Who*. This is then emblazoned with the headline "GIRLS TALK." These two images of lead female characters are not exclusively seductive or sexual images suggesting a male heterosexual stimulation, but offer a sense of knowingness and agency, connoting leadership and direction.

Consequently the discussion that follows examines the female-oriented narrative address of *Torchwood*, and then moves on to consider direct male homosexual engagement and the ambivalence of stimulation to bisexual and gay audiences.

Gwen Cooper and the Female Gaze

I would argue that female identification within *Torchwood* is played out in the manner of the female gaze. The construction of Gwen Cooper's character in the series premiere episode titled "Everything Changes" reveals strong evidence of this (discussed later). While Laura Mulvey's notion of the male gaze[36] has been the prime area of investigation with regards to the area of film studies, I would like to suggest that a female gaze is apparent in *Torchwood*, in the setting up of identity strategies and revealing prioritized viewing positions, extending contexts discussed earlier with regards to the soap opera.

Laura Mulvey's analysis of Hollywood film concerned the objectification of women, framed and subject to the masculine gaze which revealed the concept of "to-be-looked-at-ness." This suggests that women are constructed by male hierarchies within the film industry, and they are represented as objects of desire. However, as Liesbet Van Zoonen tells us, "Mulvey's dark and suffocating analysis of patriarchal cinema has lost ground to a more confident and empowering approach which foregrounds the possibility of 'subversive,' that is, non patriarchal modes of female spectatorship."[37] In this sense, female identity might be constructed outside of an adherence to masculine power and dominant viewing concerns which might be evident within the film and television industry. Also, there may be a provision for a focus on the male body as an object of desire. As David Gauntlett explains, this might progress Mulvey's ideas which "denies the heterosexual female gaze altogether [primarily discussing the] audience, both male and female [as] positioned so that they admire the male lead [character] for actions, and adopt his romantic/erotic view of the women."[38] This I would argue extends notions of female identification as discussed with regard to the soap opera, in addition to displaying evidence of active audiences, which John Fiske would suggest offers independent and subjective identification possibilities.[39] It also offers the possibility that the male body might be an object of examination, not only subject to the gaze of the female character (discussed below), but also subject to the gaze of the male homosexual viewer.

As Richard Dyer[40] argues such a focus on the male physical form as "to-be-looked-at-ness" may have commenced within contemporary aesthetics, advocating desire for the young male healthy body. Dyer cites a Levi's jeans television advertising campaign for denim in the late 1980s, which featured Nick Kamen in a laundrette. Kamen removes his clothes to reveal a well-toned body dressed only in boxer shorts, as Dyer argues this reveals "a shift in attitudes towards the male body."[41] It is significant that this commercial not only reconstructs attitudes within advertising which intensifies the male body and supposes a female heterosexual (or male homosexual) viewership in possible sexual pleasure, but also that this viewership is framed within domestic and female-oriented settings, evident within the launderette. I would argue that this supports a stereotypically female-oriented address, foregrounding notions of domesticity, at the same time situating the young male body as an object of desire. This early moment revealing shifts in representation, is not only emblematic of contemporary reconfigurations of masculinity revealing potential new viewing positions,[42] also it may be traced within diverse media generic forms such as soap opera and female-oriented science fiction such as *Buffy the Vampire Slayer* (WB Network, 1997–2003, U.S.),[43] as well as *Torchwood*.

The opening episode of *Torchwood* reveals such an objectification of the male body, framed though the identification of lead female character Gwen Cooper. Gwen discovers the covert operations of Torchwood through an encounter where she is called in her work as a policewoman to a murder scene. However Captain Jack Harkness and the Torchwood team take over from the police, and she is denied access. This creates a desire in her character to solve the murder and discover the mystery of the Torchwood organization, which have been awarded special powers by the government and operate outside normative control. As the story unfolds focusing on Gwen, a general construction might be titled "she cannot believe what she sees." Such a focus on Gwen seeing and the possibility of female agency is apparent on many levels.[44]

Notably, in the first encounter where Gwen observes the Torchwood team, looking down on them from a high position in a multi-story car park, this is literally "saturated" with female identity. Most apparent within this is the significance of the driving rain falling down on the Torchwood team, as they stand over the body of a recently murdered young man. Captain Jack Harkness comments on the downfall, telling his team that he can taste the estrogen in the polluted rain:

> There you go, I can taste it, oestrogen, definitely oestrogen, you take the pill, flush it away and it enters the water cycle and feminises the fish. Goes all the way up into the sky then falls all the way back on me. Contraceptives in the rain! Love this planet. Still at least I won't get pregnant, never doing that again!

The opening words of Jack Harkness in the series directly comments on the relationship with female identity, and issues of sexual influence. While a humorous tone is adopted in Jack's displeasure with being female (and being pregnant) in a previous life, it is the focus on female identity as strategic which reveals the gender bias. Also not only is Gwen gazing down on the Torchwood team (that she is yet to join) and her perspective is dominant, but also the two female characters within *Torchwood* (at that time), Suzy and Toshiko, are the prime agents. This is evident where Suzy uses the gauntlet (an alien device in the form of a "medieval" metallic armored glove) on the young male murder victim to briefly restore his life, and Toshiko interrogates the young man, asking who had perpetrated the murder. In this sequence, not only is female estrogen literally pouring down, but also three female characters are the prime agents of action and observation.

The priority of Gwen Cooper's female gaze continues to be a theme within the opening episode, where there is an opposition in her subjugation between "masculinized" animalistic non-sexualized objects and "feminized" male sexual objects. The former is evident when she directly gazes into the eyes of the brutal-looking Weevil (the extraterrestrial murderer) both before its capture and later at the time of its imprisonment within the Torchwood headquarters. The latter occurs when she first encounters the Torchwood team. Gwen's observance of the Weevil as an object of terror foregrounds her depth of engagement, and her attempts at understanding, yet reveals her inability to control a brutal (potentially male oriented) humanistic form. Conversely, her engagement and pleasure of viewing the Torchwood team stimulates the possibility of her agency, contextualizing issues of domesticity and sexuality.

It is not insignificant that the first member that Gwen closely gazes upon and engages in conversation with is Ianto Jones, Captain Jack's love interest, and Ianto tells Gwen, "Don't keep him waiting." This signals the potential bisexual triangle, and foregrounds Gwen's engagement with Jack, as a possible sexual encounter. Furthermore as Gwen enters the headquarters and gazes upon the Torchwood team, as they are amused in pretending that they did not know that she was arriving, her first direct encounter with Jack is significant for its parody of domesticity. Gwen has gained access to the Torchwood base through pretending that she is delivering pizza, and her appearance as a provider of sustenance bears resonance with the rigors of daily life and the soap opera, more than the drama of science fiction. In this sense when Gwen first converses with Jack, a desire to know the secret of his life and his supernatural ability is conflated with an understanding of his ordinariness. In this sense she gazes upon him as a "feminized" and domesticated male sexual object.

I would ague that the oppositional gazes represented here reveal a rejection of brutality and the uncontrollable, and support for pleasurable female-centric viewing positions. Also in these instances, the desirable male object is constructed as exotic, in his distance from normative contexts of masculinity, which may be seen as unknowable and brutal. Furthermore, the location of the "feminized" exotic male is situated within the normative domestic frame. This reveals the essential constitutive ingredient in the formation of the heterosexual female and the homosexual male dyad, stimulating the "gay guy" and the "fag hag" coupling continuum.

While a female-oriented gaze seems less apparent in the second season of *Torchwood*, as Captain Jack encounters Captain John and more explicit representations of male hypermasculine homosexual desire are foregrounded, I would argue that these representations remain objects of female desire. Furthermore, the unraveling of Captain Jack's childhood and family life offer further constitution of domesticity.

Season two opens with a provocatively titled episode "Kiss Kiss, Bang Bang." Central within this is the return of Captain Jack Harkness after a period away from the Torchwood team, and the dramatic appearance of a previous partner to Jack called Captain John. Meeting up at a night club in isolation, and deploying the generic conventions of the Hollywood Western, we see Jack engage with John in the manner of a shoot out at a saloon. Connoting masculinity, both are dressed in military apparel, with Jack in his full length contemporary army trench coat and John in a nineteenth-century captain's jacket. On first seeing each other they initially kiss passionately, then as if to rebuke this they embark on a "bar-room brawl," smashing furniture and breaking glass, punching each other violently, and drawing guns on each other. In a manner which might be considered as a sexual performance of hyperviolent masculinity involving the phallocentric iconography of loaded guns, the two paired but opposing characters intensely physically engage. While this establishes the couple as unstable, yet sexually excited by each other, they are also represented as enduring and committed. On announcing their relationship to the Torchwood team, this is affirmed:

> CAPTAIN JACK: We go back.
> CAPTAIN JOHN: Excuse me! We go more than go back.
> IANTO JONES: [concerned] In what way?
> CAPTAIN JOHN: Every way and then some.... We were together for five years. It was like having a wife.

It is significant that Ianto questions the relationship, as he is the male love interest to Jack, and we imagine that Captain John represents a threat to his possible monogamy with Jack. This establishment of the couple as highly physical, sexual and committed, however, is juxtaposed with the contextual relationship of Gwen Cooper to Jack, and her need to know more about Jack's past. In a pivotal sequence, Gwen questions Jack's integrity and endurance:

> GWEN: What did [Captain John] mean, a "time agent"?
> CAPTAIN JACK: That was in the past.
> GWEN: Oh! Here we go again. You know everything about me, Jack. Why do you keep shutting me out?
> CAPTAIN JACK: Here and now that is what is important. The work we do. The person I am now. That is what I am proud of.

This sequence foregrounds Gwen's intimate personal desire for more knowledge of Jack's past, at the same time indicating a close personal bond to him in the manner of partnership expectations. However, this reveals a disparity in the commitment offered to each other, with Jack seen as withholding and Gwen seen as fully giving.

This scenario contextualizing Jack within diverse partnerships (separately with John, with Ianto and with Gwen) focuses on his performed bisexuality, and issues of instability. This is foregrounded with a resistance to fully reveal his past. Consequently his prior role as a "time agent" is obscured from Gwen and Ianto (and the Torchwood team), and Jack resists trusting Captain John, withholding the full extent of his motives. This engenders a narrative of mistrust, and jealousy. This is evident in the words of Captain John on the subject of Jack to Gwen: "Just don't rely on him. There is a lot about him that you don't know.... He won't stay with you. He and I shared something." Also there is evidence of moving away from a troubled past, with Jack on the subject of John to Ianto: "He's a reminder of my past. I want him gone."

Such a focus on knowing or resolving, essentially, however is framed within a desire for Jack to give up his bisexual unknowable past, and move towards an affirmation of commitment to one suitor. This becomes apparent in considering Ianto's modest and sincere desire to go out with Jack, in the romantic notion of "going steady," by accepting a date with Jack where they would go to the cinema and a restaurant. Also it is evident in Gwen's focus on Jack, juxtaposing her relationship with her fiancé as less desirable than imagined commitment from Jack. Although Gwen's engagement with Jack is less obviously fulfilled than Jack's desire for Ianto (and homosexual fulfillment generally), the prioritizing of narratives of commitment, family and domesticity play a central role in the mediation of a female focused heterosexual narrative construction.

This becomes primarily evident later in the second season in an episode titled "Adam" where we discover details of Captain Jack's childhood, and his failure as a brother and a son. In a flashback sequence where Jack has been allowed to rediscover memories of his early life, Jack fails to protect his younger brother, Gray, from capture by malevolent aliens who may have been murderous, and his life has been haunted with this failing, and uncertainty as to the destiny of his brother. While at the close of the second season in the episode titled "Exit Wounds" we discover that the brother that Jack failed to protect is vengeful (and integral to the re-emergence of Captain John, who has been coerced to punish Jack), Jack is represented as responsible to make amends. In a sequence where Jack is buried alive by his brother as pennance, Jack is represented as strong and enduring concerned for family responsibility. Although Jack's brother, Gray, is culpable for the deaths of two members of the Torchwood team (Toshiko and Owen) at the close of the second season, Jack's focus on saving his "family" is central to his character's integrity.

Consequently, although Jack is signaled as bisexual and unattainable, he is represented as foundational and enduring. The character of Captain Jack Harkness is a complex mixture of desire, responsibility and unknowing. As a construction of the heterosexual female gaze, it is potentially satisfying in offering intense provocation in partnership and family potential. However, through its resistance of fixed sexual identity, it offers ambivalence to heterosexual and homosexual audiences.

Conclusion

Captain Jack Harkness as a romanticized yet unattainable figure stimulates sexual identity reconfigurations, extending the political potential of the androgynous bisexual as an icon of sexual politics (discussed earlier). While this is framed though a female-oriented gaze, *Torchwood* offers perspectives for new ways of seeing and new scope for realisation, foregrounding internal and external forces. This may be evident in the allusion "like your coat" which offers "inner" subversion within *Torchwood* which may be read as a covert homosexual text, and the generic soap opera like female-oriented frame, which offers "external" presence. However, such a tension between inner homosexual desire (as audience reading), and external female-oriented textual address (as performative stance), could be considered as dissonant. This may be evident in the prioritization of a female heterosexual perspective, which is clearly evident in the "gay guy" and "fag hag" coupling continuum. Despite this, Russell T. Davies' construction of Captain Jack Harkness in *Torchwood* as a supernatural bisexual character that is unable to die reveals permanence, and multivalence. Within this Davies has created a concretized character of diverse sexuality which, echoing the concerns of historical gay representation within drama, *literally* (in his inability to die) may not be expelled at the final curtain (in order to restore normalcy). Furthermore, this construction unravels the connection of the bisexual to AIDS, and by token challenges the association of homosexuality to impending death. Such constructions extend normative and oppressive ideas, which might restrict sexual diversity.

Notably, Russell T. Davies' ultimate provision may be a reconstitution of bisexual and homosexual lives, which resists an over reliance on sexual performance, and foregrounds romance. Although this discussion has focused on a female-centric analysis, which places gay male sexuality (and bisexuality) within a subjective focus, this offers a sensitivity rarely associated with diverse sexuality. A feminized perspective which might extend from the emerging representation of the heterosexual female interested in the homosexual male suggests commodity and use, but I would argue that this offers the framing of intensity and emotion. Although *Torchwood* does present seemingly untrammeled sexual desire, rarely is this explicitly presented; moreover, sexual desire is often framed in romantic and emotive terms.

There is an underlying thread within *Torchwood*, which supports the representation of romance as much as sexuality. Within the episode "Captain Jack Harkness" (from the first season) where we discover Jack's namesake within a nostalgic World War II setting of servicemen within a dance hall, and two men are situated within a generic narrative frame which evokes the landmark film *Brief Encounter* (1945, UK), longing and deferred fulfillment are the iconic substance of romance.[45] Furthermore, the denial of closure in the imagined couplings of both Ianto and Gwen (respectively) to Jack, and the resistance of exclusivity from Jack to keep one partner, reveals not a stereotypical reimagining of male homosexual and bisexual promiscuity, but the theatre of desire and the heroics of self denial.[46] While many would argue that historically, denial and improper relationships (such as embarking on heterosexual marriage to conform) may be the essence of hidden or repressed bisexual lives, Russell T. Davies' construction echoes the poetics of sensitivity and enforced containment in contemporary emotional terms. This I would argue re-stimulates notions of depth in feeling, rather than superficiality.

Russell T. Davies' *Queer as Folk* challenged audience perceptions of gay male sexuality, and its legacy has stimulated reconfigurations. The most notable of these within Davies' advancing oeuvre is the construction of Captain Jack Harkness. He may be coded for a heterosexual gaze, but the romance of "vivid presence" coexistent with "absence of fulfillment" stimulates further engagements, foregrounding new layers of feeling. This may echo a past of homosexual and bisexual denial and lack of fulfillment, however through new foci on tension more than resolution, the politicized romantic sexual narratives of *Torchwood* progress.

Notes

1. *Doctor Who* as a television series originally started in 1963 and ran until 1989. Russell T. Davies' reinvention of this started in 2005. See David J. Howe and Stephen James Walker, *The Television Companion: The Unofficial and Unauthorised Guide to "Doctor Who"* (London: Telos, 2003).
2. Although theoretically the character of Captain Jack Harkness could be termed as "omnisexual," in the representation of his sexual interest in alien and non-human forms of life (in addition to men and women), I am purely considering his social constructionist human potential as a character. This situates Harkness as bisexual.
3. Russell T. Davies advertises his sexuality widely in the media. See *http://www.guardian. co.uk/media/2007/oct/20/bbc.television* (accessed 28 May 2009). Also John Barrowman has advertised his sexuality in the media, and notably has been the subject of a self-reflexive documentary about his sexuality titled: *The Making of Me* (BBC, 2008, UK). See *http://news.bbc. co.uk/1/hi/magazine/7523567.stm* (accessed 28 May 2009).
4. Jonathan David White, "Bisexuals who Kill: Hollywood's Bisexual Crimewave, 1985–1998," in *Bisexual Men in Culture and Society* (New York: Haworth Press), 42.
5. John Clum, *Still Acting Gay*, rev. ed. (New York: St. Martin's Griffin, 2000).
6. The Urban Dictionary defines the term "fag hag" as "a woman who prefers the company of gay men. [It foregrounds the] marriage of two derogatory terms, fag and hag, symbolizing the union of the world's most popular objects of scorn, homosexual and woman." *http://www.urbandictionary.com/define.php?term=fag-hag* (accessed 9 June 2009).
7. In many ways Jonathan Harvey's UK sitcom *Gimmie! Gimmie! Gimmie!* (BBC, 1999) represented a parody of the "gay guy" and "fag hag" continuum.
8. Jim Colucci, *Will & Grace Fabulously Uncensored* (New York: Roundtable Press, 2004).
9. See Marisa Connolly, "Homosexuality on Television: The Heterosexualization of *Will & Grace* in Print Media," *Culture, Communication and Technology Program* (Georgetown University), Volume 3, Fall 2003. *http://gnovisjournal.org/files/Marisa-Connolly-Homosexuality-on-Television.pdf* (accessed 28 May 2009). Also see Edward Schiappa, "Can One Show Make A Difference? *Will & Grace* and the Parasocial Contact Hypothesis," *Journal of Homosexuality*, Volume 51, Issue 4, November 2006, pp. 15–37.
10. Steven Capsuto, *Alternate Channels: The Uncensored Story of Gay and Lesbian Images on Radio and Television* (New York: Balantine Books, 2000), 160.
11. See Alan Sinfield, *The Wilde Century: Effeminacy, Oscar Wilde and the Queer Moment* (New York: Columbia University Press, 1994) for discussions on homosexual identity as connected to leisure versus production.
12. See Christine Geraghty, *Women and Soap Opera: A Study of Prime Time Soaps* (Cambridge: Polity Press, 1991), and Charlotte Brunsdon, *Screen Tastes: Soap Opera to Satellite Dishes* (London: Routledge, 1997).
13. Newton E. Deiter, "The Last Minority: Television and Gay People," *Television Quarterly*, Volume XIII, Number 3, Fall 1976, 71.
14. See Steven Capsuto, *Alternate Channels: The Uncensored Story of Gay and Lesbian Images on Radio and Television* (New York: Balantine Books, 2000) for an in depth analysis of television characters.
15. Steven Capsuto, *Alternate Channels*, 110.
16. See Stuart Hall, "The Spectacle of the 'Other,'" in Stuart. Hall, ed., *Representation: Cultural Representations and Signifying Practices* (London: Sage, 1997), 223–279.
17. See Vito Russo, *The Celluloid Closet*, rev. ed. (New York: Harper & Row, 1987), and John Clum, *Still Acting Gay*.

18. Stepin Fetchit was a controversial black actor whose name was a direct reference to the term "step and fetch it" (connoting slavery), and consequently performed a reductive and subordinate stage persona. See *http://www.imdb.com/name/nm0275297/bio* (accessed 9 June 2009). Also for wider discussions on the stereotyping of black identity see Stuart Hall, *Representation: Cultural Representations and Signifying Practices*.
19. Alan Sinfield, "Closet Dramas: Homosexual Representations and Class in Post War British Theatre," *Genders* 9 (Fall 1990), 115.
20. See Steven Capsuto, *Alternate Channels*, and Steven Capsuto and Stephen Tropriano, *The Prime Time Closet: A History of Gays and Lesbians on TV* (New York: Applause Books, 2002).
21. Brett Beemyn and Erich Steinman, eds., *Bisexual Men in Culture and Society* (New York: Harrington Park, 2002), 3.
22. See Philip Auslander, *Performing Glam Rock: Gender and Theatricality in Popular Music* (Ann Arbor: University of Michigan Press, 2006).
23. Naomi Tucker, ed., *Bisexual Politics: Theories, Queries and Visions* (New York: Haworth Press, 1995).
24. See Christopher Pullen, *Gay Identity, New Storytelling and the Media* (Basingstoke: Palgrave Macmillan, 2009).
25. Brett Beemyn and Erich Steinman, eds., *Bisexual Men in Culture and Society*, 3.
26. *Ibid.*, 42.
27. Kylo-Patrick R. Hart, *The AIDS Movie: Representing a Pandemic in Film and Television* (New York: Haworth Press, 2000).
28. AIDS metaphor films often foreground viral threats to society, which may be connoted as AIDS.
29. See Edward Buscombe, ed., *British Television: A Reader* (Oxford: Oxford University Press, 2000), and Roger Silverstone, *Television and Everyday Life* (London: Routledge, 1994).
30. This might be related to a series of national television adverts in 1987, and a "poster and leaflet campaign [which commenced] with the slogan [of] "Don't Aid AIDS" [later changing (when the adverts were broadcast)] into the theme of 'Don't die of ignorance.'" See *http://www.avert.org/pictures/aidshistory2.htm* (accessed 5 November 2005).
31. See Christopher Pullen, "Non-Heterosexual Characters in Post-War Television Drama: From Covert Identity and Stereotyping, Towards Reflexivity and Social Change," in Dimple Godiwala, ed., *Alternatives Within the Mainstream II: Queer Theatre in Postwar Britain* (Cambridge: Cambridge Scholars Press, 2007), 272–297.
32. Christine Gledhill, "Genre and Gender: The Case for Soap Opera," in Stuart Hall, ed., *Representation: Cultural Representations and Signifying Practices* (London: Sage, 1997), 337–386, p. 349. Also the reference of single drama in opposition to soap opera is an extension of Gledhill's ideas.
33. Christine Geraghty, *Women and Soap Opera: A Study of Prime Time Soaps* (Cambridge: Polity Press, 1991), 40.
34. *Ibid.*, p.47–48
35. *Torchwood Magazine* 2 April 2008, front cover. Published by Titan Magazines, London.
36. Laura Mulvey, "Visual Pleasure and Narrative Cinema," in T. Tony Bennett, Susan Boyd-Bowman, Colin Mercer and Janet Wollacott, eds., *Popular Television and Film* (London: Open University, 1985), 206–215.
37. Liesbet Van Zoonen, *Feminist Media Studies* (London: Sage,1994), 97.
38. David Gauntlett, *Media, Gender and Identity: An Introduction* (London: Routledge, 2002), 39.
39. John Fiske, *Television Culture* (London: Routledge, 1994).
40. Ricard Dyer, *The Matter of Images*, second reprint (London: Routledge, 2000), 124.
41. *Ibid.*, 123.
42. See David Gauntlett, *Media, Gender and Identity*, and Peter Lehman, *Masculinity: Bodies, Movies, Culture* (New York: Routledge, 2001).
43. See Rhonda Wilcox, *Why Buffy Matters: The Art of Buffy the Vampire Slayer* (London:

I. B. Tauris, 2005), and Elana Levine and Liosa Parks, eds., *Undead TV: Essays on Buffy the Vampire Slayer* (Durham: Duke University Press, 2007).

44. Also see Tania Modeleski, *The Women Who Knew Too Much: Hitchcock and Feminist Theory* (New York: Routledge, 1988) for foundational discussion on the agency of females in Hollywood cinema.

45. Christopher Pullen, *Gay Identity, New Storytelling and the Media*, 162.

46. It is important to note that in the third series of *Torchwood*, the love triangle of Ianto, Gwen and Jack comes to a close with the death of Ianto. Significantly (in the third series) Jack is represented as more closely coupled with Ianto, and passionately kisses him at the moment of his death. However following the heterocentric drive of *Torchwood*, the closing scene of this episode (episode 4 of 5) foregrounds Gwen's emotive connectivity to both Ianto and Jack, rather than Jack's desire for Ianto. This denies an exclusive homosexual representation, and provides continuing evidence of the narrative force within *Torchwood*, further prioritizing the "female (heterosexual) gaze."

THIRTEEN

Fashioning Masculinity and Desire
SARAH GILLIGAN

Costume is used within *Torchwood* to construct a visual narrative discourse of gendered identity and sexuality that is increasingly centered upon the spectacular. The contemporary urban setting of a newly regenerated Cardiff, coupled with the narrative device of time travel through the "rift" enables a blurring between past, present and future. In turn, as the series has progressed and developed, the use of costume has extended beyond supporting character construction, to bring the pleasures of both contemporary fashion and costume drama to a sci-fi drama. Within this essay I will argue that in functioning as a spectacular intervention, masculine dress (in particular) within the program is characterized by a sartorial style that enables the spectator to revel in the visual pleasure of the objectified male and also in the "bliss" of the textile.[1] As Christine Holmlund discusses, contemporary masculinity is characterized by a series of interlocking, multiple masquerades that are enabled through a combination of costume props and the representation of the male body.[2] Therefore through a close textual analysis of the use of costume in selected episodes from season one and two of *Torchwood*, I will discuss the ways in which Owen and Ianto embody different versions of contemporary masculine sartorial style and that through the costuming of Captain Jack and Captain John not only is the spectator offered the pleasures of the flowing coats and retro military dress that construct the male as object of the gaze, but they are enabled a more fluid representation of masculinity. The pleasures of costume in the series are not solely confined to the representation of the objectified male, thus I will argue that in fashioning such new male heroes, desire is repeatedly displaced from the face and body onto the clothes themselves by self consciously fuelling the pleasures of clothes fetishism for the spectator.

As Jane Gaines argues, costume functions as an important "storytelling" element of mise-en-scène, supporting our understanding of character traits, emotions and motivations through a dress plot of changing garments and appearances.[3] Characters' literal and metaphorical journeys, conflicts and transformations are signified through the visual narrative. As well as supporting the dominant demands of story and plot, costume also articulates "a language of its own."[4] This visual language may disrupt and transcend the dominant narrative through melodramatic excess, in which garments speak more loudly than dialogue. Thus a tension therefore exists between costume serving the dominant demands of the narrative and the extravagant possibilities of design.[5] Yet costume's capacity for spectacle means that it does not solely function as a means of signifying elements of identity. It can create "spectacular interventions that interfere with the scenes in which they appear and impose themselves onto the characters they adorn."[6] Associated with frivolity, spectacle and in turn femininity, fashion and costume design privileges the aesthetic over the verbal, through its primary concern with surface appearances and vanity. While there is a growing body of scholarship on cinematic costume,[7] TV drama and costume has been granted very little academic attention, perhaps in part because TV drama has tended to (borrowing from Bruzzi, 1997, in a different context) look "through" rather than "at" costume and fashion.[8] Costume frequently remains subservient to the demands of character, setting and plot, functioning primarily to signal time period, or delineate characters rather than draw attention to itself in its own right. As TV drama (like popular cinema), becomes ever increasingly preoccupied with spectacle, the visual pleasures of costume and its intersection with the body are self consciously offered up to the spectator in texts such as *Torchwood, Sex and the City* (HBO, 1998–2004, U.S.) and *Mad Men* (AMC, 2007–present, U.S.).

This conflict between costume's subservient role versus its capacity to act as a spectacular intervention is evident from the opening scenes of the first episode of *Torchwood* ("Everything Changes"). In the case of Gwen, costume adheres to the normative relationship between costume and script, in which her police uniform clearly visually signals her status and investigative role within the narrative. Shot in the pouring rain, the camera remains in a mid-shot, drawing attention to Gwen's face, rather than her costumed body. Such camera work forces the spectator to focus on the moment of drama, rather than allowing the clothes to intrude. In contrast, the Torchwood team are immediately signaled as a disruption to the narrative. The police are required to exit the scene as the team arrive and initially the spectator is placed with Gwen through a shot-counter-shot sequence as they pass her. Yet as Jack, Owen, Tosh and Susie enter the crime scene the point of view camera work changes to showcase the team. Backlit by their vehicle the four are revealed in long shot each adorned in black, the rain causing the fabric (especially Owen and Tosh's leathers) to glisten creating a fetishistic charge. As they each confidently stride, shoulders back (in a shot that echoes texts such as *Spooks* [BBC, 2002–2008, UK] and *Hustle* [BBC, 2004–2009, UK]), the team revel in their to-be-looked-at-ness. The spectacle of their entrance is further highlighted as the camera cuts to reveal a POV shot from Gwen's perspective that draws attention to their garments as the silhouetted figures walk away, to then stand over the crime scene, the flood lights drawing attention to the contrasting cut of Owen and Jack's clothes.

What is particularly interesting in terms of this opening scene as a costume moment in the visual narrative discourse is that it offers the male, far more so than the female characters up as the object of the gaze. As Tosh virtually blends into the lines of the adjacent building, Jack is not only the object of Gwen's gaze, but also returns the gaze, looking directly at her (and by implication us). When men are presented for the female gaze, the dominant structures of male looking and woman as object are violated and there must be some attempt to counteract this violation.[9] This as Richard Dyer notes (of cinematic representations) often centers upon the "star's own look — where and how he is looking in relation to the woman looking at him." To Dyer, when the male is objectified he is usually represented averting his gaze, not in modesty, but because he is self-absorbed. Dyer argues that while the face and the body of the male may be there to be gazed at, the mind is "on higher things, and it is this upward striving that is most supposed to please." Unusually though, Jack returns Gwen's look, engaging her gaze. Rather than asserting his phallic power, the narrative self consciously further complicates the strategies of gendered representation through Jack detecting and commenting on estrogen in the rain: "Contraceptives in the rain. Love this planet! Still at least I won't get pregnant, never doing that again!"

The comment (coupled with the team's ability to bring a crime victim back from the dead through the use of alien technology) both constructs Jack as an enigma and signals the text's adherence to sci-fi conventions. Through blurring reality and fiction, together with past and present in the construction of futuristic fantasies and anxieties, sci-fi texts overtly offer the spectator pleasures of escapism and transcendence. In the case of *Torchwood*, not only is the representation of time blurred through the rift, with episodes crossing periods from "late Victorian, to the 1920's, '40s, '80s" to "the fictional 51st century,"[10] but the fantastic otherworldly aspects of aliens, cyborgs and shape shifters collide with the contemporary landscape of Cardiff. Within cinematic sci-fi texts, fashioning the future is not simply the preserve of costume designers, but also couture designers and tailors such as

Paco Rabanne, Hardy Aimes and Jean Paul Gaultier have let their imaginations run wild in creating gaudy, sexy and functionalist images of futuristic clothing within films such as *Barbarella*, *2001: A Space Odyssey*, and *The Fifth Element*. In contrast, with its contemporary setting, the costuming within *Torchwood* is more high street than couture incorporating recognizable fashions, brands and gadgets.[11]

In the "The Fashion Hub" feature in *Torchwood Magazine*, costume designer Ray Holman's discussion of costuming the *Torchwood* team focuses primarily upon the logistics, technicalities and narrative role of the clothes, rather than their fashionability, style or capacity for spectacle.[12] Costume is marked as serving a narrative function in delineating character: Owen as the "urban warrior," Ianto the "city slicker" and Jack "the matinee idol."[13] Functionality and availability are cited by Holman as key factors in the appropriation of brands such as Diesel, G-Star, Zara, Gap, Next and Marks and Spencer in costuming of Owen and Ianto.[14] The purchase of branded and high street garments (as opposed to original costume designs) and the acknowledgement of such can be seen to function to both add realism and create multiple points of identification, desire and aspiration for the spectator.

In the knowledge economy of the digital age, the nature of work and labor is ever changing and no longer demands the same physicality as it did 20 years ago. The importance of specialist knowledge and technological expertise over shear brawn means that the "geek" is no longer the subject of ridicule, but revered and allowed to be "cool."[15] Therefore masculine identity can be seen to be inscribed upon clothes, rather than the muscularity of the body. As Pamela Church Gibson discusses, in the 1990s "new action heroes appeared, more sartorially aware and able to combine sharp dressing with fisticuffs and worse."[16] The *Torchwood* team are particularly interesting as a continuation of this shift in representations of contemporary masculinity through combining specialist knowledge, action and style in which Owen and Ianto represent two contrasting modes of masculine identity and sartorial style.

As the "urban warrior" Owen's costuming has remained largely consistent through season one and two with a wardrobe dominated by leather jackets and long sleeved t-shirts. To Holman, due to the plot developments in series two it was important for Owen's look to remain consistent to "remind you who he was."[17] The urban warrior aesthetic is furthered through the use of practical clothing such as Tuf boots (as used by the military), coupled with denim and a camouflage print jacket (such as in the bar scene of the premiere episode). The look though is characterized by fitted tailoring, notably short jackets, often with the collar turned up. Together with Owen's tousled "bed hair," the look is carefully constructed to appear effortless and casual in the same mode as pervades contemporary fashion advertising for designer brands such as Prada, Gucci and Diesel. Combined with his lavish city living "loft" apartment and frequenting bars looking for one-night stands, Owen is constructed as the cocky, arrogant, narcissistic post–Lad culture embodiment of the metrosexual male.[18] In contrast, Ianto is characterized initially by his pared down, dark wool suits, crisp shirts and dashes of color — for instance, his deep red tie when he is first introduced in episode one. The sober formality of the look is in keeping with his "butlerish" role at the hub,[19] but is marked by a transformation towards an increasingly spectacular look. Taking a "traditional approach" to costume analysis, Craig Batty[20] argues that within cinematic narratives there are two separate, but intertwining threads, that of the physical (external thread) and the emotional journey (internal thread).[21] Costume therefore has the potential to set the plot in motion as a marker of narrative intention and development in which the character's emotional transformation is externalized via the use of costume. Initially seeming to signify sobriety, simplicity, conformity and restraint, the man's tailored suit functions to construct an image of the idealized male body. As Anne Hollander discusses, modern suits are cut to the proportions of the male of Classical antiquity and thus "suggest a male body that tapers from broad shoulders and a muscular chest, has a flat stomach and small waist, lean flanks and long legs."[22] The wool suit will "follow and complement the shapes and movement of the wearer's body, without bucking and rippling."[23] For Ianto, his suit both enables movement, but simultaneously creates a protective shield. His inner vulnerability and emotionality is protected by the layers of fabric that allude to a tougher exterior. As Ianto is both given a more prominent role and enabled the expression of his desire for Jack, his transformation is signified through slicker and stylish suits and increasingly showy garments and colors. In addition to more frequently removing his jacket to reveal his shirt, his wardrobe becomes increasingly dominated by a palette of rich pinks, purples and reds in his ties, waistcoats and shirts. Such colors intrude visually within the narrative, drawing attention to his face, body and actions. The function of the lightly starched shirt with folded collar draws attention to the neck and jawline, to "produce a commanding set of the head on the heroic shoulders."[24] Thus through his costuming Ianto adheres to Hollander's notion of the suited male as one which is "recut and the ideal man recast" characterized by honesty, virtuousness, "courtesy, schooled wit and refined arrogance" without having to reveal the "true fiber and caliber of his individual soul"[25] In turn the cut of Ianto's suit fits so well, he appears (to borrow from Hollander) "even more natural when dressed."

In contrast to Owen and Ianto's contemporary modes of masculinity, the representation of both Captain Jack Harkness and Captain John Hart enables a return to a different mode of masculinity. Through their characterization as time agents, they are granted a more fluid, more overtly eroticized masculine identity. In the case of the *Torchwood* episode "Captain Jack Harkness," the desire to make characters "sexy," "gorgeous," "young and attractive" is key to the visual narrative. While the hair, makeup and period dresses of the female characters may offer the most obvious source of visual pleasure, the male costuming including that of Jack, is also key in constructing a "fresh, sparkling and really sexy" look.[26] As Richard Dyer says of Heritage cinema, "One of the defining pleasures of the [Heritage] films is looking at men wearing nice clothes. If all the clothes expressed were restriction and discomfort, they would be a lot less pleasurable to look at, to imagine yourself touching or wearing them."[27] The male costumes in the *Torchwood* episode not only offer the visual pleasures of the uniformed male, but through the historical setting (like Dyer's discussion of Heritage cinema) offer retro uniforms and period haircuts that contrast with the "buzzed down" looks of contemporary military personnel. As fans have noted and discussed in detail, Jack's military costuming is not wholly historically accurate, nor does it adhere to the correct air force rank structure.[28] Together with attempting to copy the look of characters such as Jack and the processes of curatorial consumption, discussing the details, flaws and continuity errors of texts can be seen as one of the many ways in which fans express their knowledge, loyalty and devotion.[29]

Yet despite the potential historical inaccuracies of his costuming, Jack's look functions to evoke, rather than represent, the past. In doing so, his costuming enables gender and sexual fluidity that becomes central to the narrative in the episode "Captain Jack Harkness." The break in the rift that shifts Jack and Tosh to a wartime tea dance enables the past to be represented in a similar way to the Gainsborough melodramas of the 1940s such as *The Wicked Lady* (1945) in which the past is a safe place for feelings to reside.[30] As Sue Harper discusses, in such films the spectator is offered multiple pleasures, scattered throughout the narrative, "by a series of intense sensual moments which constitute the past."[31] History becomes inscribed through the mise-en-scène as a source of sensual pleasure.[32] The scene where Captain Jack / Captain Jack dance and subsequently kiss is clearly grounded within the generic conventions of such historical melodramas. The emotional excess and desire for the pair to kiss is heightened, only to be disrupted by the intersection of contemporary "reality" and Jack's need to sacrifice desire for "duty." As a contemporary representation of (an alternative) history, rather than confining the spectator to fantasies of unrequited desire,

Jack is permitted his final kiss. While the text still "punishes" Jack through his return to the constraints of his pseudo family — the Torchwood team — such sacrifice is integral to the narrative structure and pleasures of the historical melodrama.

The pleasures for the spectator of both historical / period dress and homoeroticism are overtly offered up for the spectator in the first episode of season two: "Kiss Kiss, Bang Bang." Where homoeroticism bubbled and was largely relegated to the fantasies of slash fiction writers and fleeting moments in series one, such representations were integral to the hype and publicity surrounding the broadcast of series two. The meeting of Captain Jack Harkness and Captain John Hart, overtly self consciously and playfully alludes to the conventions of the western through the mise-en-scène of the bar, the shot-counter-shot sequence of Jack entering the bar, the close up of his flowing coat and boots and the confrontation of the pair. The virtual fire on the wall playfully evokes the symbolism of melodrama as the two passionately kiss. Such a representation overtly eroticizes the male characters and creates crossover appeal for the straight female and gay male spectator, yet such gender ambiguity and eroticism (arguably) needs to be made safe from the threat of homoeroticism for the straight male spectator. As Richard Dyer and Steve Neale have both argued action, spectacle, sado-masochism and phallic props are used within cinematic texts to disavow the homoerotic "threat."[33] This cinematic convention is playfully represented as the pair brawl in the bar cut to a soundtrack of Blur's "Song 2," yet through their intertwining bodies and subsequent casual conversation the fight functions to further erotize the pair rendering the (ironic) attempts to disavow homoeroticism futile.

The seemingly "historical" costuming of Captain John both aligns and differentiates him from Captain Jack. While both characters evoke military connections and an association with the past through their costuming, John's pseudo Napoleonic look can be seen to be more overtly masculinized than that of Jack. Most obviously, John adopts an almost hysterical use of weaponry as phallic props. The long sword fastened to his belt, swings side to side as he walks and is combined with a gun holster and double pistols that he holds phallic erect in a (failed) attempt to disavow homoeroticism and re-heterosexualize Captain John. In addition, John's coat is notably worn undone, drawing the spectator's gaze through the brocade lines to the taut muscularity of his body adorned his tightly fitting t-shirt. As Dyer argues, the visualization of the male muscular body can act as a "natural" signifier of "male power and dominance."[34] Yet as Yvonne Tasker observes (after Dyer), the construction and performance of the male body that "shows" muscles, "draws attention to both the restraint and the excess involved in "being a man," the work put into the male body."³⁵ Such narcissism would serve to feminize the representation of Captain John. His body therefore remains clothed throughout, protecting and hiding the vulnerability of the actual body and self, while constructing substitute masculine amour. Thus rather than physicality and masculine identity being wholly inscribed upon revealing the bare flesh of the muscular body, the representation of John adheres to Tim Edwards' proposition (in a different context) of seeing the male's physicality via clothes. In doing so "intensely phallocentric" representations are created in the peek show of "now you see it, now you don't [... of] his manhood."³⁶ With its lack of fat, tensed muscle, "flesh and bone can pass itself off as a kind of armour."³⁷ In turn, the male body creates a defense between the inside and outside, in which through the hardness of the body the idealized male is constructed as wholly masculine, rather than possessing the softness attributed to femininity.

Through the casting of James Masters as Captain John, his clothed body does not reveal a bulked up, muscular body, but a very slender, almost androgynous body. Although not within the scope of this chapter, the star presence and inter-textual associations for fans of Captain John / Masters as Spike from *Buffy* are both loaded with meaning and worthy of further consideration. As a mode of masculine representation though, such a body adheres to Church Gibson's discussion of contemporary masculinity in which such slender male bodies pervade fashion magazines and cinema and are "designed to appeal to a younger audience."³⁸ As John sits in the bar waiting for Jack, the low key lighting draws attention to his cheekbones and the camera repeatedly draws attention to his lithe body in the scenes in which he appears. In representing John in such a way, he adheres to the tendency within popular culture of the "fracturing and sexualizing of the male body."³⁹ This not only objectifies him for the spectator, but also functions to construct and perpetuate notions of the fashionable male body in contemporary popular culture. The lean, taut body is evident in texts such as *Fight Club*,⁴⁰ but also as a clothed body in texts such as the representation of Neo in the *Matrix* films, or David Tennant in *Doctor Who*. Yet the intersection of clothes and the body differs in the case of Captain John through his representation as a "nasty" bad boy character, who will "go for anything that moves."⁴¹

While the intersection of clothes and the body functions to eroticize Captain John as the object of Jack's (and many fans) desires, Jack's military great-coat becomes an object of desire in itself. In functioning as a spectacular intervention, Jack's coat is self consciously raised to the level of fetish through the repeated "entrance" and fragmented movement shots that draw attention to the coat through repeated close ups to the hem of the coat. Holman acknowledges (although does not elaborate upon) the need for multiple versions of Jack's coat including a "running coat."[42] The coat does not only allow movement, but the tailoring and fabric themselves are showcased through the process of movement. Rather than a typically fetishized fabric such as leather or PVC that reflects the light, the soft, dark fabric of the coat absorbs the light both drawing attention to Jack's face and the fabric itself.[43] The fabric's capacity to swathe, drape and flow creates a sexual charge that disrupts and overwhelms the narrative. As Claire Pajaczkowsaka discusses, cloth through being woven is both "a grid, a matrix of intersecting verticals and horizontals, as systematic as graph paper, and yet it is soft, curved and can drape itself into the three dimensional fold."[44] Jack's coat through its spectacle therefore adheres to Pajaczkowsaka's notion that "the extremes of objectification and engulfment feature insistently and repeatedly in our experience and understanding of textiles" in which there "are surfaces and planes which are known to exist but which are not accessible to view."[45] The fabric thus both blurs the boundaries of the body and also frames the body through layers, it is at once both heavy and seemingly transparent through its movement. Central to the appeal of cloth is its place between touch and sight, distance and proximity, the seen / unseen and the known / unknown.[46] Anne Hamlyn (in a different context) argues that "fabric acts to conceal and cover objects and persons while, at the same time, disclosing them — hinting at their presence."[47] The wrapping gives the object "a certain mystery, vitality, and seductiveness. Fabric is malleable. It lends itself to wrapping, draping, and swathing." It restricts direct access to the naked object, but it also has the ability to suggest, enhance, and draw attention to what it covers over and adorns.[48] While John's coat draws attention the lines of his body, encouraging the spectator to linger on his taut torso, Jack's coat draws attention to more layers of fabric. Thus through the layers and movement of the cloth Jack potentially not only becomes feminized and eroticized, but the spectator is actually also repeatedly drawn to the pleasure of the textile itself as a fetishized object of desire. The bliss of the textile in its capacity to conceal, reveal, move and weave entrances the spectator. The garment renders Jack's body a mystery. His body, like his character, is enigmatic concealing secrets that have traveled through time and are only hinted at through moments and glimpses that intrigue the spectator, as Jack and his remaining team carry on — starting from the end.

Notes

1. The female costuming within the show is also worthy of discussion, but beyond the constraints and focus of this chapter.

2. Christine Holmlund, "Masculinity as Multiple Masquerade: The 'Mature' Stallone and the Stallone Clone," in Steve Cohan and Ina Rae Hark, eds., *Screening the Male: Exploring Masculinities in Hollywood Cinema* (London: Routledge, 1993), 222.

3. Gaines focuses her discussion upon cinematic costuming. See Jane Gaines, "Costume and Narrative: How Dress Tells the Woman's Story," in Jane Gaines and Charlotte Herzog, eds., *Fabrications: Costume and the Female Body* (New York and London: AFI / Routledge, 1990).

4. Sarah Street, *Costume and Cinema: Dress Codes in Popular Film* (London: Wallflower Press, 2001), 4.

5. See "Costume and Narrative: How Dress Tells the Woman's Story," in Jane Gaines and Charlotte Herzog, eds., *Fabrications: Costume and the Female Body*.

6. Stella Bruzzi, *Undressing Cinema: Clothing and Identity in the Movies* (London and New York: Routledge, 1997), xv.

7. For further work on costume and cinema see the following: Stella Bruzzi, *Undressing Cinema: Clothing and Identity in the Movies* (London and New York: Routledge, 1997); Sarah Street, *Costume and Cinema: Dress Codes in Popular Film* (London: Wallflower Press, 2001); Pam Cook, *Fashioning the Nation: Costume and Identity in British Cinema* (London: BFI, 1996); Sarah Gilligan, "Becoming Neo: Costume and Masculinity in the Matrix Films," in Peter McNeil, Vicki Karaminas and Catherine Cole, eds., *Fashion in Fiction: Texts and Clothing in Literature, Film and Television* (Oxford: Berg, 2009); Sue Harper, "Historical Pleasures: Gainsborough Costume Melodrama," in Christine Gledhill, ed., *Home Is Where the Heart Is* (London: BFI, 1987); Sue Harper, *Picturing the Past: The Rise and Fall of the British Costume Film* (London: BFI, 1994); Pamela Church Gibson, "The Rough with the Smooth: Male Costuming in Contemporary Hollywood," in Rachel Moseley, ed., *Fashioning Film Stars: Dress, Culture, Identity* (London: BFI, 2005); Pamela Church Gibson, "Fashion, Fetish and Spectacle: The Matrix Dresses Up—And Down," in Stacey Gillis, ed., *The Matrix Trilogy: Cyberpunk Reloaded* (London: Wallflower Press, 2005); Pamela Church Gibson, "Queer Looks, Male Gazes, Taut Torsos and Designer Labels: Contemporary Cinema, Consumption and Masculinity," in Bruce Babington, Anne Davies, and Phil Powrie, eds., *The Trouble with Men: Masculinity and Contemporary Cinema* (London: Wallflower Books, 2004); and Pamela Church Gibson, "Film Costume," in Pamela Church Gibson, Pamela Hill and John Hill, eds., *The Oxford Guide to Film Studies* (Oxford and New York: Oxford University Press, 1998).

8. Two notable exceptions are: Piers D. Britton and Simon J. Barker, *Reading Between Designs: Visual Imagery and the Generation of Meaning in The Avengers, The Prisoner, and Doctor Who* (Austin: University of Texas Press, 2003), and Stella Bruzzi and Pamela Church Gibson, "Fashion is the Fifth Character: Fashion Costume and Character in *Sex and the City*," in Kim Akass and Janet McCabe, eds. *Reading Sex and the City* (London: I.B. Tauris, 2004).

9. Richard Dyer, "Don't Look Now: The Male Pin-up" (1982) in *The Sexual Subject: A Screen Reader in Sexuality* (London and New York: Routledge, 1992), 267.

10. See Ray Holman, "Torchwood 3," on Costume Design. *http://www.costume-designer.co.uk/cv/torchwood-3/*

11. Such strategies are also evident within sci-fi cinema, for instance: Airwalk boots, Nokia and Samsung phones (the *Matrix* trilogy); Belstaff jackets (*I Am Legend*); Converse trainers (*I, Robot*); Raybans (*Men in Black, Fantastic Four: Rise of the Silver Surfer*).

12. Simon Hugo, "The Fashion Hub," *Torchwood Magazine* 5, Titan Magazines, 2008.

13. *Ibid.*, 24–28.

14. *Ibid.*

15. The *Matrix* trilogy can be seen to be instrumental in representing this shift in popular cultural representations of masculinity. See Sarah Gilligan, "Becoming Neo: Costume and Masculinity in the Matrix Films," in Peter McNeil, Vicki Karaminas and Catherine Cole, eds., *Fashion in Fiction: Texts and Clothing in Literature, Film and Television* (Oxford: Berg, 2009). Also Sarah Gilligan, *Transforming Identity: Gender, Costume and Contemporary Popular Cinema*, currently unpublished Ph.D. thesis, Royal Holloway, University of London, 2009.

16. Church Gibson focuses her analysis in particular upon *Face/Off* and *Fight Club* with

additional reference to films such as *Pulp Fiction*. See Pamela Church Gibson, "Queer Looks, Male Gazes, Taut Torsos and Designer Labels: Contemporary Cinema, Consumption and Masculinity," in Bruce Babington, Anne Davies, and Phil Powrie, eds., *The Trouble with Men: Masculinity and Contemporary Cinema* (London: Wallflower Books, 2004), 180.

17. Simon Hugo, "The Fashion Hub," *Torchwood Magazine* 5.

18. Further discussion of metrosexual masculinity see (among others): Mark Simpson, *Male Impersonators: Gay Men Performing Masculinity* (London and New York: Routledge, 1994). Also, Mark Simpson, "Here come the mirror men," *The Independent*, 15 November 1994. Available online at *http://www.marksimpson.com/pages/journalism/mirror_men.html*. Also, Tim Edwards, *Cultures of Masculinity* (London and New York: Routledge, 2006).

19. Holman cited in Simon Hugo, "The Fashion Hub," *Torchwood Magazine* 5, Titan Magazines, 2008, p. 28.

20. Craig Batty, "You Are What You Wear: Clothes as a Means of Understanding Character," conference paper presented at Fashion in Fiction: An International Transdisciplinary Conference, University of Technology, Sydney, Australia, 26-27 May 2007.

21. Also see Jane Gaines, "Costume and Narrative: How Dress Tells the Woman's Story," in Jane Gaines and Charlotte Herzog, eds., *Fabrications: Costume and the Female Body* (New York and London: AFI / Routledge, 1990).

22. Anne Hollander, *Sex and Suits: The Evolution of Modern Dress* (Brinkworth: Claridge Press Ltd., 1994), 83.

23. *Ibid.*, 88.

24. *Ibid.*, 90.

25. *Ibid.*, 9.

26. See *http://www.bbc.co.uk/torchwood/sites/makingofseries1/tw_making_s1_ep12_alien.shtml*

27. Richard Dyer "Nice Young Men Who Sell Antiques: Gay Men in Heritage Cinema" (2000), in Ginette Vincendeau, *Film / Literature / Heritage: A Sight and Sound Reader* (London: BFI, 2001), 46.

28. See for instance *http://community.livejournal.com/torch_wood/914279.html*

29. For further discussion of fan culture with particular reference to sci-fi fans see: Henry Jenkins, *Textual Poachers: Television Fans & Participatory Culture* (London and New York: Routledge, 1992); Camille Bacon-Smith, *Science Fiction Culture* (Philadelphia: University of Pennsylvania Press, 2000); Cheryl Harris and Alison Alexander, eds., *Theorizing Fandom: Fans, Subculture, and Identity* (Ann Arbor: University of Michigan Press, 1998); and Matt Hills, *Fan Cultures* (London and New York: Routledge, 2002).

30. See Sue Harper, "Historical Pleasures: Gainsborough Costume Melodrama," in Christine Gledhill, ed., *Home Is Where the Heart Is* (London: BFI, 1987), and

Pam Cook, *Fashioning the Nation: Costume and Identity in British Cinema* (London: BFI, 1996).

31. Sue Harper, "Historical Pleasures: Gainsborough Costume Melodrama," in Christine Gledhill, ed., *Home Is Where the Heart Is* (London: BFI, 1987), 173.

32. *Ibid.*, 178.

33. See Richard Dyer, "Don't Look Now: The Male Pin-up" (1982), and Steve Neale, "Masculinity as Spectacle" (1983), in *The Sexual Subject: A Screen Reader in Sexuality* (London and New York: Routledge, 1992).

34. Richard Dyer (1982) 'Don't Look Now: The Male Pin-up,' (1982), in Screen, *The Sexual Subject: A Screen Reader in Sexuality* (London and New York: Routledge, 1992), p. 274.

35. Yvonne Tasker, *Spectacular Bodies: Gender, Genre and Action Cinema* (London and New York: Routledge, 1993), 119.

36. Tim Edwards, *Men in the Mirror: Men's Fashion, Masculinity and Consumer Society* (London: Continuum, 1997), 42. Also, Edwards notes, while performativity is supposedly all about the breaking down of sex / gender binaries, performativity repeatedly "reveals the body beneath the performance" (p114).

37. Anthony Easthope, *What a Man's Gotta Do: The Masculine Myth in Popular Culture* (London and New York: Routledge, 1992), 52.

38. Pamela Church Gibson, "Queer Looks, Male Gazes, Taut Torsos and Designer Labels:

Contemporary Cinema, Consumption and Masculinity," in Bruce Babington, Anne Davies, and Phil Powrie, eds., *The Trouble with Men: Masculinity and Contemporary Cinema* (London: Wallflower Books, 2004), 177.
  39. Sean Nixon, *Hard Looks — Masculinities, Spectatorship and Contemporary Consumption* (London: Palgrave Macmillian, 1996), 201.
  40. Pamela Church Gibson, "Queer Looks, Male Gazes, Taut Torsos and Designer Labels: Contemporary Cinema, Consumption and Masculinity," in Bruce Babington, Anne Davies, and Phil Powrie, eds., *The Trouble with Men: Masculinity and Contemporary Cinema* (London, New York: Wallflower Books, 2004).
  41. See *http://www.bbc.co.uk/torchwood/sites/makingofseries2/series2_episode1.shtml*
  42. Simon Hugo, "The Fashion Hub," *Torchwood Magazine* 5, p. 24.
  43. In a similar way to Neo's coat in *The Matrix*. See Pamela Church Gibson, "Fashion, Fetish and Spectacle: The Matrix Dresses Up — And Down," in Stacey Gillis, ed., *The Matrix Trilogy: Cyberpunk Reloaded* (London: Wallflower Books, 2005). Also see Sarah Gilligan, "Becoming Neo: Costume and Masculinity in the Matrix Films," in Peter McNeil, Vicki Karaminas and Catherine Cole, eds., *Fashion in Fiction: Texts and Clothing in Literature, Film and Television* (Oxford: Berg, 2009), and Sarah Gilligan, *Transforming Identity: Gender, Costume and Contemporary Popular Cinema,* currently unpublished PhD thesis, Royal Holloway, University of London, 2009.
  44. Clare Pajaczkowsaka, "On Stuff and Nonsense: The Complexity of Cloth," *Textile: The Journal of Cloth and Culture*, Volume 3, Issue 3, Fall 2005, p. 233.
  45. *Ibid.*, 224.
  46. *Ibid.*
  47. Ann Hamlyn, "Freud, Fabric, Fetish," *Textile: The Journal of Cloth and Culture*, Volume 1, Issue 1, 2003, p. 11.
  48. *Ibid.*

FOURTEEN

Sexual Relations and Sexual Identity Issues: Brave New Worlds or More of the Old One?
SHERRY GINN

Marleen Barr believes that feminist science fiction and fantasy explore three themes — heroism, community, and sexuality/reproduction[1] — and my previous work on science and fantasy explored these themes.[2] Although some of the more recent science fiction and fantasy television series have touched upon Barr's themes, their depictions have been limited. This is especially true of the mixed messages with respect to sexuality.

Female sexuality has been addressed in many science fiction and fantasy programs, including *Buffy* (20th Century–Fox Television, 1997–2003, U.S.), *Babylon 5* (Warner Bros. Television, 1994–1998, U.S.), *Battlestar Galactica* (NBC Universal Television, 2004–2009, U.S.), *Farscape* (Jim Henson Productions, 1999–2003, U.S.), and *Firefly* (20th Century–Fox Television, 2002, U.S.). Women on these shows were quite likely to think and talk about sex, and initiate and consummate their sexual relations, which they clearly enjoyed. Nevertheless, this sexual activity was generally contained within the bounds of monogamous or heterosexual relationships. A notable exception to this trend was the character of Chiana on *Farscape* who had no reservations about sex whatsoever and was presented as such. Produced by Jim Henson Productions, *Farscape* combined human actors with puppets and impressive visual effects, in a storyline that combined action-adventure and romance and broke many of the so-called conventional rules of science fiction. The plot revolved around an American astronaut named John Crichton who was transported across the universe through a wormhole and had to find a way of staying alive. He was taken aboard a living ship, named

Moya, and the series followed his adventures adjusting to this alien universe. One of the female characters he encountered was named Chiana. Abandoned by her race, she had to use any means to survive and if that included using her body then she did so. Chiana was very sexy; she was aware that Crichton was sexually attracted to her, as most males were. However, Crichton refused Chi's sexual overtures because he had fallen in love with a soldier named Aeryn Sun. Other female members of Moya's crew, including Aeryn, made derogatory comments about Chi's sexuality, even referring to her as a "slut." Considering that these comments came from women who were sexually active themselves, they mirror the double standard that even women possess with respect to female sexuality. It seems to be acceptable for sex to occur within a relationship if you are female, but not outside of a relationship, and certainly not for the sheer pleasure of it.

Blatant female sexuality stands in contrast to male sexuality as depicted in science fiction and fantasy television. The majority of male characters are free to indulge in sexual escapades, including casual encounters, and no one comments in a derogatory fashion. Examples include James T. Kirk on *Star Trek* (Paramount Television, 1966–1969, U.S.) and William T. Riker on *Star Trek: The Next Generation* (Paramount Television, 1987–1994, U.S.). Both men had sexual relationships with human and humanoid women as long as their versions of *Star Trek* were on the air. These relationships were casual encounters for the most part; neither man developed long-term relationships with their sexual partners.

Regardless of whether the sexual encounters are casual or romantic, the sexuality of both male and female characters is almost exclusively heterosexual; even the vampires on *Buffy* appeared heterosexual in their attachments. For example, both Angelus and Spike had an apparent sexual relationship with Drusilla, a vampire, and Buffy, a slayer. Major science fiction and fantasy programs, such as *Star Trek* in all of its incarnations, rarely presented any view of sexuality that was not hetero, although they did explore androgyny in at least one episode and a symbiotic species called the Trill could be joined with both male and female hosts. This fact was explored in more detail in *The Next Generation* episode "The Host" when Beverly Crusher fell in love with a Trill scientist named Odan. It was considered a great honor to be joined with a Trill and, although Trill did not possess sex or gender, they could be joined with either a male or female host. As hosts died the Trill were implanted into new hosts, with the new host possessing all of the memories of the former. In this particular episode Odan is killed and the Trill must be implanted quickly into another host. The only one available is female. Although Odan continued to declare his/her love for Beverly, she was unable to "see" beyond the exterior female host to the Odan that she actually loved. Beverly told Odan that she could not take such changes, a clear indication of the importance of physical appearance on sexual attraction. Beverly was unable to entertain the idea of sexual activity with a female body.

On the other hand, *Babylon 5* was one of the earliest programs to show bisexuality and homosexuality. Susan Ivanova was bisexual and had sexual relationships with both men and women over the course of her tenure on the station.[3] Joss Whedon deftly explored sexuality between women in both *Buffy* and *Firefly*. Whereas homosexuality was clearly countenanced on *Babylon 5*, the issue was only jokingly referred to and never depicted on screen.[4] Thus the obvious homosexual[5] encounters depicted in *Torchwood*, were greeted with great enthusiasm. This series broke many previous taboos about sexuality, such as having male characters openly involved with other male characters. In addition, female characters engage in sexual activity usually without disparaging remarks and characterizations leveled at them.

Torchwood: Sexy, Dark, and Dangerous[6]

Torchwood, its producers say, incorporates sex and violence into its programming without being about sex and violence. *Torchwood* also examines issues contained in both sexual and nonsexual relationships. Whereas the major character, Captain Jack Harkness, would be labeled bisexual in our world, he refers to himself as omnisexual in his. Russell T. Davies notes that several of the characters are fluid in their sexuality, and it is through these characters that *Torchwood* can examine homosexual and bisexual relationships.[7] Furthermore, *Torchwood* broke one of the "cardinal rules" of series television, that of having series characters sexually and/or romantically involved with each other. My initial excitement over this decidedly "sexy, dark and dangerous" show is now tempered with trepidation as I'd argue that much of the overt sexual overtones of the series play into the usual stereotypes about gender and sexuality. Russell T. Davies has stated that science fiction and fantasy's aim seems to be to preserve heterosexuality, and one of his primary goals is to break down those barriers, to eliminate that heterosexuality.[8] Nevertheless "[a]lthough greater exposure to gay culture may lessen the public's discriminatory attitudes toward gay people, it becomes problematic when the media sources are the central means by which the general public learns about gay people in a depersonalized way,"[9] as though art, film, television and other media can "be valued only as sexual propaganda."[10] True, the numbers of gay characters on television has increased dramatically over the last 4 decades. GLAAD noted that several networks' programming contained characters that would be defined as homosexual or discussed the issue of homosexuality.[11] Nevertheless, the majority of these are portrayed by heterosexual actors and written, directed, and produced by heterosexuals as well (Benshoff; Burston; Hanson; Dyer; Keller; Russo).[12] *Torchwood* is the rare, very rare, example of a program starring an openly gay actor. The other actors on the program, who occasionally engage in sexual acts with members of their own gender, are heterosexual.

This fact has been criticized repeatedly, most notably in critiques of the gay porn industry. Although gay porn has a large fan base, the actors who star in these productions profess their heterosexuality, stating that they engage in sexual activity with men only on screen. Such comments serve to reinforce the distinction that has been made for centuries about the role that men play in sexual encounters with other men, i.e., the active vs. the passive role. Greenberg's exploration of the ways in which homosexuality has been constructed throughout history as well as in contemporary culture reinforces this distinction.[13] According to Greenberg, homosexual activities, depending upon the time and/or culture, have been accepted openly. In certain contemporary cultures (e.g., South Sea Islanders, Native American, African) such relations are not only considered normal, but are considered educational with young male members of a particular culture being sexually apprenticed to older men. However, with age it is no longer acceptable to assume the passive, or female, role in sexual encounters, particularly intercourse. Heterosexual males who engage in active homosexual acts would not, and do not, consider themselves to be gay, although others might, and do. As a matter of fact the concept that there are homosexual *people* is a fairly modern concept. This issue has been explored in much detail (e.g., Foucault, Greenberg)[14]; these authors note that a variety of historical trends, notably the class conflicts arising from the Industrial Revolution, led from sexuality's being redefined from the act to the actor. As the medical profession sought ways to explain the behavior of such actors, fear and loathing of the person replaced the feelings of those who did or who did not engage in the action. The labels applied to homosexuals then have ranged from abnormal to monstrous to unnatural, and their depictions in contemporary television and cinema continue to reinforce those labels (Benshoff, Dyer, Gever, Parmar, and Greyson, Keller, Keller and Jones, Russo).[15]

Captain Jack Harkness, the dashingly handsome con-man, was clearly bisexual when introduced in the *Doctor Who* episode "The Empty Child."[16] Jack expressed sexual interest in both men and women, often in a humorous fashion, but this was clearly one way in which to calm fears by *Doctor Who*'s fans or sponsors.[17] This humor leads us to wonder about Jack until his interest in the Doctor as well as in the Doctor's companion Rose Tyler informs us that Jack is sexually attracted to males, and not afraid to show it or do "it" either. In this episode the Doctor, Jack and Rose must enter a restricted area in order to resolve their current crisis, and a man that Captain Jack knows, whom he calls Algie, is on guard duty.[18] Rose assumes that she will be able to distract Algie long enough for the Doctor and Captain Jack to sneak past. Rose acts quite shocked when Jack tells her that Algie would not be interested in her, although we already knew it by Jack's actions with him at the officer's club. Perhaps she is shocked because Jack flirted very openly with her when they first met. Nevertheless, Rose's shock and surprise upon learning that Jack likes men and women is puzzling; after all, she is a 21st century woman, living in a country much more open to gays and Lesbians than contemporary U.S. culture. The Doctor gives her a little history lesson, albeit of a future human history, as he tells her of how humans spread across the galaxy, seeking new life and then having sexual relations with it. Captain Jack does not really understand the concept of gay, straight, or bisexual either. The term used to describe Captain Jack is omnisexual; we are not quite sure what that means other than the fact that Jack is clearly sexually attracted to the male and the female of the various species he encounters throughout time and space.

Sex, Blood, and Violence: Rock On![19]

Numerous people involved in *Torchwood*, from Russell T. Davies to Eve Myles, assert that the show is about the relationships.[20] At the very heart of Torchwood are the relationships that Captain Jack has with each of his team. But Davies states that the heart of Torchwood is Gwen Cooper. Jack's mission is to do whatever is necessary to save planet Earth. Gwen's mission is ensuring that Jack understands that people are affected by Torchwood's mission. In effect, she must humanize Jack.

Gwen Cooper's addition to the Torchwood team has caused her to grow in ways she would never have dreamed possible when she joined the Cardiff police. For one thing the very nature of her new job means that one part of her life is now cut off from her lover, Rhys Williams. Two seasons of episodes as well as several books have now allowed us to see the depth of Gwen's attachment to Rhys, and his to her, which eventually culminated in marriage (see "Something Borrowed"). Nevertheless the deep and abiding love, and respect, she holds for him has not kept her from being unfaithful to him both sexually and emotionally. We do know that Gwen loves Jack and that Jack loves her: Russell T. Davies, Julie Gardner and others have emphatically stated that Gwen and Jack love each other (Gardner: "They absolutely love each other").[21] Fan reactions are decidedly mixed on this issue; the majority supports a Jack — Ianto relationship.

Russell T. Davies and other members of the production staff certainly meant to sexualize Gwen's relationship with Owen Harper. The tension between the two was evident from the beginning of season one, culminating in "Countrycide." The intensity of the relationship could be likened to a volcano erupting: once the fires died down, nothing was left but ash, not even friendship. This was coupled with Gwen's obvious distress at deceiving Rhys and Owen unexpectedly falling in love with Diane ("Out of Time").[22] Gwen and Owen did eventually develop a congenial working relationship; it would be difficult not to considering the amount of time they spend in each other's company.

As if it was not bad enough that Gwen was involved sexually with Owen, while living with and professing her love for Rhys, and pining for Jack, she fell in love with and had a sexual relationship with another man, James, in the novel *Border Prince*.[23] Although Gwen does not realize that the relationship she has with James is the result of mind control, to her the situation was more than real. My comment upon first reading this was "how many more men is Gwen going to have sex with?" Other fans made similar comments.[24] Why do they have to sexualize her in such a fashion? And, I would argue, that is the problem with the sexuality of *Torchwood*. The sexuality is one aspect of the series to which we are drawn. But the problem is attempting to peel away the layers of the sexuality; to, in effect, deconstruct the meaning of this sexuality. Should we analyze the sexuality within the constraints of 21st century society? Or should we analyze it within the constraints of Jack's society?

In Jack's world sexuality appears to be about object choice, hence his self-designation as omnisexual: one who has sexual relations with both the male and the female of a species. Recall Tosh's statement early in season one: "I've been watching his moves. He'll shag anything that's gorgeous" ("Day One"). In our world Jack is considered bisexual, in that he will have sex with both men and women, although within the confines of the series he only has sex with Ianto. The dynamics of the Jack-Ianto relationship have evolved over the course of two seasons. One suspects, given that Ianto clearly has sexual feelings for a woman, that his earlier relationship with Jack was purely sexual and purely of necessity ("Cyberwoman"). He would do anything to become a member of Torchwood Three as that is the only way in which he could save the woman he loved. Jack forgives Ianto's disloyalty to him, recognizing the reasons behind the act: Jack after all is a romantic at heart. And his relationship with Ianto, while sexual, becomes increasingly romantic in season two.

Salmon and Symons note that slash fiction, which is written and read primarily by women, situates the relationship between male protagonists within a female-wish-fulfilling fantasy realm that they call a *Romantopia*.[25] The Jack and Ianto relationship fits into that fantasy. It certainly seems to appeal to the female members of the Torchwood audience, who are overwhelmingly in favor of the Jack-Ianto pairing, and not the Jack-Gwen pairing.[26] Wouldn't the Gwen-Rhys relationship be more characteristic of the type of relationship many women profess to desire: a caring man, who is clearly besotted with her, is handsome and witty, and who cooks and cleans as well?

Nevertheless Jack's sexuality does not detract from his masculinity; cultural constructions of the male homosexual as effeminate clearly do not apply to Jack.[27] Nor does Jack's sexuality appear to cause problems for the people he encounters, with a few exceptions. As noted earlier, Captain Jack does not really understand the concept of gay, straight, or bisexual when he is presented in *Doctor Who*. Later, on *Torchwood* he will comment on humans and their quaint little categories when Torchwood encounters, what else, an alien sex monster ("Day One").

Owen Harper, who is not a prince when it comes to sexual conduct,[28] makes disparaging remarks about Jack in general (e.g., "period military wear is not the dress code of a straight man")[29] and Jack and Ianto, in particular, on occasion ("you're just his part-time shag").[30] No one seems to care or bother with the remarks. Gwen understands that Jack and Ianto have a relationship with one another. It is another thing to "see" it and she reacts with shock and embarrassment when bursting into Jack's office and finding the two in a torrid embrace. As several of my students, both male and female, remarked: "I don't care what they [homosexuals] do. I just do not want to see it."[31]

Season two's episodes clearly "pushed the envelope." In a *Starlog* interview prior to the start of the season, John Barrowman stated that there would be a sequence during the second season that would be, "and I'm going to put this in really blunt terms — every sci-fi boffin's dream come true."[32] Jack's encounter with Captain John Hart, someone from his past, played by the magnificent James Marsters, is sexy even to those of us who are heterosexual in orientation ("Kiss Kiss, Bang Bang") Jack's relationship with Ianto, as mentioned previously, also undergoes a change: well, actually "they dabble," according to Ianto. In response to Martha Jones' query, "How is [Captain Jack's] dabbling?", Ianto replies, "Quite innovative and verging on the avant-garde" (See the episode "Reset").

This comment is disturbing. Not the fact that Jack is gay, but that a potentially positive and successful depiction of gay people on television is being undermined. *Torchwood*'s writers are sending out mixed signals. Yes, Jack is bisexual. He enjoys sex with both men and women, as well as with males and females of other species. Rather we have been teased with Jack's wedding photo, which looks to be from the 19th century, and his obviously emotional reaction to it. We think that Jack has romantic feelings toward Gwen, but is willing to "let her go" since she obviously cares for Rhys. When first introduced Jack tells her that she really is the only one of them with anything resembling a normal life and she should keep it that way.

It is my assertion that Jack's relationship with Ianto reinforces the stereotype of the promiscuous gay male, one capable of sexual relations anytime, anywhere. The fact that Ianto's female lover was transformed into a cyberperson, and that his primary reason for joining Torchwood was to figure out a way to save her, suggests that he and Jack are evenly matched in their belief that sexual activity is sexual activity. The view is put forward that dabbling is okay between friends; however serious emotional feelings are reserved for heterosexual couples. As Keller notes, "Invisibility defines the experience of gays and lesbians where our personal lives and specifically our relationships are considered unspeakable or at least unimportant.... There is real reticence to examine the subject in detail. This is true of the portrayal of same sex intimacy, and the public is particularly squeamish about intimacy between men."[33] Hence Jack and Ianto can dabble because it is clear that the primary relationships in the series, even Jack's, involve heterosexuality. That is, Jack had a wife sometime in the past, a female lover Estelle ("Small Worlds") with whom he was in love, along with his current feelings for Gwen. The unrequited relationship with Gwen has Jack acting the part of the heroic male, who gives up the woman he loves for her own happiness.

In many respects *Torchwood* reinforces the futility of love. Jack certainly knows that love is not forever however much we might profess our undying love for our significant others. Jack is very aware of unrequited love as his comments to Martha Jones with respect to the Doctor suggest.[34] Martha Jones is leaving her position as the Doctor's companion because she loves him; she knows he will never love her, not in the same way. As Martha and Jack talk of what it is like to "fancy someone who does not fancy you," they look at each other and Jack says, "You too?" Many of *Torchwood*'s episodes explored this issue, notably "Cyberwoman," "Small Worlds," "Greeks Bearing Gifts," "Out of Time," "Captain Jack Harkness," "To the Last Man," "Fragments," and "Exit Wounds." Both Tosh and Owen bear much of the brunt of the knowledge that love is painful. It is only late in season two ("Fragments") that we learn why Owen acts the way that he does with respect to women. He is not a nice man, in that he uses women and is frequently unkind, especially to Tosh, who loves him. Although he falls in love with Diane ("Out of Time"), when she treats him just like he has treated his many sexual conquests, he goes quite mad. It is difficult to feel pity for him, or understand his madness ("Combat"). He acts like he is the only person who has ever had a broken heart, as if he has not done the same thing to the women in his life.

What about those members of the audience who are heterosexual and admittedly are looking at the series through the lens of heterosexuality? Burston, a gay journalist, admits to being turned on by pictures of naked women, even lesbian women.[35] Such an admission perhaps surprises those people who view sexuality as a dichotomy: you are either heterosexual or you are homosexual. How could a gay man possibly find any woman sexually attractive? Turn that around and you have the obverse: how can heterosexual women find gay men attractive? Let's face it, John Barrowman is an attractive man, and he is popular with the female viewers,[36] even though he is openly gay. The character he plays however can and does enjoy women as well as men. Captain Jack would be, is, and has been, capable of sexually engaging a woman. An encounter with him would be sexually satisfying, and helps us understand the obvious sexual attraction of the viewer to the series' characters. Fortunately for us the sexuality of the characters is situated within the substrate of the program, and it does not take itself too seriously.[37] Thus the focus of the show is *not* on the sexuality even as those themes are explored by the writers.[38] Myriad themes are explored and certainly *Torchwood* is not the first science fiction and fantasy series to explore contemporary issues within the bounds of the genre.

"NO! It's got to be a man"[39]

Whereas the ratings for *Torchwood* have been more than respectable in both the UK and the U.S., negative comments have been made about the overt sexuality of the show, particularly the homosexuality.[40] Most of the comments on the BBC America website are positive and when someone does make derogatory comments with respect to the gay relationships, the other bloggers react quite forcefully.[41] *Torchwood* fans are quite vocal in support of the show. Both male and female bloggers (who have self-identified themselves by gender or who have obvious gender-specific names) are physically attracted to Captain Jack and prefer that Jack and Ianto's relationship develops further.

But these reactions come from fans of the show. Whatever the reason for watching *Torchwood* in the first place, most viewers are clearly not offended by the sexuality of the characters or the sexiness of the storylines.

But what about the reactions of those people who are not fans of the program? How would they react? To explore this issue a simple study was conducted in order to examine college students' reactions to the obvious sexuality, particularly the homosexuality, of the series.

Students enrolled in general psychology classes during the fall semester 2008 served as subjects for this analysis. The project was approved by the Rowan-Cabarrus Community College Institutional Review Board and all students gave informed consent prior to participation. Students watched the first episode of the second season, "Kiss, Kiss, Bang, Bang," and then answered general demographic questions, questions about sexual identity, questions relating to the episode's violence and sexuality, and other questions designed to solicit their opinions about homosexuality. (see Appendix a). This sample consisted of 41 women and 26 men; one person did not identify their gender. Ages ranged from 18 to 49, with the average being 21.34 years. The majority of participants were either Caucasian/White or Black/African American, with the remainder identifying themselves as Mixed Racial, Native American, Hispanic, or Other. No one in the sample identified him or herself as exclusively homosexual; 94 percent (n = 64) identified themselves as exclusively heterosexual. Only 3 participants (4 percent) identified themselves as bisexual; two of these were women and the other person was the respondent who did not identify their gender. Sixteen percent of the sample (n = 11) indicated that they had engaged in sexual activity with a member of the same gender. Thirteen respondents (19 percent) had a family member who was homosexual, although 12 respondents (18 percent) were unsure. Fifty-nine respondents (87 percent) had friends who were homosexual. Fifteen percent (n = 10) of the sample believed homosexuality to be personally offensive. The primary reason for this response was usually based upon religious beliefs. Eighty-five percent (n = 58) did not think that homosexuality was offensive; a few respondents indicated that they were unsure, and that they did not care one way or the other. Forty-one percent (n = 28) of the sample thought that homosexuals should be allowed to marry, with 31 percent (n = 21) saying no, and 28 percent (n = 19) saying they were unsure how they felt about this issue. Many of the respondents watched programs with either homosexual actors, such as *Ellen*, or that portrayed homosexual characters, such as *Will & Grace*, *Grey's Anatomy*, *Queer as Folk*, etc. Some respondents seemed to be unsure as to whether the actor or the character was gay.

Respondents were asked for their reaction to the scene where Jack and John kiss as well as their reaction to the fight scene following the kiss. For each scene respondents were to rate their response on a scale from 1 to 5 for the reactions surprise, shock, disgust, excitement, and anger, with larger numbers indicating a more intense response. There were no differences between men and women with respect to their average rating. Respondents were a little surprised (3.19), shocked (3.03), and disgusted (3.08) at the kissing scene. They were not excited (2.28) by the kissing scene but they were not angered (2.21) by it either. Reactions to the fighting scene were: a little surprised (3.17), a little shocked (3.03), not disgusted (2.21), not excited (2.47), and not angered (2.07). Respondents were also asked if they noticed any other sexual activity in the episode. Fifty-four respondents said that they did notice other instances of sexual activity, 3 specifically said no, and the remaining 11 did not reply to the question. Respondents were asked to indicate the types of sexual activity they noticed. Their responses indicated that they considered Jack's flirtatious remarks with members of the team to be examples of sexual activity. Most respondents also mentioned Jack's relationship with Ianto, especially when Jack asked Ianto for a "real" date. In addition respondents mentioned Captain John's sexual banter with Gwen and Tosh, and how he called Ianto "eye candy."

Certainly these results should be interpreted cautiously. Although none of the subjects stated that they had seen *Torchwood* prior to this screening, 22 (32 percent) indicated that they did know John Barrowman was gay. I do not know if I might have inadvertently mentioned this fact, or if the respondents made this assumption on the basis of the scene with James Marsters (and I did not ask them if they knew about James Marsters' sexuality). Nevertheless these preliminary results indicate that today's young people are more accepting of homosexual behavior as depicted on television. This may be related to the fact that more and more positive images of homosexuality are available in today's media.

"We all end up alone"[42]

Science fiction is just one of many genres that allow for examination of contemporary social, cultural, and political themes, even as those themes are disguised within future spaces or future places. Although *Torchwood* is set on a very 21st century Earth the issues of that same 21st century Earth are showcased against alien artifacts, alien technology, and a decidedly uncommon hero. *Torchwood* is indeed romantic, sexy, and dark; the characters' lives illustrate issues that are relevant to the society in which they, and we, live. The issues of female and male sexuality were illustrated throughout season one and two of the program. Reactions to *Torchwood*'s sexuality were almost overwhelmingly positive, on both sides of the Atlantic, and in other countries as well.[43] Such reactions indicated that people, whatever their personal sexual object choice, were willing to watch a television program with openly gay characters who have sexual relations with one another. Nevertheless I believe that sexuality, as presented in *Torchwood*, is fraught with danger: mixed messages that detract from the celebration first experienced at a television series with an openly gay actor portraying a man who could, and did, enjoy sexual relations with both the male and female of the various species he encountered throughout the galaxy. Russell T. Davies stated that his mission was to stop the emphasis on the heterosexuality that pervades science fiction television. If that is the case, then there is still some way to go. Giving the heart of *Torchwood* to Gwen Cooper and apparently the heart of Captain Jack to Gwen serves to reinforce those mixed messages and that pervasiveness he so desires to eliminate.

Notes

1. See Marleen Barr's work in Marleen Barr, *Alien to Femininity: Feminist Theory and Speculative Fiction* (New York: Greenwood Press, 1987). See also Marleen Barr, "Feminist Fabulation; or, Playing with Patriarchy vs. the Masculinization of Metafiction," *Women's Studies*, 14, no.2, 1987, pp. 187–191. Marleen Barr, ed., "Future Females: The Next Generation: New Voices and Velocities," in *Feminist Science Fiction Criticism* (Lanham, MD: Rowman and Littlefield, 2000). Marleen Barr, *Lost in Space: Probing Feminist Science Fiction and Beyond* (Chapel Hill: The University of North Carolina Press, 1993).

2. My previous works include: Sherry Ginn, *Beauty, Brains and a Good Right Hook: Warrior Women on the Forefront De/Re-Constructing Gender*, paper presented at the annual meeting of the Popular Culture Association, Boston, MA, 2007. *Envisioning Future Space through the Eyes of the Women of Farscape*, paper presented at the annual meeting of the Popular Culture Association, Atlanta, GA, 2006. *Women in the Whedonverse of Firefly and Serenity*, paper presented at the annual meeting of the Popular Culture Association in the South, Savannah, GA, 2006. *Our Space, Our Place: Women in the Worlds of Science Fiction Television* (Lanham, MD: University Press of America, 2005).

3. See "Divided Loyalties," *Babylon 5* (Warner Bros. Television, 1997, U.S.).

4. See "Racing Mars," *Babylon 5* (Warner Bros. Television, 1997, U.S.).

5. I use the term homosexual in its sexual sense: having sexual relations with someone of your gender. I do not believe that a person should be defined in terms of their sexual preferences, any more than I believe a person should be defined in terms of their gender. I understand that the terms gay and Lesbian can be used both ways, to refer to people as well as to sexual object choice, likewise, the term queer. Because a complete discussion of queer theory is beyond the scope of this chapter, the interested reader is referred to books by either Jagose or Wilchins. See Annamarie Jagose, *Queer Theory: An Introduction* (New York: New York University Press, 1996) and Riki Wilchins, *Queer Theory, Gender Theory: An Instant Primer* (Los Angeles: Alyson Books, 2004).

6. Russell T. Davies, creator and executive producer, quoted in the special feature *Welcome to Torchwood* on the Series 1 DVD boxed set.

7. See Stephen James Walker, *Something in the Darkness: The Unofficial and Unauthorised Guide to Torchwood Series Two* (London: Telos Books, 2008).

8. I believe that Russell T. Davies undercut his argument about sex in science fiction television when he allowed Lisa to be so obviously sexualized in "Cyberwoman" (1.4). He said that the production staff had many discussions about the way in which Lisa should be depicted; they were going for attractive and sexy, for elegance without being crass. One reviewer stated

that she looked like a Las Vegas showgirl (Lowry), and I agree. See Brian Lowry, "Torchwood," *Variety*, September 3–9, 2007, p. 59.

9. Sheng Kuan Chung, "Media Literary Art Education: Deconstructing Lesbian and Gay Stereotypes in the Media," *Jade* 26, 2007, p. 100.

10. Ellis Hanson, ed., *Out Takes: Essays on Queer Theory and Film* (Durham: Duke University Press, 1999), 11.

11. See "Sexual Issues," in *Touchstone*, October 2007, p. 41.

12. See Harry M. Benshoff, *Monsters in the Closet: Homosexuality and the Horror Film* (Manchester: Manchester University Press, 1997). Paul Burston, *What Are You Looking At?* (London: Cassell, 1995). Ellis Hanson, ed., *Out Takes: Essays on Queer Theory and Film* (Durham: Duke University Press, 1999). Richard Dyer, *Now You See It: Studies on Lesbian and Gay Film* (London: Routledge, 1990). James R. Keller, *Queer (Un)Friendly Film and Television* (Jefferson, NC: McFarland, 2002). Vito Russo, *The Celluloid Closet: Homosexuality in the Movies* (New York: Harper & Row, 1981).

13. David F. Greenberg, *The Construction of Homosexuality* (Chicago: The University of Chicago Press, 1988).

14. See *Ibid.*, and Michel Foucault, *The History of Sexuality: Volume I: An Introduction*, translated by Robert Hurley (New York: Random House, 1978).

15. See Harry M. Benshoff, *Monsters in the Closet: Homosexuality and the Horror Film* (Manchester: Manchester University Press, 1997). Richard Dyer, *Now You See It: Studies on Lesbian and Gay Film* (London: Routledge, 1990). Martha Gever, Pratibha Parmar, and John Greyson, eds., *Queer Looks: Perspectives on Lesbian and Gay Film and Video* (New York: Routledge, 1993). James R. Keller, *Queer (Un)Friendly Film and Television* (Jefferson, NC: McFarland, 2002). James R. Keller and Anne G. Jones, "Brokeback Mountain: Masculinity and Manhood," *Studies in Popular Culture* 30, 2008, pp. 21–36. Vito Russo, *The Celluloid Closet: Homosexuality in the Movies* (New York: Harper & Row, 1981).

16. "The Empty Child," *Doctor Who* (BBC, 2005, UK).

17. See Stephen James Walker, *Inside the Hub: The Unofficial and Unauthorised Guide to Torchwood Series One* (London: Telos Books, 2007).

18. "The Doctor Dances," *Doctor Who* (BBC, 2005, UK).

19. John Barrowman, Series 1 DVD, Disk 3, Special Features: *The Team and Their Troubles*.

20. See Special Features on *Torchwood*: and *Torchwood: The Complete Second Season* (BBC Video, BBC Worldwide Ltd., 2008).

21. See Special Features on *Torchwood: The Complete First Season* (BBC Video, BBC Worldwide Ltd., 2008).

22. Tosh, with her unrequited love for Owen, must have really liked telling Gwen that Owen was sleeping with Diane. Doesn't anyone else wonder about HIV/AIDS, because as far as I can tell no one on the show ever mentions birth control, much less STDs. Gwen does think about having children (*Slow Decay*) and is apparently using birth control at this time. See Andy Lane, *Slow Decay* (London: BBC Books, 2007).

23. Many will assert that these novels are not "canon," but they provide a more in-depth look at the *Torchwood* universe (much as the myriad *Star Trek* and *Star Wars* novels do for their fans).

24. See Captain Jack's blogs: *http://www.bbcamerica.com/content/262/s2_captainsblog.jsp*

25. Catherine Salmon and Dan Symons, "Slash Fiction and Human Mating Psychology," *The Journal of Sex Research* 41, 2004, pp. 94–100.

26. See Captain Jack's blogs: *http://www.bbcamerica.com/content/262/s2_captainsblog.jsp*

27. For an excellent discussion of the issue see David F. Greenberg, *The Construction of Homosexuality* (Chicago: The University of Chicago Press, 1988).

28. Gary Russell, *The Torchwood Archives* (London: BBC Books, 2008).

29. See "Day One."

30. See "Captain Jack Harkness."

31. As a scientist I feel compelled to list the methods I employed in researching this chapter. I watched every episode of *Torchwood* and the Captain Jack *Doctor Who* episodes at least

twice, as broadcast on BBC America or the Science Fiction Channel, or on my personal copies of the DVDs. In addition, I viewed every Special Feature and Commentary on each *Torchwood* DVD as well as the commentaries on each Captain Jack *Doctor Who* DVD and the Special Feature on Captain Jack on *Doctor Who: The Complete First Series* (BBC Video, 2005, UK). I read several of the *Torchwood* books, published by BBC Books. I also purchased and read any other material on *Torchwood* available in the U.S. Furthermore, I read all of Captain Jack's blogs available on the BBC American website (26 as of February 2009) along with the commentary by the fans for each blog. I searched the Internet for sites related to *Torchwood* (with that as my search term). Many years of research have taught me that the first 5 pages or so are the ones that will be most useful; the majority of such content is repetitious. Likewise, I searched YouTube, but most of the material I used for this chapter came by restricting my YouTube search to Torchwood Fan Videos (see note below). Finally I utilized my student's reactions to one episode of *Torchwood*; those reactions and the methodology will be presented later.

32. Joe Nazzaro, "Call Him Captain Jack," *Starlog* 359, October 2007, pp. 28–31.
33. James R. Keller, *Queer (Un)Friendly Film and Television* (Jefferson, NC: McFarland, 2002), viii.
34. See "The Sound of Drums," *Doctor Who* (BBC, 2007, UK).
35. See Paul Burston, *What Are You Looking At?* (London: Cassell, 1995).
36. Kent Gibbons, "Torchwood," *Multichannel News*, 27 August 2007, p. 22.
37. Brian Lowry, "Torchwood," *Variety*, September 3–9, 2007, p. 59.
38. See the Series 1 DVD Special Feature, *Welcome to Torchwood*.
39. Carys Fletcher, possessed by the alien sex monster, says this to Gwen, upon discovering that Gwen is a woman (see "Day One").
40. Stephen James Walker, *Something in the Darkness: The Unofficial and Unauthorised Guide to Torchwood Series Two* (London: Telos Books, 2008).
41. When *Torchwood* first aired, fan reactions, as evident by commentary on Captain Jack's blogs, were mostly positive. A few people posted negative comments to the effect that there was too much sex on the show and that the homosexuality should be toned down. Other bloggers, some of whom self-identified their sexuality and their gender, reacted to the negative comments. Some reacted forcefully by telling those who made negative comments to just be quiet (in rather more rude language than that). Others tried to be more diplomatic. Some tried to educate those who made the negative comments. Most of those who made the negative comments never commented again.
42. See "End of Days," the season one finale.
43. Stephen James Walker, *Something in the Darkness: The Unofficial and Unauthorised Guide to Torchwood Series Two* (London: Telos Books, 2008).

Appendix A: Torchwood *Survey (Spring 2008)*

1. What is your Gender? ____Male ____Female

2. What is your age:_____

3. What is your ethnicity? _____

4. Do you work: ____Yes ____No

5. If yes, how many hours per week? _____

6. Are you married?____Yes ____No
   If not, are you involved in a relationship with someone?
   ____Yes ____No

Fourteen. *Sexual Relations and Sexual Identity Issues* (GINN) 179

7. How would you characterize yourself? ____exclusively heterosexual
____exclusively homosexual ____bisexual

8. Have you ever engaged in any type of sexual activity with a person of the same gender as you? ____Yes ____No ____I am not sure

9. Have you ever seen the television program *Torchwood* before today?
____Yes ____No
Did you know that the actor who plays Captain Jack is gay?
____Yes ____No

10. What was your reaction to the scene between Captain Jack and Captain John kissing?

Surprise	___none at all	___just a little	___quite a bit	___knocked me over
Shock	___none at all	___just a little	___quite a bit	___knocked me over
Disgust	___none at all	___just a little	___quite a bit	___knocked me over
Excitement	___none at all	___just a little	___quite a bit	___knocked me over
Anger	___none at all	___just a little	___quite a bit	___knocked me over

11. What was your reaction to the scene of them fighting, after the kiss?

Surprise	___none at all	___just a little	___quite a bit	___knocked me over
Shock	___none at all	___just a little	___quite a bit	___knocked me over
Disgust	___none at all	___just a little	___quite a bit	___knocked me over
Excitement	___none at all	___just a little	___quite a bit	___knocked me over
Anger	___none at all	___just a little	___quite a bit	___knocked me over

12. Did you notice any other instances of sexual action/attraction in the episode? Explain. If you cannot remember the characters' names, simply describe them or the scene.

_____
_____
_____
_____
_____

13. Do you watch any television programs in which openly gay actors portray the characters (like *Ellen*)?
____Yes ____No ____I am not sure
If yes, which program? _____

14. Do you watch any television programs in which the characters on the program are openly gay (like *Will and Grace*?)
____Yes ____No
If yes, which program? _____

15. Does the concept of homosexuality offend you?
    ____Yes   ____No   Why or why not?

_____

_____

_____

_____

_____

16. Should gay couples be allowed to marry?
    ____Yes   ____No   ____I am not sure how I feel about it
17. Do you know anyone who is gay or lesbian?
    ____Yes   ____No   ____I am not sure
18. Are any of your family members gay or lesbian?
    ____Yes   ____No   ____I am not sure

Fifteen

"Loving the Alien": The Erotics of Technology

Paul Winters

In its March 7, 2005, issue, *Entertainment Weekly* ran a rather gratuitous, dismissive review of the second season of *Torchwood*, a review in which Ken Tucker concluded that "[a]s with P.G. Wodehouse novels and Robbie Williams songs, you have to be either British or adolescent to commit to this stuff; for the rest of us, it's a head-scratching lark."[1] Tucker's stated problem with the show is that it is "tonally weird," meaning that the outlandishness of the plots, the apparent "cheesiness" of the special effects, and the grand statements of the show do not combine well with the show's "bloodletting ... explicit sex ... [and] florid, romance-novel subplots." Tucker furthermore characterizes *Torchwood* as "breezy" and "genially sleazy," which perhaps at least partially reveals the subtext of his review. Tucker ultimately gives *Torchwood* a "B" in his review, but, the tone of his review dismisses the series in a way that is contemptuous of the show's fans, as the quote above illustrates.

When *Torchwood* is discussed in the popular media, it is generally in reference to the perceived kinky sexuality on display in the show. Indeed, in that very review, a risqué exchange from the "Meat" episode between Captain Jack Harkness and Gwen Cooper in which Gwen asks Jack if he has ever eaten alien meat gets salacious play, and most reviews and articles focus to some degree on the Harkness character's open bisexuality. Of course, framing the show as a outré genre exercise relieves the critic from actually engaging with what the series is attempting to do, which is not to say that *Torchwood isn't* an outré genre exercise, but rather that I believe that what *Torchwood* is trying to do is different enough to cause unease among mainstream reviewers in the popular media, if not viewers. That fact, I'd argue, accounts for the "tonal weirdness" that Tucker and other critics have noticed, and it is the subject of this essay.

Created for the BBC by Russell T. Davies, *Torchwood* looks and feels different from any previous science fiction television show, and I would like to examine those differences, what they mean, and how they help us to understand the work that science fiction does in the popular imagination. In interviews, Davies — who also created the series *Queer as Folk* (Channel 4, 1999–2000, UK) — claims that his main influences for creating *Torchwood* are the American shows *Buffy the Vampire Slayer* (20th Century–Fox Television, 1997–2003, U.S.), *Angel* (20th Century–Fox Television, 1999–2004, U.S.), and *The X Files* (20th Century–Fox Television, 1993–2003, U.S.). These influences at least partially account for *Torchwood*'s uniqueness among science fiction television shows; the supernatural story lines, the self-contained stories told within the framework of an overarching mythology, and the deliberate appeal to a cult audience among them.

The Torchwood Institute was established by Queen Victoria in episode two of *Doctor Who*, "Tooth and Claw,"[2] the series to which *Torchwood* was created as a sequel. The purpose of the institute was to investigate supernatural and alien occurrences. More importantly, Torchwood exists to collect alien technologies that have fallen through the rift in the space-time continuum that has opened up in Cardiff, Wales. I will argue that the sexual and the emotional fluidity of the characters and the specific storylines help to structure an emotional response to technology in the viewer through the cross-transfer of erotic energy between sexual and technological desire. Desire for the "other" in a sexual sense and desire for technology become one and the same. I will argue that this approach provides a special insight into the way(s) in which science fiction in general structures the feelings, to use Raymond Williams's term, of the audiences of these texts. Williams meant by the term "structure of feelings" the way(s) in which culture helps to make our ideas and emotions manifest to us as "realities."[3]

Torchwood is a text that is rich in strangeness. Of course, what more would one expect from creator Russell T. Davies, who graduated from a career in children's television to the groundbreaking, remarkably sexually frank and explicit *Queer as Folk*, and who followed that series with a miniseries called *Bob and Rose* (ITV, 2001, UK), about a gay man who falls in love with a woman, and *The Second Coming* (ITV, 2003, UK) about a common man who discovers that he is the messiah.

John Barrowman, who plays Captain Jack Harkness in *Torchwood*, says of Davies:

> Russell is probably the one writer around today who really has no fears of what people think. And he writes everything as it happens in society. Rather than having things that are glossed over and pretending that they don't happen, Russell writes about them, because as he says "I write about the way people live."[4]

Davies himself says:

> Making the impossible work — I do like doing that. A gay man falling in love with a woman. Jesus coming back. Any *Doctor Who* story. *Mine All Mine*, about a man who inherited a town.... I like taking big, high-concept ideas and pulling them down and making them real. The impossible can become very believable. Every story is ordinary people in extraordinary circumstances. Even if you take falling in love, which, although it's very common, feels extraordinary when it happens to you.[5]

I consider there is a desire to play around with people's expectations in Davies, which makes his successful career in mainstream television all the more remarkable, although it should be noted of the aforementioned *Bob and Rose* that "despite very strong reviews the ratings were disappointing."[6] The desire, perverse or otherwise, to play with expectations makes Davies a perfect candidate to work in genre. It helps in particular to be working in science fiction, a genre that welcomes strangeness, even perversity on some levels, and invites cult fandom in its audiences.

Torchwood's rift in the space-time continuum serves several functions in the show. First, it provides the alien technologies, aliens themselves, and characters and adventures spanning both the past and the future, all of which make up the subject matter of the show, the adventures of the Torchwood gang. As Jack explains in the first episode ("Everything Changes"), "There's a rift in space and time running right through the city. The Weevils didn't come in a spaceship. They kind of just, slipped through. All sorts of things get washed up here. Creatures, time-shifts, space junk, debris. Flotsam and jetsam." Weevils are alien monsters that play a role of irrational creatures of appetite in opposition to the human creatures of "reason." Also, the rift raises practical, pseudoscientific, and philosophical questions about the nature of time and memory, some of which also contain a very strong emotional component, seen especially in the episode "Out of Time," about the lives of three travelers who come through the rift from 1953 and have to deal each in his or her own way with the change in time. In addition, the rift creates a threat to the stability of Cardiff, and by extension, the entire world. In the series opening, Jack says, "The 21st Century is when it all changes, and you've gotta be ready." This threat includes not just annihilation and destruction, but also the breakdown of the social order, a constant enough threat to the series to constitute a running theme. In addition, though, the rift functions symbolically, as the characters in the show work through the actual loss and the potential threat of loss that make up the subtext of the series.

In other words, the rift provides a destabilizing, decentering influence on the show, the characters, and the narrative, an influence that threatens the members of the team to the core of their being as it also threatens their world. In fact, the threat of losing their subjectivity as they play with their alien toys and sport around Cardiff on their adventures is the Sword of Damocles for the people who work at Torchwood attempting to keep Cardiff and the world safe. But that potential for dissolution is what drives most of the plots and serves as an overarching theme. As Gwen says in the second episode (perversely titled "Day One"), "You've been hidden down here too long, spending so much time with the alien stuff, you've lost what it means to be human." Later in the same episode, Gwen's worth to the team is revealed to be the fact that she is more in touch with her humanity than the rest. Jack says to her, "Do one thing for me. Don't let the job consume you. You have a life. Perspective. We need that." The episode from which those quotes are taken concerns a young woman named Carys who is possessed by a mysterious alien gas that gives her an insatiable sexual desire. Helping Carys restore her subjectivity is the task that Gwen gives herself on her first day on the job at Torchwood. Of course, the threat of the loss of their subjectivity provides the grounds for which that subjectivity is established. Gwen says to Jack, "This isn't about meteorites or gases. We have a trapped girl, and we've got to save her. When I was with her in the cell Carys told me she was losing. We have to find a way to keep her fighting, remind her to hold on to who she is." Of course, Jack responds with an incredulous stare, but he later comes to see the value in this approach.

At first glance, there seems to be two counter discourses running through the series, the discourse of the rift, which represents the potential for irrationality, dissolution, and loss, and the discourse of technology, which represents the potential for reason, wholeness, and integration. The two discourses could also roughly be labeled feminine and masculine. But to do so, one would have to confront the inherent contradictions within such labels. Michel Foucault, in his discussion in *The History of Sexuality, Volume I* of the science of sexuality, notes the constitution of the techno-scientific discourse of sexuality is based on a paradoxical desire to both mask the truth and bring it to light. He says, "Misunderstandings, avoidances, and evasions were only possible, and only had their effects, against the background of this strange endeavor: to tell the truth of sex."[7] In any given episode, the universe of *Torchwood* and the subjectivity of individual characters is left teetering in the balance between the two discourses. Not surprisingly for a series that bears all of the hallmarks of the millennial anxiety of the post-9/11 world, the main mood of the show is suspense, between actions, ethics, narratives, and even identities, sexual, gender or otherwise. All meaning, all denomination is ultimately suspended in the *Torchwood* universe, leaving the viewer to decide what is and what it means. It should be noted that while the media brand Captain Jack Harkness "openly bisexual" and his own teammates speculate about the nature of his sexuality, Jack himself has never identified sexually in any specific way, while each member of the rest of the team has been subject to erotic activities with both same sex and the opposite sex partners. Like Lisa in the episode "Cyberwoman," Jack straddles a rift between identities, and, as in their adventures, the rest of the characters tend to follow his lead.

But Jack isn't alone. People, places, and things in *Torchwood* are endowed with a strange multiplicity. Is the city of Cardiff itself the drab place that causes characters to exclaim, "Aliens? In Cardiff?" On the other hand, is it the dazzling and mysterious jewel of the overhead nighttime shots? Is Captain Jack Harkness alive or dead? Is his past our future? Is Rhys Williams Gwen's somewhat dim fiancé, or is he the resourceful hero of the "Meat" episode who finds a way for the team to infiltrate the illegal meat ring and takes a bullet for Gwen? Is Gwen in love with Rhys, or is she Captain Jack's soul mate? Is she the kind of person who would lie about her job and her affair with Owen to the man she loves, tell him the truth out of a guilty conscience, and then give him an amnesia pill so he will forget her confession, or is she the conscience of Torchwood who always considers the ethical possibilities in any of their actions, and insists that she will NOT give Rhys an amnesia pill so that he will forget Torchwood and his part in the "Meat" episode? Is Tommy Brockless of "To the Last Man" the hero who goes back to 1918 and saves the universe, or is he the troubled coward who is shot for desertion once he gets there? Are the individual citizens of Cardiff like Beth in "Sleeper" just ordinary people going about their business, or are they actually alien sleeper agents, given false memories and programmed for the destruction of the human race?

Consider the conundrum of Captain Jack Harkness traveling back in time to the early 1940s, where he meets Captain Jack Harkness — another doomed soldier from the past — and the two of them falling in love (in the episode "Captain Jack Harkness"). The kiss they share at the end of the episode became an internet sensation, amassing views in the hundreds of thousands on YouTube and other blogs and video sharing sites, while it was also the first exposure many in the United States had to the series. Jack and Toshiko go through the rift and get stuck in a Cardiff dance hall during a German blitz in World War II, and Jack confesses to Tosh that he was a "con-man" back then who was working "under cover" and took the identity of the dead soldier after the war. Of course, this being *Torchwood* and Jack being Jack, this is the way he tells her: "It's not my name. It's his. I took his name. But I didn't realise he was so hot!" Like the cowboys in *Brokeback Mountain* (2005, U.S.), the idea of two dashing heroes falling in love apparently carries a specific type of erotic charge, and not just for the gay men in the audience. However, in an episode that is already heavily inflected with the sense of loss and the past, the Captains Jack share a moment that is always already lost, one Jack being a time traveler and the other doomed to die in his next mission, investing their tenderness with an added poignancy. In addition, one Jack's present is another Jack's past, a Gordian knot that makes the conundrum of time travel that much more mind-boggling.

Part of the erotic charge of *Torchwood* also inheres in these perplexities, mysteries, and paradoxes. It isn't merely the possibility of alien sex that the series holds out for its viewers, but also the possibility of sex rendered alien, the possibility of difference compounding difference. This aspect of the series bears the influence of slash fiction. Dale Rosenberg outlines this project in her essay "Confessions of a Lesbian Feminist Slasher," in which she calls what she does "mutant porn," a description that might go a long way towards describing the psychosexual aspects of *Torchwood* as well.[8]

Rosenberg argues:

> Slash challenges gender assumptions and social ideas about masculinity and femininity, both in its content and in its distribution. It's a sexually explicit form of fiction written primarily by and for women depicting men. It's a way for women to relate to one another sexually while objectifying the male body without objectifying actual people.... It's a fictional appropriation of male sexuality for women's enjoyment.[9]

Slash fiction is a form of fan writing about two assumed heterosexual male characters in novels, films, television series, and comic books falling in love and developing a sexual relationship. It is written and consumed mostly by and for women, many of them lesbians.[10]

According to Catherine Salmon and Don Symons:

> Like mainstream genre romance novels, slash is written almost exclusively by and for women. It originated in the mid–1970s when female Star Trek fans began to write and disseminate narratives in which Kirk and Spock fall in love and become lovers. As time went by, virtually every cop, spy, adventure, and science fiction television series featuring two male partners was "slashed" (i.e., slash stories focusing on the main characters were written and disseminated) by some of its female fans.[11]

In her discussion of slashing the *Harry Potter* series, Marianne MacDonald points out that not only is the sexual identity of the two characters a problem, "there are many love stories between two people of the same sex in which sexual identity or orientation isn't mentioned, let alone pondered or contested."[12] Russell T. Davies discusses the fact that he changed the gender of a character from male to female, which made the relationship the character developed with Toshiko Sato in the episode into a lesbian relationship. Mary, the alien, was originally written as a man, but Davies changed the gender at the instigation of his producer. Davies says in a commentary that he made the change deliberately with as little alteration to the script or the story as possible. He states that he did not want to deal with Tosh "coming out of the closet" and much like the characters in slash fiction, did not want her sexuality to be an issue at all.

Another thing *Torchwood* shares in common with slash fiction is that the sex depicted is never sex for its own sake. Salmon and Symons studied slash fiction in relation to female mating psychology, and they determined that "[i]n slash and mainstream romances alike, sex occurs within a committed relationship as part of an emotionally meaningful exchange."[13] While there may be more or less emotionally resonant sex depicted in *Torchwood*, sex is almost always treated as a messy adjunct to emotion, which in *Torchwood*, as in life, contains its own perplexities, mysteries, and paradoxes. Take, for instance, the following scene from the episode in which Davies changed the gender of the character, "Greeks Bearing Gifts," which concerns the relationship between Tosh and an exiled political prisoner from another planet. Tosh is feeling alienated and taken advantage of by her coworkers, and while she realizes that she has unresolved feelings for Owen, she senses that there is more to Gwen's and Owen's relationship than they are letting on. Mary seduces Tosh by offering her a pendant that allows Tosh to read people's minds. Tosh struggles with whether or not to give the pendant to Torchwood or to keep using it for her own ends. Mary, however, is using Tosh for *her* own ends, and when Tosh tells her about her plan to give the pendant to Torchwood, Mary reveals herself to Tosh. Changing the gender of the character hasn't fundamentally altered what the episode is about, but it has called attention to what was at stake sexually all along. "Yours is a culture of invasion," Mary says to Tosh, and she could easily be talking about love as well as war. What is the pendant allowing Tosh to do, if not to invade the thoughts of others? The Trojan Horse to which the title of the episode refers and which the pendant represents is not what it causes you to find out about others, but rather what it causes you to find out about yourself. Tosh asks Jack at the end of the episode about this knowledge —"How can I live with it?"— to which Jack responds, "There are some things we're not supposed to know." None of these questions would be asked as effectively without the image of Tosh confronting the alien with whom she has been sleeping, though, and her realization, "So I'm shagging a woman and an alien."

Davies says in the DVD bonus feature "*Torchwood*: Sex, Violence, Blood and Gore": "I think that science fiction is very much the preserve of heterosexuality, and I'm very keen to push that further and to knock down those barriers."[14] But there is a sense in the series that identity in general, not just sexual identity, is something fragile, tentative, and contingent. "Adam" explores this idea by using the device of an alien being that is literally a creature of memory; he can only exist if people remember him. Adam inserts himself into the Torchwood team, just as the show inserts him into the opening title sequence. The identity of each member of the team is affected by this insertion. Gwen forgets her engagement to Rhys; Tosh finds herself in a relationship with Adam and spurns Owen's advances; Owen has become timid and ineffectual, mooning after Tosh as she carries on with Adam, and Jack must confront a painful episode in his own past in which he holds himself responsible for his younger brother's death. Ianto Jones reads his own diary and discovers no mention of Adam. Like the aliens in *Dark City* (1998, U.S.) attempt to do with John Murdoch in order to find the secret of the human soul, Adam turns Ianto into a serial killer in order to keep him quiet. Adam and Ianto have a heated exchange that ends with a same-sex kiss. The episode itself ends with a return to normal of sorts, but it is one that is dependent on the destruction of Jack's one remaining good memory of his father and his doomed younger brother, and on the team all taking amnesia pills in order to forget Adam completely.

The characters in *Torchwood* must deal with emotional consequences not just of the sex they have or would like to have, but of everything they do in Torchwood. When Jack sets the Weevil free in Cardiff in "Combat," he and Tosh watch it get beaten and kidnapped. Tosh asks Jack, "Just so I know where we stand — we would never deliberately put a human being through that but Weevils are fair game? Is that right?" The men in the "fight club" fight the Weevils because of dissatisfaction with their lives; the episode deals extensively with the emotional fallout from the dissatisfaction in the lives of Owen and Gwen. After his time in the cage, in which despondent over the loss of Diane, the pilot from 1953 with whom he fell in love in "Out of Time," Owen offers himself to the Weevil to be killed just as the man whose body Jack and Tosh find in the warehouse had done earlier, Owen says to Jack, who has told him the doctors say he can go home now, "Mm, doctors. What do they know, eh? I didn't want saving. For a few seconds in that cage, I was totally at peace. Then you lot blundered in. Do you always know best, Jack? Is that what you believe?" The "doctors" to whom he refers sarcastically in this quotation, of course, include him. At the end of the episode, Owen discovers the Weevil inside himself, as he causes the Weevils in the basement of the Hub to cower from his sneer.

Aliens are blank screens on which the characters, and by extension the audience, can project their emotional needs. Similarly, technologies in the series exist mostly as mirrors for human desire. There is a rule in Torchwood (which, much like the Prime Directive in *Star Trek*, exists only to be broken), that none of the technologies they encounter are to be removed from the Hub. In the first episode, as Jack sits in a pub telling Gwen about this rule, the camera cuts to the various members on the team, each with his or her purloined technology. The technologies they steal reveal much about the desires of each character. Tosh takes a device that allows her to translate complete books just by coming into contact with them, and Susie, who turns out to be a serial killer testing the resurrection glove, takes the glove, a device over which the Torchwood team has little control. Owen takes a spray that renders him sexually irresistible. He picks up a woman in a bar using it, and is then confronted by her boyfriend. Owen sprays himself again, and the woman's boyfriend is overcome with lust, giving Owen the series' first same-sex kiss. Clearly, the relationship between technology and human beings in this clip has the power to complicate notions of gender and sexual identity, and I don't think that it is insignificant that the first turn the series takes away from the science-fictional preserve of heterosexuality Davies talks about is related to technology.

In her groundbreaking work, "A Cyborg Manifesto," Donna Haraway discusses how technology can channel desire into challenging dualisms inherent in Western culture, in which "[i]t is not clear who makes and who is made in the relation between human and machine."[15] A consequence of this confusion, according to Haraway, is that "our connection to our tools is heightened."[16] Haraway concludes her manifesto in a way that describes the way(s) in which *Torchwood* constructs human selves and relationships when she says, "There is no drive in cyborgs to produce total theory, but there is an intimate experience of boundaries, their construction and deconstruction."[17] The characters in *Torchwood*, the aliens and the alien technologies they encounter, even time and memory, the building blocks of narrative, all are active participants in this intimate experience of boundaries, and the construction and deconstruction of all sorts of boundaries, I believe, is, more than any other aspect of the series, responsible for the strangeness that people experience in viewing *Torchwood*.

Notes

1. Ken Tucker, "Work that Bawdy," *Entertainment Weekly*, March 7, 2008, p. 79.
2. "Tooth and Claw," *Doctor Who* (BBC, 2006, UK).
3. See John Higgins, *Raymond Williams: Literature, Marxism, and Cultural Materialism* (London: Routledge, 1999).
4. See *http://www.russelltdavies.com/#/torchwood/4521448404* (accessed 20 July 2009).
5. See "Russell T. Davies: One of Britian's Foremost Television Writers," *The Independent Online*, October 26, 2006. *http://www.independent.co.uk/news/people/russell-t-davies-one-of-britains-foremost-television-writers-421182.html* (accessed March 20, 2008).
6. Gary Couzens, October 5, 2005, DVD Times: *http://dvdtimes.co.uk/content.php?contentid=57072* (accessed May 4, 2009).

7. Michel Foucault, *The History of Sexuality, Volume 1: An Introduction,* translated by Robert Hurley (New York: Random House, 1980).
8. Dale Rosenberg, "Confessions of a Lesbian Feminist Slasher," *Off Our Backs*, October 1, 2007, pp. 51–52.
9. *Ibid.,* 52.
10. Dale Rosenberg, "Confessions of a Lesbian Feminist Slasher," *Off Our Backs*, October 1, 2007, pp. 51–52.
11. Catherine Salmon, and Don Symons, "Slash Fiction and Human Mating Psychology," *The Journal of Sex Research*, February 2004, p. 94.
12. Marianne MacDonald, "Harry Potter and the Fan Fiction Phenom," *The Gay and Lesbian Review*, January-February 2006, pp. 28–30.
13. Catherine Salmon, and Don Symons, "Slash Fiction and Human Mating Psychology," *The Journal of Sex Research*, February 2004, p. 94–100.
14. See the DVD special feature "*Torchwood:* Sex, Violence, Blood and Gore," *Torchwood* Series 1 DVD.
15. Donna J. Haraway, "A Cyborg Manifesto: Science, Technology, and Socialist-Feminism in the Late Twentieth Century," *Simians, Cyborgs, and Women: The Reinvention of Nature* (London: Free Association, 1991).
16. *Ibid.,* 178.
17. *Ibid.,* 181.

SIXTEEN

Cyberwomen and Sleepers: Rereading the Mulatta Cyborg and the Black Woman's Body

ELSPETH KYDD

In the second episode of *Torchwood*, "Day One," Gwen Cooper (Eve Myles) passionately kisses a young woman possessed by an alien who is in search of human sexual experiences. This exchange is witnessed by the others in the team. Owen (Burn Gorman) comments on his expectations of Gwen's hetero-normativity, while the omnisexual, futuristic Jack (John Barrowman) replies: "you people and your quaint little categories." *Torchwood*'s approach to sexual difference is liberal, blurring the boundaries of conventional expectations and discarding traditional moral values. The "quaint little categories" are subject to revision, and categorization around difference is constantly under question. Like the categories of sexual desire that Jack is referring to, *Torchwood* also questions the "quaint little categories" of racial and ethnic difference, presenting a multi-cultural society in the early stages of encounters with various forms of extraterrestrial, mythical and temporal Others. On closer examination, however, the categories that are under question still retain a certain force, as the series comes to rely on conventional tropes of racial and ethnic representation.

One of these tropes, the stereotype of the tragic mulatta, gets replayed in *Torchwood* through the hybrid alien-human or cyborg-human embodied in a black woman. In particular the characters of Beth Halloran (Nikki Amuka-Bird) in "Sleeper" and Lisa Hallett (Caroline Chikezie) in "Cyberwoman" evidence how alien invasion is both racialized and feminized, with black women representing the threat of invasion through their physicality, their sexuality and their reproductive capacity. Ultimately, these characters function as tragic mulattas: hybrids between identities who bring crisis and conflict to the normative human community and who are fated to meet a violent end.

The racial narrative of *Torchwood* is linked to the fear of alien invasion or intrusion into human life: this threat is implied in the opening of each episode as we are reminded that Torchwood is "arming the human race against the future." Torchwood's mission to scavenge alien technology and to prepare the defenses against alien attack, resonates with a tradition within British science fiction that links the alien menace with post-imperial anxieties around the geo-politics of power and the fear of difference. This fear of alien invasion is traceable through the earlier manifestations of *Doctor Who* (BBC, 1963–1989; 2005-present, UK), in particular the episodes of the 1960s, such as the aptly named "The Invasion,"[1] in which Cybermen plan to colonize the planet, entering society through the sewer tracks of London and "we are therefore encouraged to view London as the paradigmatic representation of Earth."[2] This serial is in keeping with a focus, during the years of the second Doctor (Patrick Troughton), on narratives of invasion/intrusion. Invasion or intrusion narratives resonate with post–Imperial fears in at least three clear ways; first, invasion fears echo a tradition of a reverse colonization scenario that has its origins in the early SF writing such as H. G. Wells' *The War of the Worlds*.[3] In narratives of this type, a direct parallel is made between British imperial history (as Wells's narrator puts it "we must remember what ruthless and utter destruction our own species has wrought ... upon its own inferior races") and the threat of alien invasion: "Are we such apostles of mercy as to complain if the Martians warred in the same spirit?"[4] Second, James Chapman sees this fear of invasion as reflective of a "contradictory sense of national awareness. On the one hand, it expresses a sense of paranoia and insecurity: the nation is vulnerable to alien (for which read foreign) invasion.... On the other hand, it also suggests a perverse sense of national self-importance and prestige: as long as alien invaders deem it necessary to take over the British Isles as a prelude to their conquest of the Earth, the illusion of Britain as a great power is maintained."[5] Finally, the intrusion scenario, the penetration of aliens into national life not so much as an invading force but as a contaminating presence, resonates with fears of the swamping of imagined national purity by immigrants, and the presence of difference already there. This reflects racial anxieties where, "The conventional interpretation of SF/horror intrusion narratives of this sort is to characterize the monster as a form of 'Other' that represents cultural anxieties around race and immigration."[6]

The Torchwood institute is an overt commentary on *Doctor Who*'s imperial subtext. Formed in response to Queen Victoria's encounter with the tenth Doctor (David Tennant) and Rose (Billie Piper) in "Tooth and Claw,"[7] the representatives repeat pro–Empire and nationalistic propaganda, rationalizing their mission to protect the empire and the Earth from the alien threat.

This is most clearly evident in "The Army of Ghosts"[8] when the Doctor, accompanied by Jackie Tyler (Camille Coduri), first encounter Torchwood. Yvonne Hartmann (Tracey-Ann Oberman), the representative of the London base, explains their mission: "Anything that comes from the sky we strip it down and we use it for the good of the British Empire." Jackie questions this, claiming that "there is no British empire." The reply "not yet" produces an interesting slippage, placing the empire not as part of a British past, so much as an aspiration for the future, clearly foregrounding the link between *Torchwood*'s ideology of colonization and the classic context of imperial domination.

The Doctor's conflict with Torchwood can then be read as his anti-imperial sentiment; he rejects their xenophobia, their theft of alien technologies, and their choice to use violence to deter the potential invaders such as the Sycorax in "The Christmas Invasion."[9] Jack, at least in part, rejects this nationalism and claims a different agenda in his leadership of Torchwood, as he explains to the Doctor in "The Sound of Drums": "The old regime was destroyed at Canary Wharf.... I rebuilt it, I changed it, I did it for you...."[10] Jack modernizes the Torchwood mission, attempting to replace imperialist xenophobia and to be in keeping with the fantasy of contemporary multicultural Britain.

If the fear of invasion is manifested in the 1968 *Doctor Who* serial as an extraterrestrial cyborg race penetrating the heart of the empire through the sub-terrestrial sewage tunnels, how are we to read the contemporary invasion narrative which is echoed in the rationale behind *Torchwood*? If London is still the center of humankind which alien invaders must take hold of first, in episodes such as "Aliens of London," "World War Three" and "The Christmas Invasion"[11] what then is Cardiff? If, in *Doctor Who*, London represents the imperial center, the point of focus for the alien attack on the earth, then Cardiff represents a decentralization and refocus on the port city of the new millennium: a place where Weevils and other marginalized aliens, in Jack's words, just "slip through" or "wash up." ("Everything Changes"). The rift through Cardiff is a narrative device to justify the setting — locating the action in the location of production. But is also opens up room for interpretation; Cardiff's "rift in time and space" becomes metonymic for an urban space of access for intrusions through the national borders and threats to the imagined purity of the nation.

Historically, the port cities of Britain have been the focus of anxieties around the entrance of undesirable others through sea traffic. In particular, the threat of black seamen from the colonies settling in the urban areas such as Cardiff have led to racial tension and racist rhetoric around keeping the nation pure. This fear was articulated from the 1890s to World War I when there was an increased settlement in Cardiff due to more colonial seamen serving in the British fleet. By 1925 there was a "Special Restriction (Colored Alien Seamen) Order" designed to limit access of seaman and to repatriate them when numbers increased. The rhetoric that surrounded this fear of numerous "colored" men in the ports often took on a sexualized dimension, with anxieties about reproduction of mixed race children: "By 1929 the *Daily Herald* was already reporting that 'hundreds of half-caste children with vicious tendencies' were 'growing up in Cardiff as the result of black men mating with white women' while 'numerous dockland cafes run by colored men of a debased and degenerate type are rendezvous for immoral purposes.'"[12]

Torchwood references this earlier history of Cardiff in flashback, when Jack is found stabbed to death in the streets of Cardiff in "Fragments," and then captured by Torchwood operatives. He is seen to inhabit the underworld of the seaport, one of the many, marked by difference, who "slip through" the port or "wash up" on the rift. In this sequence Cardiff is shown visually as the historical port city negotiating its various forms of difference that have "slipped through." Thus, as the invasion of London resonates with fears of swamping of colonial others of the center, so the "washing up" in the port of Cardiff of, as Suzie (Indira Varma) describes it, the "Weevils and bollocks and shit" ("Everything Changes") represents other displaced fears of multicultural contamination, borders in crisis and in need of the rigorous policing of the Torchwood institute.

As the fears of mixed race offspring suggest, there is also a sexualization of this narrative, as the fear of mixed race reproduction increases the anxieties around alien contamination. Thus, as the threat of alien invasion reflects the racial anxieties around the end of empire, it is also feminized in interesting ways. In the first season of *Torchwood*, in particular, the alien threat takes the form of a woman and the narrative centers around the investigation of the female body for evidence of invasion. In season one, women who are part alien, violated or infected by aliens, or corrupted by a too close proximity to aliens include: Suzie ("Everything Changes" and "They Keep Killing Suzie"), whose work at Torchwood causes her to turn to manipulation and murder; Carys (Sara Lloyd Gregory), whose body is taken over by a sex-starved gas-like extraterrestrial; Lisa, the hybrid cyberwoman; Jasmine (Lara Phillipart, "Small Worlds"), the little girl chosen by the mythical fairies, and the alien Mary (Daniela Denby-Ashe, "Greeks Bearing Gifts"), who has assumed human form and seduces Toshiko (Naoko Mori) to gain access to the Torchwood building. In contrast the men who figure as antagonists are generally humans corrupted and desiring power, for example the rapist Ed Morgan (Gareth Thomas, "Ghost Machine"), caught through temporal psychic evidence; Ewan, the leader of the rural cannibals (Owen Teale, "Countrycide"); or Mark, the fight clubber victimizing the Weevils (Alex Hassell, "Combat").

The *Torchwood* team and their guest stars represent a multicultural society; working within the organization are a diverse group in terms of gender, ethnicity and sexuality. Yet even within this, the sense of racial difference still plays into the development of the certain characters. Although there is no black woman among the *Torchwood* regular cast, there are a number of significant guest roles. These characters embody varying fears around the nature of racial and gendered difference and present the black woman's body as a site of contestation. In particular, the characters of Lisa, Beth, and Martha Jones (Freema Agyeman) and to some extend, Suzie, embody varying levels of difference concealed. At least three types of Otherness are utilised, which are all specifically founded in the generic conventions of science fiction. Martha's difference stems from her time traveling adventures with the tenth Doctor, Beth's difference is her alien nature hidden beneath her human psyche, Suzie's lies in the manipulation of the forces of resurrection, and Lisa is the more visually apparent Cyborg. These black women are concealing their alien nature; a camouflage that is similar to the act of racial passing. As figures of passing, one identity covers another, but in such a way as to put in dispute the nature and essence of both the categories in question. These characters are hybrids, existing in a continuum between the alien other and the human, and they play through the existential crisis of in-betweenness.

Throughout the course of the episodes in which they appear, each character is tested and investigated for traces of the Other: the search for evidence of difference beneath the human exterior. Each character embodies an existential crisis in trying to deal with the knowledge and the physical challenge of the alien presence within the body. The narrative resolves with each character making a choice that will, on some level, resolve their crisis of hybridity and return them to a more normal state. Martha regains control, Beth becomes the tragic mulatta, sacrificing her life to protect the humans she no longer considers herself to be. Suzie's desire to fight mortality ends with her death, and Lisa attempts and fails to return herself to a human state. Her failure is grotesque and overwrought, and, although she is no longer the hybrid human-machine that threatened human survival, in her weakened human condition she is killed by the team. It is to these last two examples that we will now turn, to explore the black woman tragic mulatta trope.

In "Sleeper," Beth Halloran is an alien sleeper agent living an apparently normal human life. During an encounter with two burglars she unknowingly and brutally attacks them. The Torchwood team discover that she was responsible, despite the fact that she retains no memory of the incident. An investigation into her nature follows, revealing her to be an alien "sleeper" agent, part of a sleeper cell. Rather than a response to an outside threat, the struggle against invasion is embodied through the black woman character who also fulfills the role of the tragic mulatta, caught between her human feelings and desires, and her alien programming.

The first part of the episode includes a lengthy investigation into Beth's alien nature and this investigation incorporates racial as well as gender difference. After conventional methods of physical examination have failed, the team use an alien "mind probe" to look for the manifestation of the hidden evidence of her alien nature. Jack explains that the mind probe "drills down through your consciousness, so if there's anything hidden it will pop to the surface." The sequence continues with images of blood, etc., intercut with close-ups and extreme close-ups on Beth's body. Shots of eyes and skin function as an examining gaze, pathologizing difference as a series of symptoms to be diagnosed through close viewing and examination as well as through the technological medium of the mind probe. Although narratively, the difference that is being sought is a biologically Othered alien, the visuals of the scene also allow us to view racial difference and to see the parallels between the biologically defined projections of racial difference, of skin and phenotypical characteristics, and the fantasy of the extraterrestrial life form.

The alien probe is successful and difference is revealed. After much pain to the human Beth, both a physical and a psychological shift occur. The skin on Beth's arm parts to reveal a red implant that is both weapon and communication device. The alien now recites a phrase in a language not identifiable to any but Jack who translates it as "name, rank and serial number." Like many tragic mulattas before her, Beth is passing. One identity has effectively concealed another, putting both her human and alien selves into identity crisis, blurring the boundaries of difference and creating a liminal anxiety for the representatives of the normative group.

This discovery of the contaminating alien presence in the body is a metaphor for a common trope in tragic mulatta fiction, the reversal of fortune scenario. In many early examples of tragic mulatta stories the mulatta character discovers an unknown racial difference and loses both social standing and position and her sense of identity and self. This reversal draws the audience into the crisis of the character that appears to be white, or in this case human, but must face the challenge of Otherness, at the same time as giving the racial/alien difference a white/human face.[13] Beth's artificially created identity battles with the "real" submerged identity, creating the hybrid character.

Now Beth recognizes her difference, she plays out the role of the existential mulatto, negotiating the crisis of identity around both what, as well as who, she is.[14] Her developing friendship with Gwen allows for an exploration of the feelings of duality; she claims to have "always had a nagging feeling I don't fit in." With her human characteristics in ascendency and her love for her husband Mike (Dyfed Potter) to foreground her human emotions, she fights her alien programming, gaining temporary control of her arm implant in order to track others in her sleeper cell. The others in her cell activate, shedding all human characteristics and single-mindedly fulfilling their alien mission. Unlike Beth, these characters — portrayed as absolutes (first completely human, then completely alien) — are embodied by white humans. Thus, the racial parallel to alienness is visibly at the fore in Beth's character that embodies the crisis of difference. Beth is the hybrid, she retains human emotions, in particular her connection to Mike. She aids the team in tracking the other aliens and by doing this she becomes a "figure of mediation" another characteristic identified by Hazel Carby as relating to representations of the fictional mulatta.[15]

Beth fulfills many of the stereotypical traits of the mulatta heroine: the reversal of fortune, mediation between two groups, and the requisite existential crisis. She also embodies the gender specific elements of the role as the mulatta; the mixed race woman who is, on the one hand, over-sexualized, and on the other non-reproductive. Drawing from the myth of mixed race infertility, many tragic mulatta characters in traditional fiction and film were unable to reproduce, or embodied heightened anxieties around reproduction. Although Beth does not show the attributes of the over-sexualized mulatta, she does, at one point, refer to having children as something lost to her through her discovery of her alienness.

The tragic mulatta myth has its origins in American fiction, from the abolitionist era when the mixed race character was used as a rhetorical method for gaining sympathies of a white reading public for a character to whom they could relate.[16] Subsequent manifestations of the character of the mulatta have appeared throughout literary and filmic representation, serving different allegorical purposes, but linked by the anxieties produced by their boundary blurring status. The existence of the mulatta serves to call into question the legitimacy of racial categorization and racist systems based on those categories. The tragic mulatta translates and appears less frequently in British fiction although the fear of "half-caste pathology"[17] is part of the historical trajectory of race relations. *Torchwood*'s stylistic appropriation of elements of popular American television extend to the unconscious inclusion, appropriation and refitting of certain stereotypical representations.

Beth's most clear affiliation to the mulatta myth comes with her assumption of the tragic fate. The resolution of the existential and identity crisis of the mulatta is an automatic and assumed failure to pass or to gain legitimacy within the group she aspires to infiltrate. Lynne Edwards examines the updating of the mulatta myth in *Buffy the Vampire Slayer* (20th Century–Fox Television, 1997–2003, U.S.) and sees a recent manifestation of the character as "not necessarily racially mixed ... or actively trying to pass for white, but she is still on a quest for legitimacy."[18] Beth at first appears legitimized in her marriage to the human, white male Mike, which is the ultimate goal of the aspirant mulatta. Yet, in the SF world of *Torchwood*, Beth's race at first appears not to be an issue, but her extraterrestrial status alienates her from human peers. Yet, in her liminal state, alien identity becomes a metaphor for racial difference as she embodies human characteristics to mask an alienness that is inassimilable.

The tragic mulatta's fate is to end in death, and Beth's suicide fits this pattern. In her own words, she is "not human enough," to fit in on Earth and not to pose any danger to those around her. When she threatens Gwen, she forces Jack and the others to shoot her, rather than to freeze her, store her in the vault and hope for an impossible cure. This ending is inevitable from the start of the episode and it finds a cathartic resolution; her threat is neutralized, she is punished for her uncontrolled murder of Mike, and her act of self-sacrifice offers emotional closure to the narrative. She is even seen as noble in this; her death attests to her humanness, her denial of difference and her final attempt to gain legitimacy in the human/white world.

The first-season episode "Cyberwoman" brings the issues of race and gender forward in the representation of the character of Lisa Hallett, stuck in a partial phase of conversion to a Cyberman. In her status between human and Cyberman Lisa is the quintessential hybrid, neither one thing nor the other, embodying the classic identity crisis of the mulatta. She is also presented in a highly charged sexual manner with the exotic ideal of the partially clad woman with fetishized machine parts attached.

Like Beth, Lisa is the object of the investigating gaze, as the camera lingers over shots of her body attached to the cyber-conversion unit, then pulling out to reveal the whole image of her laid out at an angle on the machine. The cyber-expert Dr. Tanaizaki (Togo Igawa), invited by Ianto (Gareth David-Lloyd) and Lisa to help her, examines Lisa, excitedly running his hands over her exposed skin and metal-covered breasts. He asks Ianto about the percentage of flesh to machine. Ianto's discomfort with this objectification is evident as he corrects Dr. Tanaizaki from describing Lisa as "it." Unlike Beth, Lisa is presented in a highly erotic manner, accentuating the exoticism of the combination of machine and partially clothed woman. Also unlike Beth, the investigation is not into the concealed nature of her difference, but into the visibly evident markers of human-machine. Lisa is gendered, raced, and individualized, in identity crisis, exoticized, interrupted, and stuck between identities.

As discussed previously, the Cybermen have their origins in the 1960s episodes of *Doctor Who*, embodying the post-imperial and contradictory fears of invasion. They appeared most frequently during the period of the second doctor occurring in four serial narratives during 1967–1968. They then returned once with the fourth Doctor (Tom Baker) in 1975 and four times in the 1980s in conflict with the fifth, sixth and seventh Doctors (Peter Davidson, Colin Baker, Sylvester McCoy). In this period their function shifted from invaders: "In the 1980s, assimilation of the human race was the main aim of the silver giants; if they could not destroy humanity then they would try and adapt it to suit their needs."[19] This assimilation fear marks a change in the understanding of difference, from the violent threat of invasion, to anxiety around how the internalization of alien Otherness affects the understanding of self. This shift is important for the *Torchwood* scenario, as it is the failure to assimilate Lisa, the interruption and the in-betweenness that makes the episode of interest.

Yet Lisa is not the only human to resist the process of cyber-control. As early as "Tomb of the Cybermen"[20] in 1967 the black servant character Toberman (Roy Stewart) is taken over by the Cybermen only to resist their control after they kill his employer, Kaftan (Shirley Cooklin). It is through his devotion to Kaftan, spurred on by the urging of the Doctor, and the combination of physical strength and supposedly primitive psyche that Toberman resists cyber control in order to protect the humans. In the episodes of the contemporary series, resistance is embodied in the women characters. The encounter between Cybermen and human women becomes a failure to integrate. Women resist the process; Lisa gets stuck in between, Yvonne Hartman in "Doomsday"[21] is already patriotically pre-programmed ("I did my duty for queen and country!") and is therefore not re-programmable, and Mercy Hartigan (Dervla Kirwan) in "The Next Doctor"[22] shows an emotional strength that exceeds the limits of cyber control.

Cyber conversion operates with the intent to eradicate signs of difference, eliminating individuality as well as markers of race and gender, although simultaneously normalizing gender as male — Cyber*men*. Yet this control is resisted most by those who are different from the normative white male. The attributes of racial and gender difference allow these characters to avoid the process of assimilation. They maintain an affiliation to a racial and/or gendered identity marked by an excess of difference that cannot be conquered as easily as the individualized psyches of their former-human cyber counterparts. Toberman and the women who fail the cyber conversion are also linked by both sexuality and emotion, which are destructive to technological standardization of the Cybermen. In various episodes of the series, from the weapon created by Tobias Vaughn (Kevin Stoney) to stimulate emotions in "The Invasion" to the tenth Doctor's cancellation of the emotional inhibitors in "The Age of Steel"[23] (2006), Cybermen are defeated by a return to or imposition of feeling. The inassimilable women and black man, are therefore stereotypically associated with the power of emotion to overcome technological programming.

It is also the excess signification of women's and black male sexuality that is resistant to cyber-programming. The eroticization of Lisa as both woman and racial Other makes her an appropriate embodiment of the resisting hybrid. Getting stuck between a woman (half of a committed, mixed race, heterosexual couple) and an asexual, but masculine appearing, machine, her erotic nature becomes heightened and she is more than ever set up as the object of the gaze. As with the tragic mulatta that Beth becomes, Lisa's sexual and reproductive functions are called into question. As Donna Haraway suggests, "Cyborg replication is uncoupled from organic reproduction"[24] and Cybermen replicate themselves through the merging of the mechanical with the organic, and the appropriation of human bodies. Thus, the conversion table substitutes for both sex and birth. Lisa is stuck in this phase and therefore permanently eroticized. As a woman, she embodies the potential of organic reproduction while paradoxically failing at technological replication by resisting the cyber conversion. Ultimately, female and black sexuality is inassimilable into the white, or perhaps silver, patriarchal matrix of cyber-technology.

The violence and confusion of Lisa's identity crisis is evident in her conflict with the Torchwood team; at first she wants to be human, but when she is freed from the conversion table she attempts to upgrade Dr. Taniazaki, killing him in the process. She fights the team with the intention of rebuilding the cyber-race, but finally chooses to attempt humanity for Ianto's sake. But even this attempt to become human, her rejection of her cyber-self, is accomplished through a method worthy of a classic Cyberman. Her final act to regain her humanity is to appropriate the body of another individual and colonize it for her own purposes. It is not accidental that the body available to her is that of a pretty young blond woman, caught in the wrong place, delivering a pizza and stumbling on Torchwood's hidden underground complex. Lisa is re-embodied as the idealized white woman; if Donna Haraway has declared that she would "rather be a Cyborg than a goddess,"[25] Lisa makes a different choice. Lisa's "goddess," however, is a grotesque parody, as her brain is encased behind a Frankenstein-style head scar which is still bleeding, while the discarded cyber-body lies dead close by. She reaches out to

Ianto when he finds her in this state, claiming that he never loved her for her looks. Like Beth, she fails to reintegrate with humanity; there is no cure for the hybrid. Her aspiration for the legitimacy of humanity, for whiteness even, is a monstrous failure, and her death inevitable.

So, *Torchwood* utilizes a multicultural cast of supporting characters, but on closer examination there are some troubling aspects to this multiculturalism. Interracial couplings are normalized in the narrative, incorporated as part of the scheme of British/Welsh life; Ianto and Lisa, Beth and her husband Mike, Mark and Sarah Brisco (the couple the team encounter in "They Keep Killing Suzie"), perhaps even Tosh and Owen in a potential that is never realized. Yet, what happens to these couples? They are violently destroyed, either from within or outside, but ironically through the agency of the troubled black or ethnic woman. Lisa's theft of the pizza girl's body ensures her death by the team, the Brisco family are victims of Suzie's machinations, violently destroyed under the bloody graffitied banner of "Torchwood." Beth's accidental (and grossly phallic) stabbing of Mike not only kills him, but makes her suicide necessary, her human side unable to bear the guilt. Owen and Tosh die, the relationship unconsummated, and they bear no blame for their own destruction; they die bravely in the line of duty, the boundary blurring coupling unfulfilled. So *Torchwood* normalizes interracial couples, making them an acceptable part of life in multi-cultural Britain, only to subject them to a violent death at the hands of a racially othered woman, representing a harbinger of an imminent or potential invasion. The source of that invasion shifts; from space, from the blackness beyond death or atavistically, from deep within one's own nature. The alienness of these invaders represents the difference that cannot be incorporated and that will always exceed the fantasy of inclusion; if classic femininity is inassimilable into Patriarchy or patriarchal models of technology, then racially Othered femininity is even more so.

Notes

1. "The Invasion," *Doctor Who* (BBC, 1968, UK).
2. Nick Caldwell, "A Decolonizing Doctor? British SF Invasion Narratives," *MC: A Journal of Media and Culture* 2, no. 2, 1999. See *http://www.uq.edu.au/mc/9903/who.php* (accessed February 6, 2009).
3. H. G. Wells, *The War of the Worlds*, in David Y. Hughes, ed., *War of the Worlds: Oxford World's Classics* (New York: Oxford University Press, 1995).
4. *Ibid.*, 9.
5. James Chapman, *Inside the TARDIS: The Worlds of Doctor Who* (London: I.B. Taurus, 2006), 5.
6. *Ibid.*, 66–67.
7. "Tooth and Claw," *Doctor Who* (BBC, 2006, UK).

8. "Army of Ghosts," *Doctor Who* (BBC, 2006, UK).
9. "The Christmas Invasion," *Doctor Who* (BBC, 2005, UK).
10. "The Sound of Drums," *Doctor Who* (BBC, 2007, UK).
11. See "Aliens of London," *Doctor Who* (BBC, 2005, UK), "World War Three," *Doctor Who* (BBC, 2006, UK) and "The Christmas Invasion," *Doctor Who* (BBC, 2005, UK).
12. Paul B. Rich, *Race and Empire in British Politics* (Cambridge: Cambridge University Press, 1990), 131.
13. Jules Zanger, "The Tragic Octoroon in Pre–Civil War Fiction," Werner Sollors, ed., *Interracialism* (Oxford: Oxford University Press, 1998), 284–290.
14. Judith Berzon, *Neither Black Nor White: The Mulatto Character in American Fiction* (New York: New York University Press, 1978), 119–139.
15. Hazel Carby, *Reconstructing Womanhood* (Oxford: Oxford University Press, 1987), 89.
16. Werner Sollors, *Neither White Nor Black Yet Both* (Cambridge, MA: Harvard University Press, 1999), 220–245.
17. Paul B. Rich, *Race and Empire in British Politics*, 120–144.
18. Lynne Edwards, "Slaying in Black and White: Kendra as Tragic Mulatta in *Buffy*," David Lavery and Rhonda Wilcox, eds., *Fighting the Forces: What's at Stake in Buffy the Vampire Slayer* (Lanham, MD: Rowman & Littlefield, 2002), 90.
19. Lincoln Geraghty, "From Balaclavas to Jumpsuits: The Multiple Histories and Identities of *Doctor Who*'s Cybermen," *Atlantis: Journal of the Spanish Association of Anglo-American Studies* 30, issue 1, 2008, p. 87.
20. "The Tomb of the Cybermen," *Doctor Who* (BBC, 1967, UK).
21. "Doomsday," *Doctor Who* (BBC, 2006, UK).
22. "The Next Doctor," *Doctor Who* (BBC, 2008, UK).
23. "The Age of Steel," *Doctor Who* (BBC, 2006, UK).
24. Donna Haraway, "The Cyborg Manifesto: Science, Technology and Socialist-Feminism in the Late Twentieth Century," *Simians, Cyborgs, and Women* (New York: Routledge, 1991), 150.
25. *Ibid.*, 181.

Seventeen

No Consent Necessary: A Feminist Perspective on Non-Consensual Penetration

CARRIE DUNN

Author's note: For my definition of what makes an act consensual, I am holding that a person consents if he or she agrees to it by choice, and he or she also has the freedom and capacity to make that choice. It is only really since the 1970s that non-consensual sexual activity has been addressed by sociologists, politicians and society at large, since feminists drew attention to the issue.

The first major work on the matter of rape was Susan Brownmiller's 1975 *Against Our Wills*,[1] which argued that men rape women as a conscious, mutual decision between all men across the world at all times to ensure their dominance. One's position in history, society and culture is irrelevant; this occurs everywhere. Those men who do not rape know that their power over women has already been secured by those men who do. Rape is a process of intimidation by men to keep women in a state of fear.

Lynne Segal discusses Susan Griffin's 1971 article for *Ramparts* magazine, in which Griffin admits, "I never asked why men raped; I simply thought it one of the many mysteries of human nature."[2] Griffin argues that men are encouraged to rape women as a symbolic expression of power. As Segal points out, though, rape only becomes a matter of importance when feminist critiques are applied to it.[3] She concludes, "There are still men today, pronouncing legal judgments, treating wounded women, writing psychological tracts, laughing with their peers, who downgrade women's suffering at the hands of men."[4] Indeed, as we shall see in this essay, there are still men and women within the patriarchy producing and writing television series downgrading women's suffering at the hands of men.

Brownmiller shows that rape isn't an isolated crime like robbery or murder, but part of a systematic process of demoralization and degradation, hence its use as a war tactic. Kate Millett discusses typically "female" personality traits such as passivity, masochism and narcissism, and concludes that women are expected to be passive, to suffer, and to be sexual objects.[5] Segal reminds us of the myth that rape is a rare event in modern society, debunked by feminism: "Rape is a common event, often planned by the rapist, who usually has a wife or girlfriend, and attacks a woman he knows."[6] She analyzes the lack of sympathy accorded to rape victims as a demonstration of cultural misogyny: "Police, hospital and judicial treatment of rape victims were rapidly revealed to be frequently hostile to the assaulted woman, more protective of the 'rights' of the rapist (of his self-proclaimed 'misreading' of a woman's rejection as assent) than the rights of a woman — at any time, in any place — to say 'no' to sex."[7] This is what we see in *Torchwood*. We never see the impact of the non-consensual penetration on the woman; usually we only see how it affects those around her.

David Gauntlett argues that in the latter part of the 20th century, mass media has made gender identities more fluid. Stifling stereotypes have been ignored in favor of opening up a new realm of possibilities for all, regardless of gender. He enthuses:

> The traditional view of woman as a housewife or low-status worker has been kick-boxed out of the picture by the feisty, successful "girl power" icons. Meanwhile the masculine ideals of absolute toughness, stubborn self-reliance and emotional silence have been shaken by a new emphasis on men's emotions, need for advice and the problems of masculinity.[8]

One would expect a 21st-century series like *Torchwood* to promote more fluid, flexible gender identities. Certainly *Torchwood* is famous for its sexual fluidity. Every member of the team has had sexual relationships with members of the same and opposite sexes, and sometimes other species. Jack flirts with most people, but is in some kind of relationship with Ianto. Gwen is engaged to Rhys but kisses Carys ("Day One") and has an affair with Owen. Ianto was in love with Lisa and then transfers his love to Jack. Having slept with Suzie and Gwen (as well as men "if it makes it easier," according to "Everything Changes"), Owen ignores Tosh but falls in love with Diana when she comes through the rift. Tosh's relationships are doomed — first with a time-travelling alien in female human form ("Greeks Bearing Gifts"), then with Tommy ("To the Last Man"), then with Adam ("Adam"). However, the gender binary division remains strong throughout; sexuality may be fluid, but gender is not. One can be male or female, and that is the extent of the possibilities.

The gender binary division is evident from the very first episode ("Everything Changes"). The first time we see the Torchwood team, it consists of two men and two women—Jack and Owen, Suzie and Tosh. Gwen is also in the scene, paired in a gender binary with her colleague Andy.

In his very first scene and first section of dialogue, Captain Jack deplores the changing chemical make-up of rain, as estrogen enters the water cycle and "feminizes" creatures. "Still, at least I won't get pregnant, never doing that again!" Evidently this is not a possibility anyway. Jack, in his military dress, is both masculine and male, and firmly on the XY side of the binary divide. From what we know of Jack's previous life, we can assume that his pregnancy occurred either on another planet or another dimension, where the gender binary division is not as definitive as it is on Earth.

Later, Gwen returns home to her boyfriend Rhys. Their relationship proves a vital focal point over the rest of the series—none of the rest of the Torchwood team have partners, and Jack admires Gwen's domestic stability.

"Day One" begins with a focus on Gwen's home life; she and Rhys on a night out bowling and then having dinner before work interrupts and she has to leave. She joins the team in investigating a crash site, and they enter into some gender-baiting dialogue vaguely reminiscent of *The Taming of the Shrew*.

"Don't mess with me, little girl," says the army officer protecting the scene. Jack objects to his terminology: "She's no little girl—from where I'm standing, all the right curves in all the right places." Having asserted Gwen's adulthood and femininity, he then infantilizes and subordinates her by taking her hand and leads her through to the scene. She and Owen begin to bicker: "Make yourself useful, sweetheart, pass us the big chisel from the toolbox," says Owen, whose request for a "large tool" is another assertion of his phallic mastery over her. Gwen attempts to reclaim her autonomy by telling him to use her name: "Not sweetheart—Gwen. One syllable. Sure you can manage it." Owen refuses to recognize her personhood by taunting her some more with possible "terms of affection" he could use in place of her name: "Not sweet-cheeks? Freckles? New girl?" Gwen's response is: "It's a shame your tool's not big enough for the job." She throws him the chisel but misses, and it hits the rock; possibly a sly reference to females being stereotypically bad at throwing.

When the gender binary is so strongly enforced, and certain characteristics are classified as "female" and others as "male," it is unsurprising that stereotypes emerge throughout. When even the sexually liberated Jack bickers with his ex-boyfriend John about which of them was "the wife" in their relationship (in the season two opener "Kiss Kiss, Bang Bang"), we see that in the world of *Torchwood* there is a very clearly delineated male/female divide in all relationships. John explains to Ianto that they were trapped in a time loop, making two weeks the equivalent of five years.

> JOHN: So we were together for five years. It was like having a wife.
> JACK: You were the wife.
> JOHN: You were the wife.
> JACK: No, you were the wife.
> JOHN: Oh, but I was a good wife!

Sadly John doesn't elaborate on what made him a "good" wife; that is left to our imagination. What is evident is that in a world with static male-female binary oppositions, there is also a very strong male-female dominant-subordinate power dynamic operating. These are played out through *Torchwood*'s themes of sex and violence, which play important roles in *Torchwood*, as might be expected from adult-focused drama. However, a disturbing element that emerges time and again over the course of the two seasons is the lack of agency participants in either sexual or violent encounters have over what they are doing, leaving them to be penetrated or to penetrate another without them making any conscious decision about the situation; most often, somebody forces them into it. Of the multiple examples that could be used to illustrate this point, I shall look at three episodes in particular, examining how the non-consensual penetration is introduced and presented — "Everything Changes," "Adam," and "Sleeper."

Episode one, "Everything Changes," as the very first episode, sets up the framework for episodes to follow. We are introduced to the idea of the resurrection glove, as the team bring the stabbed John Tucker back to life, and gain no useful information — he did not see his assailants, and he did not see anything after he died. The thought of no life after death causes him great distress in his final few seconds — seconds of torment he would not have had if Torchwood and the glove had not intervened.

Later, the police discuss the murder, which is the third in a series; the previous two victims were women, who were stabbed in the front, while he was stabbed in the back. This could certainly be read as having sexual connotations — women must be penetrated from the front, men from the back.

Gwen begins to enter spaces that she is meant to keep out of. First she goes beyond the sealed-off area of the hospital and encounters a Weevil. She attempts to question him and elicit information, meaning the porter follows her up to see what she is doing. Angered, the Weevil attacks him; and Jack seizes Gwen to drag her to safety, while the rest of the team capture the Weevil. The porter, of course, cannot be saved.

Her next invasion is of the Torchwood base, except this is not an unwanted and unwarranted penetration, but a manipulation. She abuses her powers as a police officer to get information from the pizza delivery shop, but what she thinks is ingenuity is actually playing into Jack's trap to lure her in. Once she realizes they were expecting her, she wants to leave, but Jack will not let her. She tells him, "I think I'd better go," and he replies, "Oh, I think we've gone past that stage." Her agency is removed. Jack will decide what happens to her from now on. She tries to invoke some autonomy and protection by reiterating her status—"What happens to me? I'm PC Gwen Cooper. You can't do anything." Jack responds only by telling her to look at the Weevil, and when she is unsure, Suzie encourages her to follow him. After a few minutes, Gwen complains, "I'm getting tired of following you," and Jack refuses to believe her—"No, you're not. And you never will." Her own opinions and feelings are irrelevant; Jack is omniscient and he has decreed that she will be part of the team now.

Gwen and Jack go for a drink and discuss Torchwood's work. She asks why they are trying to solve murder cases, and he explains that they are not—they are just resurrecting victims to test the glove. They are intruding into crime scenes and intruding into corpses to test their technology, by which Gwen is appalled—not because they are resurrecting the dead, but because they could be finding out about the crime that has been committed, and she vows that she will tell the authorities about their dereliction of duty. Jack smiles and tells her that she won't remember—like any self-respecting sex predator, he has added retcon and sedative to her drink to wipe her recollections of Torchwood.

While Gwen is drinking a cocktail of psychotropic drugs, Owen is downing shots of spirits in a noisy bar and scouting for potential sexual partners. He approaches a blonde woman and begins to talk to her; she is standoffish, which he interprets as saying "no" when she really means "yes." He tells her that he has an early start in the morning and "can't be bothered with all the chat," and sprays himself with pheromones. She immediately kisses him, and drags him out of the bar. Her boyfriend follows shortly afterwards, in a rage with his girlfriend and with Owen, whose tactic to defuse the situation is to use the spray again, making him irresistible to the boyfriend too.

At the end of the episode, Jack asks Gwen if she would like to become part of the team, and she agrees that she would like to. However, judging from what we have seen of Jack already and his willingness to dupe people and interfere with their minds, it seems unlikely that saying "no" to his offer would have been an option.

In "Adam," an episode midway through the second series, ideas about the nature of memory and the act of remembering are brought into play. Team member Adam appears from nowhere, and Gwen doesn't recognize him. When he touches her, he implants sepia-tinted memories into her mind, and all of a sudden she knows who he is. He does the same to Tosh, but he implants memories of a sexual relationship between them. Tosh immediately begins to kiss him, and Adam promises her a celebration that evening. In this version of *Torchwood*, Owen is in love with Tosh, who is cruelly dismissive of him, and Gwen and Jack behave increasingly flirtatiously — all because of Adam's meddling with their memories.

When Gwen returns home, she doesn't remember Rhys; she threatens him with a gun and rings Jack for assistance. The team run to her flat, and when she lets them in, Jack is puzzled — "It's Rhys!" Gwen claims that she's never seen him before in her life, and Rhys gets angry with Jack, blaming him for Gwen's bizarre behavior — "What have you done to her? ... I know the kind of sick games you play, pills that make you forget!" While Rhys is right about Jack's own hobby of meddling with people's memories, he is wrong about it being his fault in this particular instance. Adam defuses the situation by taking Gwen back to the hub, while Jack reassures Rhys that they will put things right — "right," in this circumstance, means manipulating Gwen's memories back as Rhys wants and recalls them.

Owen can see no signs of "alien intervention" as he examines Gwen; and meanwhile Jack is rooting through Rhys's memories, forcing him to narrate his relationship with Gwen. Adam touches Gwen's hair and tells her that what Rhys is saying is true, thus implanting Rhys's perceptions of their relationship in her mind.

While Weevil-hunting, Jack is tormented by visions of his father, and is then surprised by Adam's appearance there alongside him in the present. Adam claims to have travelled there with him, touches his shoulder, and Jack "remembers." Adam elicits more information from Jack by touching his shoulder and asking questions, and then putting him into something resembling a hypnotic reverie, recalling his early life.

Ianto becomes suspicious of Adam when he realizes that he has not written about him in his diary and Adam makes him "remember" murdering a string of young women. Ianto is broken by this false knowledge of his crimes, and tells Jack, "I'm a monster." Jack gives him a lie-detector test as he narrates the murders, and each case is classified as truth. Jack refuses to believe it, and reviews the footage of the base over the preceding hours, and sees Adam forcing the memories into Ianto's mind. When Adam realizes that he and his modus operandi have been discovered, he imposes himself on Jack's last memories of his father and his brother Gray, so that when he takes whatever tablets he needs to take to wipe Adam from his mind, he'll also forget his family.

Though these are all examples of non-consensual, non-sexual penetration, non-consensual sexual penetration also occurs. While Rhys is kissing

Gwen in an effort to remind her of their relationship, Adam and Tosh are also kissing as a prelude to sex. After his discovery, Adam justifies his actions to Jack by saying that he has helped them all — "[Toshiko] has never been this confident." Jack guides the team to recover their original memories, and tells them all to take a drug so that they can go back to who they are, destroying Adam. Tosh weeps, saying: "I'm going to lose so much.... He loved me. And I loved him. It's no different from real memory." Jack tells her, "He forced it on you. You have to let it go." He is talking about the "love" being forced, but the disturbing element of her consent to sex being equally forced is overlooked.

"Sleeper" is one of the clearest examples of Jack's impulse to exercise his power. Torchwood are investigating a case where burglars are attacked on their intrusion into a house. The team suspect the female half of the couple, and decide to interrogate her.

Rather than using the tactics Gwen was ostensibly employed for — that is, "soft skills," and being able to relate to people on an empathetic level — Beth is kidnapped by Torchwood, a bag is placed over her head, and they take her to the base. Jack interrogates her aggressively, while she cries and says she doesn't understand. Jack refuses to entertain her explanation, and decides to run tests. When Beth asks what kind of tests, Gwen speculates on blood tests, and tells her with all the sympathy she can muster, "They're doing these tests whether you like it or not, Beth. Don't make it any harder on yourself."

Beth is tied down, and Owen begins to put needles into her arm. Each needle snaps, and Beth asks, "Haven't you got a nurse to do this?" Gwen tells her that Owen is a doctor; prior to this, Beth had had no reassurance as to Owen's competence. He then tries to use a scalpel, which also breaks. Owen asks her about her medical history, which is non-existent, and Jack demands to know what planet she is from, telling her that she is an alien. He wrestles the handcuffed Beth into the cells so that she can see a Weevil, and she begs to be able to prove that she is not an alien.

Jack tells the team that he can prove that she is an alien, and his method of doing this is to use a mind-probe, which on its previous usage caused the subject's head to explode. Beth, of course, is not in the room or privy to this information; in fact, when she enters, Gwen reassures her that the test is safe. When Beth is strapped into the chair, Gwen explains that Tosh will control the probe, Owen will monitor her vital signs, Ianto will bring her water, and she will stay by her side. Having set up this entire situation, Jack refuses to be part of it — "I'll be watching," he says. He instructs Tosh to begin the probe, which inflicts agonizing pain on Beth, who begs them to stop. "Go deeper!" demands Jack, and when Tosh objects, he shouts, "Do it!" Gwen pleads with Jack to stop; he shouts at Tosh twice to go deeper still, and she obeys. The mind-probe hits "a buried component — she couldn't have been aware of it." Jack's aggressive attitude towards Beth, who was entirely ignorant, is shown to have been unreasonable. Only then does Jack give them permission to stop the probe.

These three episodes contain just some examples of individual agency being removed and another person imposing behavior on them. So why is this acceptable for mainstream, prime-time television consumption?

In the cases of Owen's pheromone spray and Tosh's relationship with Adam, both these sexual encounters occur because one participant tricks and manipulates the other(s) into thinking they have made the choice to have sex. But it would seem that as this situation has occurred on more than one occasion, in more than one episode, and no comment has been made on it, because the unwitting partners had been forced into thinking they had made the choice, the show's narrative does not regard it as rape. Adam may be a villain and Owen may be on the side of good, but either way, their status as men gives them the desire and authority to assert their dominance. Of course, in a show depending so heavily on science-fiction tropes, these incidents could not occur in real life, but even in cases where lesser degrees of coercion and manipulation are involved, the perpetrator is guilty of rape.

However, just as *Torchwood*'s narrative believes that coerced consent is still consent, so too does the general public have a warped view of what constitutes a "real" rape. A 2005 Amnesty survey[9] found the prevalence of beliefs that women make themselves more susceptible to rape if they wear short skirts, if they walk alone at night or even flirt with men; indeed, one-third of respondents said that women who flirt with a man who later rapes them have themselves to blame for the attack. A 2006 study by End Violence Against Women showed that 40 percent of young people know girls whose boyfriends have coerced or pressurized them to have sex.[10] Owen and Adam's actions make them rapists. They had no possible grounds for thinking that their partner(s) genuinely and freely consented to sex, but because they made their partner(s) think they liked it, it is acceptable television viewing. Indeed, Joanna Bourke's research indicates that one in every eight Hollywood movies contains a rape scene, so watching violation and violence is clearly the kind of leisure pursuit producers think viewers want.[11]

Jack's role in the team varies according to the situation, but when they are dealing with Beth, he is a puppet-master figure. He forces Beth into having her mind probed, and he has apparently removed Tosh's agency to reject his command to probe deeper. Tosh's discomfort at her actions is evident, but saying no to Jack is not an option. Not only is this a form of non-consensual penetration by proxy, it is reminiscent of the Milgram experiment, which measured the willingness of study participants to obey the orders of an authority figure, even if the actions that resulted from those orders were against their personal moral code.

> The extreme willingness of adults to go to almost any lengths on the command of an authority constitutes the chief finding of the study and the fact most urgently demanding explanation.... Ordinary people, simply doing their jobs, and without any particular hostility on their part, can become agents in a terrible destructive process. Moreover, even when the destructive effects of their work become patently clear, and they are asked to carry out actions incompatible with fundamental standards of morality, relatively few people have the resources needed to resist authority.[12]

This is still the case today. A team of researchers at Santa Clara University repeated Milgram's experiment in 2008 and got the same results, as did psychologist Dr. Abigail San for a BBC documentary.

"It's not that these people are simply not good people any more — there is a massive social influence going on," said San in a BBC interview.[13] Just as these real-life people are influenced by a man in a white coat telling them what to do, so too is Tosh influenced by a man in a military coat. When we find out later in the second season that Tosh owes her liberty and possibly her life to Jack and Jack alone, his power over her and her willing acquiescence becomes even more disturbing — possibly even a case of Stockholm syndrome, where a hostage is loyal to her captor. Bourke tells us that historically:

> Some types of people are deemed to be unable to consent ... in the first place. For them, consent does not apply. Slaves, for instance, were simply not human enough for the concept of "consent" to be relevant. Slave women were regarded as the absolute property of another person and were incapable of acting as individual agents.[14]

When Jack loses his temper at Tosh using her initiative, he shouts, "When I want you to think for yourself, I'll tell you" ("Cyberwoman"). In the meantime, she is his instrument, obeying his orders, entirely under his command.

Non-consensual penetration in *Torchwood* is acceptable because the powerful dominant male is meant to be our hero. We are meant to identify with him; we are meant to approve of his actions. If the non-consensual penetration is sexual, it is acceptable if the perpetrator made his partner(s) think they liked it; and we as viewers aren't troubled by any fall-out from the rape afterwards. If the non-consensual penetration is violent, it is acceptable if the perpetrator thinks the victim is guilty of a crime, but he can keep his own hands free of blood by making his staff into the torturers — perhaps indicating that he could not bring himself to commit the act himself, knowing that it is morally and ethically reprehensible. More than this, though, looking at the Amnesty research, non-consensual penetration in *Torchwood* is acceptable because more often than not it is also acceptable in real life. Why not, then, present it on television for our viewing pleasure?

Notes

1. Susan Brownmiller, *Against Our Will: Men, Women and Rape* (London: Simon and Schuster, 1975).
2. Lynne Segal, *Slow Motion* (London: Palgrave, 2007).
3. *Ibid.*, 198.
4. *Ibid.*, 199.
5. Kate Millett, *Sexual Politics* (London: Virago, 1977), 194.
6. Lynne Segal, *Slow Motion*, 199.
7. *Ibid.*
8. David Gauntlett, *Media, Gender and Identity* (Routledge: London, 2002), 248.
9. Amnesty International UK, Sexual Assault Summary Report, *http://www.amnesty.org.uk/uploads/documents/doc_16619.doc* (accessed 25 January 2009).
10. See *www.endviolenceagainstwomen.org.uk/.../brendan_barber_and_liz_kelly_speeches_for_web.doc* (accessed 26 July 2009).
11. Joanna Bourke, *Rape — Sex, Violence, History* (London: Counterpoint LLC, 2007), 14.
12. Stanley Milgram, "The Perils of Obedience," 1974. See *http://www.age-of-the-sage.org/psychology/milgram_perils_authority_1974.html*
13. BBC News website, "People still willing to torture," see *http://news.bbc.co.uk/1/hi/health/7791278.stm* (accessed 25 January 2009).
14. Joanna Bourke, *Rape — Sex, Violence, History*, 76.

Eighteen

Out in Space: Masculinity, Sexuality and the Science Fiction Heroics of Captain Jack

LEE BARRON

> JACK: With a dashing hero like me on the case, how can we fail?
> IANTO: He is dashing. You have to give him that.

According to Brian McHale's[1] analysis of the anatomy of postmodernist fiction, and what he dubs the literary post-modern fantastic, science fiction typifies this literary form because it is fundamentally concerned with spatial and conceptual slippage, with the erosion of discrete boundaries, between what exists and what is imagined, between differing worlds and dimensions, and between the organic and technological. To illustrate, McHale cites various examples which include invasion from space tales such as H.G. Wells' *War of the Worlds*, or sagas of men visiting other worlds such as Wells' *The First Men in the Moon* and *The Time Machine*, Ray Bradbury's *The Martian Chronicles*, and Edgar Rice Burrough's Martian and Venus adventures. While such aspects would become extensively part of science fiction cinema, such qualities were encapsulated within the long-running British science fiction television series *Doctor Who*, which originally ran on the BBC from 1963 through 1989, returning in 2005 in the hands of the television writer Russell T. Davies. Within the 2000s revamped version, in addition to new incarnations of the Doctor character, new companions and new villains was a male "co-hero" character, Captain Jack Harkness, played by the Scottish/American actor John Barrowman. Such was the appeal of Harkness that the "Captain Jack" character would subsequently feature in the spin-off series, *Torchwood*. As with *Doctor Who* (BBC, 1963–89; 2005-present, UK), *Torchwood* would also exemplify central tropes of classic science fiction outlined above, but which in addition to time travel, dimension-hopping and extraterrestrial invaders would also persistently play with sexual boundaries.

Indeed, *Torchwood* would prove to be a radical spin-off in terms of its focus and representation of sexuality, arguably to an unprecedented extent within a popular science fiction series. Consequently, *Torchwood* would combine the "alien menace" and time travel motifs pivotal to *Doctor Who* with a significant and sustained focus upon gender, sexuality, bisexuality, and centrally, homosexuality.

This essay will examine the modes by which *Torchwood* and the figure of Captain Jack Harkness combines longstanding central themes of science fiction (time travel, alien invasion, temporal displacement and uncertainty) with an avowedly non-heteronormative narrative stance that also establishes a masculine and overtly homosexual/bi-sexual heroic male figure that represents a radical televisual symbol of homosexuality and bi-sexuality (or, as Captain Jack claims, a 51st century "omnisexuality"). But, although the figure of Captain Jack is most assuredly politically progressive in terms of his blatant sexuality and visibility within a populist television genre, the mix of science fiction and "adult" themes does have consequences for the narrative in terms of tonal stability and identity.

There Is a New Hero in Town: Confronting Cultural Invisibility (In and Out of the Rift)

With reference to his previous work as a television writer, most notably in creating the ground-breaking Channel 4 gay drama, *Queer as Folk*, the UK tabloid *The Sun* greeted the announcement that Davies was heading the revamp of the long-defunct *Doctor Who* with the headline "Doctor Queer."[2] And in some senses, they were not too far off the mark. Indeed, the *Doctor Who* of the 21st century would, under Davies' vision, have more of a sexual dimension to it than the original run. Although *Doctor Who* from 1963 to 1989 arguably confronted a range of political issues such as fascism, ethnic persecution, feminism and class conflict,[3] sexuality was not paramount. The character of the mysterious and otherworldly Time Lord, the Doctor, would range from the avuncular, impish, and eccentric, but was most assuredly chaste. Even with the companionship of numerous female (and some male) companions, from (to name but a few) the resourceful Sarah Jane (Elizabeth Sladen), the warrior Leela (Louise Jameson), the Time Lord Romana (Mary Tamm), and the "streetwise" Ace (Sophie Aldred), the issue of sexuality and the Doctor was notably absent or certainly ambivalent. This changed somewhat in the one-off 1996 BBC/Fox *Doctor Who* television film in which Paul McGann's Doctor kissed his erstwhile companion, Dr. Grace Holloway (Daphne Ashbrook). And within Davies' version, a romantic narrative link between the Doctor and companions would become more manifest, particularly between the tenth Doctor and his companion, Rose Tyler (Billie Piper). Moreover, in addition to romance, the new *Doctor Who* also introduced the character of the roguish "Captain" Jack Harkness, "a time-traveling bisexual conman from the fifty-first century who teams up with the Doctor and Rose within "The Empty Child" and "The Doctor Dances."[4]

Captain Jack's introduction came in the role of the rescuer of Rose, who is perilously hanging from a rope attached to a barrage balloon drifting over Blitz-era London in the midst of a German air raid. Saving Rose with an alien tractor beam, and in possession of a Chula alien spacecraft, Jack, like the Doctor, is an otherworldly figure. Ostensibly an American volunteer with the RAF, Jack's immediate attraction is to Rose, and he initiates a process of seduction. Yet, as suggested by Jack's earlier banter with his fellow officer, Algernon (Robert Hands), who is euphemistically described as being "not Rose's type," Jack, sexually, is not so straightforward. Therefore, in addition to new Doctors and Daleks, the 2005 *Doctor Who* also introduced sex, and homosexual sex, and sexual pleasure. As the Doctor explains to Rose about Jack's approach to sexuality:

> THE DOCTOR: Relax. He's a 51st century guy. He's just more flexible when it comes to dancing.
> ROSE: How flexible?
> THE DOCTOR: ... So many species. So little time...

Accordingly, not only would the new *Doctor Who* be marked by sophisticated CGI effects and the creation of new villains (Slitheen and Reapers) to threaten humanity alongside the iconic classics (Autons, Daleks, Cybermen and the Master), but also with a distinctive and politically progressive modern sexual dynamic. As John Barrowman states of his character and orientations, "Russell had made it clear to me that Jack's character would be unlike any other in the classic *Doctor Who* series. As a result, the subtle sexual chemistry among all three characters — the Doctor, Rose and Jack — was always in play."[5]

Captain Jack would appear again within the 2005 series, and subsequently feature with David Tennant's incarnation of the Doctor, sacrificing himself in battle against the Daleks but gaining immortality when resurrected by Rose. Moreover, Captain Jack and the Doctor would even kiss goodbye in the episode "The Parting of the Ways." Thus, throughout the course of his *Doctor Who* adventures, Captain Jack progressively develops from an intergalactic shyster to a hero; and it is this latter status that formed the basis of the 2006 Julie Gardner and Russell T. Davies produced spin-off series, *Torchwood*.

Now based on Earth and serving as the leader of the Cardiff-based alien defense Institute, Torchwood Three, Captain Jack would firmly assume the mantle of heroic commander, combating extraterrestrial threats, time anomalies, the subterranean Weevils, and even Death, all principally stemming from the mysterious time/space anomaly dubbed the "Rift." But *Torchwood* would be a very different series from *Doctor Who*, with its won particular identity, with a demonstrably adult tone such as: intertextual references to science fiction and horror films (*Predator, 28 Days Later, Terminator 1 & 2, Star Wars, The Texas Chainsaw Massacre*, and with literary fantasy nods towards H.P. Lovecraft's Cthulhu mythos), allusions to the War on Terror and the practice of Rendition, and the copious abundance of violence, gore, profanity, and sexuality. With reference to the latter component, within *Torchwood* sex is a narrative constant and although the bi/omnisexuality of Captain Jack was present within *Doctor Who*, *Torchwood*'s incarnation would be far more openly sexualized from the outset. Indeed, the tonal differentiation between *Doctor Who* and its textual progeny is markedly expressed by Andy Medhurst, who dubs *Torchwood* not so much a science fiction series but rather "a post-queer, pan-sexual perv-fest."[6]

Broadcast post-watershed (9 P.M. in the UK), sexual boundaries within *Torchwood* are routinely effaced, with a host of characters in addition to Captain Jack engaging in sexual acts, and often bisexual trysts. Such a radical shift in emphasis and content (effectively removing younger *Doctor Who* fans from its audience) did not garner universal praise from critics. As one reviewer states: "The sex and violence added to justify the post-watershed slot feel tacked on, as most of the characters display an adolescent naivety and gormlessness that make it hard to engage with them on a truly 'adult' level."[7] Yet, the emphasis upon sexuality is far more potent than such a dismissal suggests. Critically, it is fair to suggest that *Torchwood* only fully hits its stride in the second season, a season which cements relationships between the ensemble and which begins to unravel the enigmas that surround the Captain Jack character and his history (or is it his future?): the loss of his brother, Gray (Ethan Brooke and Lachlan Nieboer), his recruitment to the Torchwood Institute in 1899, his background as a "Time Agent," and, crucially, his sexuality. A theme that runs throughout *Torchwood* is the suggestion of an attraction between Jack and Gwen Cooper (Eve Myles), the Cardiff-based police constable who is recruited to Torchwood. Yet for all of the potential Mulder and Scully-like "will they/won't they" tension, Jack's sexual liaisons tend not towards the bisexual or the omnisexual (although Jack does refer to some of his alien encounters — the inventive being without a mouth as one example), but the homosexual. As such, this is *Torchwood*'s major significance within contemporary culture, and especially popular science fiction. Charismatic and heroic, Captain Jack is an iconic figure who combats television heteronormativity as much as he combats Weevils, cannibals or Abaddon, the Great Devourer. So in addition to disparate worlds and temporal zones colliding and threatening Cardiff, *Torchwood* mirrors such spatial flux and "has interesting gay and straight storylines interwoven"[8] throughout it, an aspect I will return to.

Consequently, on one level, Captain Jack is a valiant character who is candid about his sexual preferences, as Toshiko "Tosh" Sato (Naoko Mori) states within "Day One": "I've watched him in action. He'll shag anything if it's gorgeous enough." True enough, but throughout the *Torchwood* narrative, Captain Jack's physical encounters are invariably with men, and they are unambiguous and frequently visually realized. Thus, from *Doctor Who* to *Torchwood*, Russell T. Davies has established a gay/Queer male hero and text which signifies a major progression within the history of gay and lesbian television representation.

With regard to this history, as Doty and Gove[9] argue, it is crucial to note that there *has* been some form of Queer representation on Western television from the 1940s onwards. For example, one of the most popular programs in the formative years of American television was *The Milton Berle Show*, which frequently featured its star in front of the camera in drag and engaging in camp antics. However, irrespective of such a dubious presence, the general critical consensus would suggest a limited representational range of gay and lesbian characters and that "queerness" on mainstream popular television has been marked by a process of distinct and pervasive heteronormativity, mirroring a social, cultural and legal invisibility.[10] As Thornham and Purvis state, within popular representations, homosexual discourse was traditionally presented in terms of secrecy, concealment and isolation. Moreover, television representations of sexuality have been structured according to a number of assumptions, that "sex" was adjudged offensive, and homosexual sex was more offensive still.[11] Subsequently, media output was typically underpinned by a distinct and pervasive heteronormative ideology. For this reason, if sitcoms and popular dramas historically did feature homosexual characters, they tended to take the form of crude gender stereotypes. Consequently, from the mid-1950s to the late 1960s, British television was still heavily committed to dramas, documentaries, sitcoms and children's programmes, which addressed audiences on the basis of an assumed heterosexuality.[12] Yet, as the 1970s progressed, there were progressive signs against such a trend. For example, the British situation comedy *Are You Being Served?* (1972–1985) similarly presented the figure of Mr. Humphries. While never being formally identified as being gay, as Thornham and Purvis point out, actor John Inman's constant and blatant innuendo was still challenging and, within such a popular genre and enduring series, highly visible. But it was the broadcasting of *The Naked Civil Servant* in 1975, a dramatization of the life of Quentin Crisp (John Hurt), which was to represent a "quantum leap" in broadcasting history with regard to the representation of male homosexuality.[13]

And yet, the primacy of heteronormativity would remain a key issue within television. Although, in terms of mainstream broadcasting, the U.S. situation comedy *Will & Grace* (NBC, 1998–2006, U.S.) was one of the only network programmes based on an openly gay protagonist, principally the character of Will Truman (Eric McCormack) — a role for which John Barrowman auditioned. Yet, although centrally representing homosexuality, Quimby argues that the narrative was never centrally concerned with "queer issues" but rather, it was a narrative about a friendship between a straight woman, Grace (Debra Messing) and a gay man[14] and subsequently a conservative text. Nonetheless, the 1999 Channel 4 broadcast of Russell T. Davies' *Queer as Folk* (re-made in the U.S. in 2000) represented a television program that manifestly did *not* conform to social conceptions of heteronormativity. As Thornham and Purvis argue, if gay identity and homosexual life had been predominantly culturally invisible on television, *Queer as Folk* alternatively fully visualized a culture and space broadly associated with male same-sex desire.[15] Within *Queer as Folk*, it would be the straight world which is obscured and as it visualized male gay life, the nightlife and scenes of visible sexual behavior. Therefore, rather than stereotypical depictions, *Queer as Folk* portrayed a range of differing gay identities: the pleasure-seeking confidence and self-assured sexuality of Stuart (Aidan Gillen), the more publicly furtive Vince (Craig Kelly) and the "coming out" of Nathan (Charlie Hunnam). *Queer as Folk* would explore the gay world both in terms of culture, principally the club scene, the personal and family issues, but crucially, it was about gay men as sexual entities, representing the centrality of sex and its myriad manifestations: from one-night stands and Stuart's workplace trysts, gay pornography and online sexual dating and unrequited love, to steady relationships. Furthermore, *Queer as Folk* included graphic gay sex scenes, male nudity and frank discussions of sex and sexual acts, representing a significant moment in countering television heteronormativity.

In the wake of *Queer as Folk*, the late 1990s and 2000s saw a number of television programmes featuring prominent gay and lesbian characters that, in differing ways, negotiate with cultural heteronormativity, shows as diverse as *Xena: Warrior Princess*, *Ellen*, *Tales from the City*, *Buffy the Vampire Slayer*, *Six Feet Under*, *Sex and the City* and *The L-Word*, and British soap operas such as *Brookside*, *Eastenders*, *Coronation Street* and *Hollyoaks*. But, as Newman states, *Queer as Folk*, via its *Doctor Who*–loving character Vince (who at one stage is presented with a birthday gift of a fully-automated K-9 by Stuart), established that Russell T. Davies "was simultaneously a major television writer and an archetypal [Doctor] Who geek,"[16] a factor that would subsequently see a distinctive "queer" dimension become part of venerable science fiction series, then more fully realized within *Torchwood*. For Peeren, the gay spaces of *Queer as Folk* speak of a "queer universe" or "another world" and she conceptualizes the spatial zones in a way that has striking parallels with *Torchwood*, and which is worth quoting at length, because as Peeren states:

> In the British original, this is Manchester's Canal Street, and in the American adaptation it is Pittsburgh's Liberty Avenue. These locations have a well-defined margin separating them from the straight world, an alien realm whose incursions into the queer universe are perceived as threatening. An alien world that does, however, offer opportunities for strategic forays across the border.... [It is a] ... queer world that can no longer be seen as strictly and safely separated, but as intermingled, crossing and blurring the lines between apparently antithetical universes.[17]

Such spatial crossing and blurring is, as stated, part of the fundamental components of science fiction, a genre which, in differing modes and expressions, frequently stages "close encounters" between different worlds and frequently places them in confrontation.[18] Within *Torchwood*, this is certainly the case, but *Torchwood* also draws out distinctive spatial/sexual parallels in its depiction of flux. The Rift, the temporal and spatial anomaly is a doorway to alien worlds and differing time zones, and the main crux of the *Torchwood* narrative is dealing with the dangers it creates, principally the threats which gain entry to Cardiff/Earth through it, and, as the episode "Adrift" establishes, the Rift can also draws people into it and disperse them across the universe. Thus, the idea of boundary slippage is central to the narrative, and it is also mirrored in its representational strategy concerning sexuality. Within *Torchwood*, the boundaries of sexual preference are equally unstable and unpredictable, so much so that characters Gwen, Owen (Burn Gorman), Ianto (Gareth David-Lloyd) and Toshiko, although formally "straight" have all periodically engaged in bisexuality. But it is of course Captain Jack who is the locus of such fluctuation, a principle that is most potently articulated within the pivotal episode, "Captain Jack Harkness," which interweaves the science fiction subjects of time travel and differing worlds with boundary-crossing sexuality.

Whereas the *Doctor Who* episodes "The Empty Child" and "The Doctor Dances" indicated a sexual relationship between Jack and Algernon, "Captain Jack Harkness" goes further. The penultimate episode of season one is thematically a time-travel/timeslip narrative which sees Jack and Tosh drawn to the apparently "haunted" long-derelict Ritz Dancehall to investigate reports of the sounds of 1940s-style music coming from within it. But, through the plot device of a Rift-produced temporal shift, they step back in time to 1941. The episode centrally concerns the issue of the effacement of boundaries, however, it mirrors such effacement with a specific sub-plot involving Jack and the real Jack Harkness (Matt Rippy), an American volunteer fighter pilot with the 133rd Squadron from whom (we learn) Jack has taken his identity. Against the background of two temporally and spatially-distinct narratives, Jack's history and sexuality is explored. The relationship between the two Jacks is initially framed upon a clichéd eve-of-battle "buddy" routine, with "Jack" urging Jack to go to his English sweetheart, Nancy (Elen Rhys), to "make tonight the best night of your life." The result of this advice confirms the real Jack's hitherto repressed homosexual desires, and, in the course of a single night, the two Jacks recognize a mutual attraction, which is acted upon and publicly articulated. For Needham, the episode confronts a further "impossibility" in the midst of the fantastical dimensions of the narrative, which is that of expressing openly homosexual desire in this 1940s era. But, the Rift enables such expression, and the relationship culminates in the two Jacks taking to the dance floor and, moments before the Rift re-opens and enables Jack and Tosh to return back to the future, the two men engage in "one of the longest gay kisses on television."[19] The ethos of the scene is one of desire, romance and loss, and the newly returned Jack sheds a tear for his lost potential love. This scene firmly establishes both the series as a text that subverts heteronormativity and establishes a multi-dimensional heroic figure who frequently saves the Earth and is not afraid to cry while doing it. Therefore, Captain Jack Harkness is "Out" but this does nothing to efface his masculinity or heroic status. Indeed, Jack is something of an archetypal hero. He is arguably a variation of Joseph Campbell's[20] classic mono-mythical heroic figure, a character who is initially a reluctant hero, but becomes one, who enters into the belly of the beast, in his case, death, only to receive his apotheosis and return with a "boon" for humanity, his immortality, which is intrinsic to his appointed role as a guardian of the Earth and which is essential in his defeat of Abaddon, and crucially, against the coming 21st century threat for which he has endeavoured to make Torchwood "ready."

Captain Jack's heroics reveal him to represent a stark combination of differing modes of masculinity, a factor which becomes more complex as the second season got underway. The opening episode of season two, "Kiss Kiss, Bang Bang" sees Jack reunited with his former Time Agent partner, Captain John Hart (James Marsters—who played another fantasy TV icon—Spike—in *Buffy the Vampire Slayer*). The episode sees Captain John Hart materialize in Cardiff through the Rift and rapidly establish his own brand of masculinity as he comes face-to-face with Captain Jack, a confrontation that is framed with inter-textual visual motifs. The meeting of the two Captains is framed with stylistic (and deliberately clichéd) references to the cinematic genre of the Western and the figure of the gunslinger. Jack enters the bar alone, pushing open the swinging double-doors "saloon-style" and the two men stand before each other, ready to draw. Yet, instead of going for their guns, the two embrace in a passionate kiss, *then* they proceed to fight to the non-diegetic strains of Blur's "Song 2," a fight that is brutal, involving fists and feet, heads smashed though glass, and a Mexican standoff with pistols, and finally, the "macho" consumption of alcohol. The effect of these scenes is that, underscoring the virile homo-eroticism of the encounter, Captain Jack is accorded a highly physical (and knowing) masculine quality, a quality that has a significant historical pedigree.

As Segal points out, a traditional view of masculinity is that *true* manhood involves toughness, struggle and conquest,[21] stemming from the early 19th century western celebration of a Spartan, athletic "muscular manliness;" and Thomas Carlyle's idealized notion of English manliness based upon the principles of "toughness of muscle" and "toughness of heart." Within *Torchwood*, Captain Jack fully corresponds with such physical masculinity. He is an indestructible fighting man, and when need be, he is ruthless (as his willingness to utilize torture in the episode "Sleepers" illustrates). However, for all of his tough masculinity, as already touched upon, Captain Jack also has an emotional core that reflects more contemporary views of masculinity. As Parker and Lyle[22] argue, recent decades have seen dramatic shifts in constructions of masculinities, the rise of the "New Man," a cultural form of masculinity focused upon visual appearance, crystallized in the media-dubbed "cosmetically conscious male"— the "metrosexual"— the socially mobile cosmopolitan man. The archetypal metrosexual displays a penchant for clothes and cosmetics and a precise look that demonstrates a sustained seam of narcissism. Though usually "straight," this 21st century man manifests a variety of cosmetic and aesthetic awareness previously associated with certain versions of gay masculinity. And, Captain Jack also demonstrably displays a metrosexual sensibility, and it is a central component of the "pan-sexual" debate that surrounds the character.

Intrinsic to Captain Jack's iconic status is his clothing and style, a retro look that roots Jack to the moment of his "creation," the assumption of the real Jack Harkness' name and RAF status. Thus Jack maintains a 1940s period uniform image, iconically signified by his blue greatcoat. With regard to the function and power of fashion, as Craik asserts, it is "through clothes we wear our bodies and fabricate our selves."[23] Accordingly, in addition to representing a stylistic visual motif of the character, within the narrative of *Torchwood* the militaristic/RAF period costume (complete with World War II service revolver) is central to the origins of the Captain Jack Harkness persona, and the fixity of what is an anachronistic image in 21st century Cardiff serves as a reinforcement and stabilizing factor of that appropriated and constructed identity.

So, although tough of muscle, look and stylish sartorial choice are central to Captain Jack's character and a key indicator concerning diegetic debates about his sexuality. As Owen states within "Day One": "Period military is not the dress code of a straight man," and the dress of other characters forms a consistent comedic thread in relation to Jack, who consistently notes the styles of others, from sardonically likening the Doctor's look to a U-Boat Captain, loving Rose's Union Jack t-shirt, to passing the pithy throwaway comment "Grey is so not her color" in relation to a female security guard at PHARM in the episode "Reset." And Jack's look is the initial point of suggestive contact between him and Ianto, the major homosexual thread that runs throughout *Torchwood*, and which is the most potent.

The roots of this attraction are revealed within the episode "Fragments," which revolves around a booby-trapped building which explodes and leaves a number of the Torchwood team trapped beneath debris. The episode takes the form of a series of flashbacks that provide details concerning how each member came to join the Torchwood Institute. Within Torchwood 3's "General Support Officer" Ianto Jones' (Gareth David-Lloyd) narrative, we learn that Ianto has been approaching Jack for a job, and we see him come to Jack's assistance to subdue a Weevil. As Jack leaves with the captured alien, Ianto calls after him: "By the way, love the coat." Although a major plotline within season one saw Ianto concealing his "Cyberwoman" fiancée, Lisa (Caroline Chikezie), the Ianto/Jack relationship forms a running thread throughout the series, with ever more telling indications that they engage in recreational and playful sexual activity (involving naked hide-and-seek, and the enigmatic "stopwatch" game). Within "Reset," former *Doctor Who* companion Martha Jones (Freema Agyeman) discusses obtaining a UNIT military cap for Ianto, a suggestion made by Jack, and inquires about their relationship:

> MARTHA: So am I right in thinking that you and he...?
> IANTO: We ... dabble.
> MARTHA: So, what's his dabbling like?
> IANTO: Innovative.
> MARTHA: Really?
> IANTO: Bordering on the avant-garde.

Interchanges like this between Ianto and Jack then develops from innuendo and suggestion into physicality, as illustrated within the episode

"Adrift," when Gwen disturbs Jack and Ianto, both naked and engaged in a sexual act. This scene potently cements a by now long-running theme, the attraction/flirtation/sexual play between the two men, and confirms and visually represents the physical expression of this attraction. Thus, from the seeds of romance sown within *Doctor Who*, *Torchwood* constitutes a far-reaching progression within the *Doctor Who* universe. It constitutes the creation of a new a heroic figure who is tough, noble and who regularly saves the both Cardiff and the world, but who also likes sex, and who has sex. But, just to remind us how much Jack does like sex, and that he is a 51st century man.

"As Chris Isherwood once said to me..."

While the *Sarah Jane Adventures* (BBC, 2007-current, UK) have marked a further *Doctor Who* spin-off that returns to the children's television tradition the Doctor originally came from, *Torchwood* has represented a radical departure. Operating within the same narrative universe, and with crossover themes and characters, it is nevertheless a very different program aimed at an alternative audience. Moreover, it has established a new icon within the *Doctor Who* pantheon, which has progressively established its own cultural identity and fan base. Nevertheless, it has not been a problem-free development. The establishment of an adult tone does mean that, particularly the first season but still evident in the second, the tone of *Torchwood* is at times unstable. This is particularly evident within episodes such as "Sleeper" that simultaneously fuse cinematic references (*Terminator* and *Predator*) with not-so-subtle hints of government-sanctioned torture and hidden urban terrorist cells. Alternatively, the episode "Something Borrowed" contains no evidence of allegory but rather plays as broad farce. Moreover, the narrative mix of sci-fi staples (time travel, alien invasion, cyborgs) with sexuality, violence and liberal profanity, is sometimes jarring and can be a little queasy — Owen's ostensible "date rape" strategy using alien pheromones to attract sexual partners for example in "Everything Changes."

Despite such criticism, *Torchwood* was granted a second season and it was this set of episodes that would see the program firmly establish its own identity, and present a unique contemporary science fiction action hero who is part Captain Scarlett, part Stuart from *Queer as Folk*. As such, Captain Jack is a noble indestructible hero who is also a pleasure seeker, who imposes no boundaries on his sexual attractions and for whom male/female/human/non-human sexual dualisms are no longer valid. Moreover, even though Gwen pledges her life to long-suffering fiancé and then husband

Rhys (Kai Owen), there is an underlining chemistry between her and Jack. So, Jack is both fully "Out," and he is also homosexual amongst other things. And yet, the dominant ethos and source of Jack's desire is invariably (thus far, at least) for men. In addition to the real Jack Harkness, Captain John Hart, and Ianto, *Torchwood* is littered with Jack's references to and reminiscences of past male lovers and potential sexual scenarios that involve men, from "End of Days": "Under any other circumstances, an exuberant Roman soldier would be my idea of a perfect morning"; saving a postman's life from an alien that obtains a chemical "high" from male orgasms in "Day One" with the line "Put your trousers back on and get out, now! It always breaks my heart to say those words"; and, most evocatively, memories of literary heroes and sexual adventures, such as dating Proust and "cruising the Kurfurstendamm" with Christopher Isherwood.

So, Captain Jack Harkness is both rugged male and period military-styled metrosexual; he is a character which performs virtuous deeds, saves the day (if not always all of the members of his team), is not averse to self-sacrifice, looks dashing *and* enjoys sex. And as such, Russell T. Davies' continuum, from *Queer as Folk*, through *Doctor Who* to *Torchwood* has done much to visualize gay representation within mainstream television, to counter media heteronormativity and to blur the boundaries between straight and Queer worlds. In the process, popular culture has acquired not merely a revamped Doctor, but also a distinctive 21st century sci-fi hero, confident in his sexuality within the *Torchwood* universe, and, crucially, a sexuality and sexual identity that extends beyond the television text. As the openly gay John Barrowman states: "I certainly never set out to be a hero to gay men and women, although I've perhaps become one, as the piles of letters and emails I regularly receive attest." And although the creation of the Captain Jack character lead, as Moreton points out, to critical charges of the imposition of a "Gay Agenda" onto *Doctor Who*, Russell T. Davies has recognised the political potential and inspiration that Jack offers. Because, in addition to entertainment and sci-fi derring-do, Davies has stated that "he loves the thought that somewhere a young boy might watch Captain Jack with his family and say, "Actually, I've got something to tell you.""[25]

Thus, Captain Jack is proudly and visibly "Out" in space, within the Rift, back and forth in various time periods, and in contemporary Cardiff. And, when getting positive images of gays and lesbians on screen is still very much a political and cultural struggle,[26] that may just be Captain Jack Harkness's greatest and most enduring triumph.

Notes

1. Brian McHale, *Postmodernist Fiction* (New York and London: Methuen, 1987).
2. Esther Walker, "After the TARDIS: Russell T. Davies," *The Independent Newspaper* (UK), 4 Oct. 2008, 40.
3. John Tulloch and Henry Jenkins, *Science Fiction Audiences: Watching Doctor Who and Star Trek*. (London and New York: Routledge, 1995).
4. James Chapman, *Inside The TARDIS: The Worlds Of Doctor Who: A Cultural History* (London: I.B. Taurus, 2006), 191.
5. John Barrowman and Carole E. Barrowman, *Anything Goes: The Autobiography* (London: Michael O'Mara Books Limited, 2008), 18.
6. Andy Medhurst, "One Queen and his Screen: Lesbian and Gay Television," in Glyn Davis and Gary Needham, eds., *Queer TV: Theories, Histories, Politics* (London and New York: Routledge, 2009), 79–88.
7. Sergio Angellini, "Torchwood — Series 1, Part 1," *Sight & Sound*, vol. 17, issue 3, 2007, 84.
8. Dinah Eng, "Gay Programming Is About More Than Sex," *Television Week*, vol. 27, issue 14, 2008, 10.
9. Alexander Doty and Ben Gove, "Queer Representation in the Mass Media," in Andy Medhurst and Sally Munt, eds., *Lesbian and Gay Studies: A Critical Introduction* (London and Washington: Cassell, 1997), 84–99.
10. Jeffrey Weeks, *Coming Out: Homosexual Politics in Britain from the Nineteenth Century to the Present* (London: Routledge, 1977).
11. Sue Thornham and Tony Purvis, *Television Drama* (Basingstoke: Palgrave, 2005), 134.
12. *Ibid.*, 136.
13. *Ibid.*
14. Karin Quimby, "Will & Grace: Negotiating (Gay) Marriage on Prime-Time Television," *The Journal of Popular Culture*, Vol. 38, No. 4, 2005, 714.
15. Sue Thornham and Tony Purvis, *Television Drama*, 142.
16. Kim Newman, *Doctor Who* (London: BFI, 2005), 113.
17. Esther Peeren, "Queering the Straight World: The Politics of Resignification in Queer as Folk," in James R. Keller and Leslie Stratyner eds., *The New Queer Aesthetic On Television* (Jefferson, NC: McFarland, 2006), 63.
18. Brian McHale, *Postmodernist Fiction* (New York and London: Methuen, 1987), 60.
19. Gary Needham, "Scheduling Normativity: Television, the Family, and Queer Temporality," in Glyn Davis and Gary Needham, eds., *Queer TV: Theories, Histories, Politics* (London and New York: Routledge, 2009), 54.
20. Joseph Campbell, *The Hero With A Thousand Faces* (London: Fontana Press, 1993).
21. Lynne Segal, *Slow Motion: Changing Masculinities, Changing Men* (London: Virago, 1997), 104.
22. Andrew Parker and Samantha Lyle, "Chavs and Metrosexuals: New Men, Masculinities and Popular Culture," *Sociology Review*, no. 15, November 2005.
23. Jennifer Craik, *The Face of Fashion: Cultural Studies in Fashion* (London: Routledge, 1994), 16.
24. John Barrowman and Carole E. Barrowman, *Anything Goes: The Autobiography*, 242.
25. Cole Moreton, "Russell T. Davies: Return of the (tea) Time Lord," *The Independent* (UK), Sunday, 6 April, 2008, 2.
26. Dinah Eng, "Gay Programming Is About More Than Sex," *Television Week*, vol. 27, issue 14, 2008, 10.

Episode Guide

Season 1
Episode 1: "Everything Changes"
Writer: Russell T. Davies; director: Brian Kelly
Original air date — 22 October 2006

Episode 2: "Day One"
Writer: Chris Chibnall; director: Brian Kelly
Original air date — 22 October 2006

Episode 3: "Ghost Machine"
Writer: Helen Raynor; director: Colin Teague
Original air date — 29 October 2006

Episode 4: "Cyberwoman"
Writer: Chris Chibnall; director: James Strong
Original air date — 5 November 2006

Episode 5: "Small Worlds"
Writer: Peter J. Hammond; director: Alice Troughton
Original air date — 12 November 2006

Episode 6: "Countrycide"
Writer: Chris Chibnall; director: Andy Goddard
Original air date — 19 November 2006

Episode 7: "Greeks Bearing Gifts"
Writer: Toby Whithouse; director: Colin Teague
Original air date — 26 November 2006

Episode 8: "They Keep Killing Suzie"
Writer: Paul Tomalin and Dan McCulloch; director: James Strong
Original air date — 3 December 2006

Episode 9: "Random Shoes"
Writer: Jacquetta May; director: James Erskine
Original air date — 10 December 2006

Episode 10: "Out of Time"
Writer: Catherine Tregenna; director: Alice Troughton
Original air date—17 December 2006

Episode 11: "Combat"
Writer: Noel Clarke; director: Andy Goddard
Original air date—24 December 2006

Episode 12: "Captain Jack Harkness"
Writer: Catherine Tregenna; director: Ashley Way
Original air date—1 January 2007

Episode 13: "End of Days"
Writer: Chris Chibnall; director: Ashley Way
Original air date—1 January 2007

Season 2

Episode 1: "Kiss Kiss, Bang Bang"
Writer: Chris Chibnall; director: Ashley Way
Original air date—16 January 2008

Episode 2: "Sleeper"
Writer: James Moran; director: Colin Teague
Original air date—23 January 2008

Episode 3: "To the Last Man"
Writer: Helen Raynor; director: Andy Goddard
Original air date—30 January 2008

Episode 4: "Meat"
Writer: Catherine Tregenna; director: Colin Teague
Original air date—6 February 2008

Episode 5: "Adam"
Writer: Catherine Tregenna; director: Andy Goddard
Original air date—13 February 2008

Episode 6: "Reset"
Writer: J.C. Wilsher; director: Ashley Way
Original air date—13 February 2008

Episode 7: "Dead Man Walking"
Writer: Matt Jones; director: Andy Goddard
Original air date—20 February 2008

Episode 8: "A Day in the Death"
Writer: Joseph Lidster; director: Andy Goddard
Original air date—27 February 2008

Episode 9: "Something Borrowed"
Writer: Phil Ford; director: Ashley Way
Original air date — 5 March 2008

Episode 10: "From Out of the Rain"
Writer: Peter J. Hammond; director: Jonathan Fox Bassett
Original air date — 12 March 2008

Episode 11: "Adrift"
Writer: Chris Chibnall; director: Mark Everest
Original air date — 19 March 2008

Episode 12: "Fragments"
Writer: Chris Chibnall; director: Jonathan Fox Bassett
Original air date — 21 March 2008

Episode 13: "Exit Wounds"
Writer: Chris Chibnall; director: Ashley Way
Original air date — 4 April 2008

Season 3

Episode 1: "Children of Earth: Day One"
Writer: Russell T. Davies; director: Euros Lyn
Original air date — 6 July 2009

Episode 2: "Children of Earth: Day Two"
Writer: John Fay; director: Euros Lyn
Original air date — 7 July 2009

Episode 3: "Children of Earth: Day Three"
Writer: Russell T. Davies and James Moran; director: Euros Lyn
Original air date — 8 July 2009

Episode 4: "Children of Earth: Day Four"
Writer: John Fay; director: Euros Lyn
Original air date — 9 July 2009

Episode 5: "Children of Earth: Day Five"
Writer: Russell T. Davies; director: Euros Lyn
Original air date — 10 July 2009

The original air dates listed refer to the UK premiere broadcast of each episode. Season 1 was initially broadcast on BBC3, season 2 on BBC2, and season 3 on BBC1.

About the Contributors

Lee Barron is a senior lecturer in the Department of Media at Northumbria University. He has degrees from Northumbria University and the University of Sunderland. His primary research and teaching interests are in the areas of cultural theory, media, and popular culture, and include celebrity, popular music, film, and television. He has published on subjects such as film soundtracks, popular music and urban myths, reality television, and celebrity studies of Elizabeth Hurley, Kylie Minogue and Angelina Jolie.

Richard Berger, PhD., is a reader in media and education at the Centre for Excellence in Media Practice, Bournemouth University, UK. He coordinates pedagogic research in the Media School at Bournemouth. His other research interests include the adaptation of literature, comic books and videogames to film and television as well as blogging, fanfic, and other forms of personal expression online. In addition he is an experienced broadcaster and journalist for BBC Online and BBC Radio, a regular contributor to the independent film magazine *The Big Picture*, and co-editor of *The Media Research Journal*.

Ria Cheyne has a Ph.D. from Royal Holloway, University of London, and is a postdoctoral fellow at Liverpool Hope University. Within contemporary culture her research focuses on popular genre forms, particularly science fiction, and representations of the body. She has written for *Science Fiction Studies*, *Extrapolation*, and the *Journal of Literary and Cultural Disability Studies*.

G. Todd Davis is an assistant professor at Kentucky State University. He specializes in nineteenth-century British literature and critical theory, with specific interests in the Gothic and queer theory. He has a passion for, some would say an obsession with, Lord Byron — the one person with whom he would like to have dinner, when the long-awaited and much-anticipated Doctor finally rescues him with the TARDIS from the drudgery of grading composition essays.

Carrie Dunn combines academia with the vast consumption of media. She is a freelance journalist, writing about media, culture and sport for many publications, including the *Times* and the *Guardian* newspapers. She lectures in journalism and communications at various UK institutions. She is studying for a Ph.D., examining female sports fandom from a narrative feminist angle.

About the Contributors

Valerie Estelle Frankel is the youngest person to receive an M.F.A. in creative writing from San Jose State University, where she currently teaches. Her works have appeared in more than 70 magazines, and her award-winning first novel, *Henry Potty and the Pet Rock: An Unauthorized Harry Potter Parody*, is out in paperback, along with its sequel. Her latest book exploring the heroine's journey is forthcoming from McFarland.

Sarah Gilligan is a lecturer in media at Hartlepool College of Further Education. She is the author of *Teaching Women and Film* and has recently published a chapter on costume in the *Matrix* films in Peter McNeil and Vicki Karaminas' edited collection, *Fashion in Fiction*. Sarah's research interests primarily focus on gender, costume and fashion in popular culture. She is working on a Ph.D. dissertation and had forthcoming publications on subjects including Gwyneth Paltrow as a fashion icon, post-heritage cinema, teen films and sci-fi cinema.

Sherry Ginn earned both her M.A. (1984) and Ph.D. (1988) in General-Experimental Psychology from the University of South Carolina. She currently teaches at Rowan-Cabarrus Community College. Her book, entitled *Our Space, Our Place: Women in the Worlds of Science Fiction Television*, was published in 2005. She is a member and/or officer of a number of professional organizations, including the Association for Psychological Science, the International Society for the History of the Neurosciences (president, 2008-2009), the North Carolina Academy of Sciences, the Popular Culture Association (chair, Science Fiction and Fantasy Section, 2009–2012), and the Southeastern Women's Studies Association (treasurer). Sherry is working on her new book on power and control in the Whedonverse, to be published by McFarland in 2011.

Andrew Ireland is the associate dean for undergraduate students in the Media School, Bournemouth University. A 2004 National Teaching Fellow in the Rising Stars category, he contributes to the strategic direction of the Media School and teaches undergraduate and postgraduate courses in television and film production. He is studying for a practice-based Ph.D. in the area of television drama. This includes an investigative remake of a contemporary drama text following historical production methods to ascertain what we've gained, and lost, through technological change.

Elspeth kydd is a senior lecturer in film studies at the University of the West of England, where she teaches in the area of theorized practice. She is both a creative practitioner in experimental documentary and a scholar with an interest in racial representation in film and television.

R. C. Neighbors is a graduate student in the English Department at the University of Arkansas, Fayetteville. His primary research interests are fiction writing, screenwriting, contemporary literature, and popular culture studies. He is planning to pursue a doctorate in literature and creative writing.

Tom Powers is a college lecturer who teaches composition courses and is the co-author, along with Marc Schuster, of *The Greatest Show in the Galaxy: The Discerning Fan's Guide to* Doctor Who (McFarland, 2007). His writing has also appeared in *Teaching for Success*, *Kaleidotrope*, and *Back Issue*.

About the Contributors

Christopher Pullen, Ph.D., is a senior lecturer in media studies at Bournemouth University. He is the author of *Documenting Gay Men: Identity and Performance in Reality Television and Documentary Film* (McFarland, 2007), and *Gay Identity, New Storytelling and the Media* (Palgrave, 2009). His general research interests relate to the representation and performance of minority identity within contemporary media, and contexts of gender and sexuality.

Daniel J. Rawcliffe is an undergraduate at Newcastle University waiting to pursue an M.Litt. under Dr. Stacy Gillis on the intersections of science fiction and queer theory. He then hopes to pursue a Ph.D. in science fiction and fantasy literature. His research interests include contemporary sci-fi, vampires, werewolves and *fin de siècle* Gothic fiction.

Courtney Huse Wika, Ph.D., is a South Dakota writer and teacher who received her graduate degrees in English with a specialization in creative writing from the University of South Dakota, and her B.A. in English and philosophy from Augustana College. Her research interests include the (in)stability of postmodern identity and the manifestation and representation of the Uncanny in contemporary texts and popular culture.

Paul Winters is the chair of the Composition and Communication program at DeVry University in North Brunswick, New Jersey, where he has taught for the last ten years. He holds an M.A. and a Ph.D. in English literature from Lehigh University with a specialization in the nineteenth-century novel and narratology. Among his interests are the studies of popular culture, science fiction, and queer theory, all of which inform both his research and teaching.

Susan J. Wolfe, Ph.D., professor and chair of Languages, Linguistics, and Philosophy at the University of South Dakota, has published articles on sexism and gender in languages and co-edited four books on lesbian issues. Her current research interests include the presentation of gendered subjectivity and the boundaries established between the human and the monstrous or the mechanical in literature, film, and television.

Index

Abaddon 25, 40, 58, 84, 98, 99, 124
Adam (character) 62
"Adam" (episode title) 26, 34, 48, 50, 60, 95, 117, 147, 187, 188, 204, 206, 207
Adams, Douglas 73
"Adrift" 46, 52, 72, 85, 93, 223
Afterlife 22, 25
"The Age of Steel" 200
AIDS 140, 141
Aimes, Hardy 156
Aldiss, Brian 73
Alien 14, 92, 114, 116; eye 46; intervention 208; invasion 35, 48, 116, 192, 194; life-forms, gendered as female 114; menace 214; Other 31; parasite 48; pheromone spray 128; posing as human 32, 128; possessed 127, 191; presence 196; sleeper agent 195, 196; threat 38, 122, 194; touch 47
Alien 102, 104
"Aliens of London" 193
Althuser, Louis 22
Amulet 39
Angel (*Buffy* character) 80
Angel (TV show) 121, 182
Annie 57
Antiheroes 121
Archie 86
Are You Being Served? 217
Aristotle 87
"The Army of Ghosts" 193
Army trench suit 136, 161
Aslan 56
Assimilation 199; *see also* Cybermen
Athena 80
Audience 11, 12, 13, 14, 15, 17, 19, 20
Author 19
Autton, Norman 52
Avon, Kerr 121

Babylon 5 13, 54, 55, 63, 165, 167
"Bad Wolf" 55, 69

Baggins, Frodo 59, 61, 62
Bakhtin, Mikhail 72, 73
Ballard, J.G. 73
Barbarella 156
Barr, Marleen 165
Barrett, Duncan 36
Barrett, Michele 36
Barron, Lee 7
Barrowman, John 20, 59, 71, 83, 95, 100, 171, 214, 224; on Russell T. Davies 182
Barthes, Roland 11, 13, 67
Basic Instinct 140
Battlestar Galactica 102, 165
Batty, Craig 157
BBC 66
BBC America 1, 173
BBC3 1
Beemyn, Brett 139
Belaqua, Lyra 54
Berger, Richard 4
Beth 35, 196, 197; forcibly investigated 209; suicide 198
Billis 49
Bisexuality 2, 72, 139, 219
Blake, William 81
Blake's 7 121
Bob and Rose 135, 182, 183
Bolan, Marc 139
Boler, Jean Shinoda 92
Botting, Fred 104, 109
Bourke, Joanna 210
Bowie, David 139
Brief Encounter 149
Brockless, Tommy 72
Brokeback Mountain 185
Brookside 218
Brownmiller, Susan 203, 204
Brunsdon, Charlotte 137
Buffy the Vampire Slayer 25, 53, 69, 80, 103, 121, 144, 160, 165, 166, 167, 182, 198, 218, 220
Burston, Paul 173

Byron, Lord 79, 80, 83, 88, 106
Byronism 80

Campbell, Joseph 56, 63, 129, 220
Cannibals 26, 195
Capsuto, Steven 137
"Captain Jack Harkness" (episode title) 51, 86, 149, 158, 172, 185
Cardiff 15, 43
Carlyle, Thomas 221
Carys 48, 49, 184, 194
Castle of Orranto: A Gothic Story 103
Chantho 86
Chapman, James 192
Chesterton, Ian 125
Cheyne, Ria 3
Chiana 165
"Children of Earth" 19, 20, 64
Christian symbolism 26, 28
"The Christmas Invasion" 193
Chula ambulance 83
Clarke, Arthur C. 73
Clerc, Susan 68, 69, 70
"Combat" 47, 118, 127, 129, 173, 188, 195
Comolli, Jean-Luc 22
Concerned Observer 12, 14
Connor, Steven 48
Cooper, Gwen 35, 90, 107, 127; descendent from Gwyneth 69; and Eugene 46; first encounter with *Torchwood* 13, 14, 16, 32, 44, 144, 154, 206; over Rhys' death 99; relationship with Owen 170; and Suzie 45, 97, 108–109
Copley, Prof. Aaron 116
Co-Presence 11
Coraline 54
Coronation Street 218
Costello, Suzie 24, 39, 44, 45, 96, 97, 98, 108, 109
Costumes 153; *see also* Harkness, Capt. Jack
"Countrycide" 26, 37, 38, 128, 170, 195
Craik, Jennifer 221
Crisp, Quentin 218
Cross-platform 66
The Crow 79
Cruise, Tom 54
Crusher, Beverly 166
Cyber-girlfriend 57
Cybermen 192, 199, 200; as gendered male 199
"Cyberwoman" 36–37, 44, 114, 125–126, 170, 172, 185, 191, 198
Cyborgs 35, 36, 39, 40, 41; replication 200

Daleks 16, 55, 83, 87, 123
Dark Angel 54
Dark City 188
Davies, Russell T. 2, 90, 92, 136, 149; and construction of Capt. Jack's character 148; creating Capt. Jack Harkness 55, 135, 213; creating characters 167, 186; creating *Torchwood* 15, 69, 121, 182; vision for *Doctor Who* 214
Davis, G. Todd 4
"A Day in the Death" 26, 27, 46, 47, 50, 51, 118, 119, 129
"Day One" 34, 48, 49, 72, 92, 95, 127, 171, 184, 191, 205, 222, 224
"Dead Man Walking" 24, 25, 27, 50, 51, 118, 119
Death 27, 40, 58, 117
de Beauvoir, Simone 113
Deiter, Newton E. 138
Dent, Arthur 121
Dentith, Simon 72
Dialogue 14, 16
Dicks, Terrance 73
Digital Spy 121
Dirty Harry 124
The Doctor 20, 49, 53, 55, 57, 59, 60, 125, 199; and companions 215; and sexuality 214
"The Doctor Dances" 215, 219
Doctor Who (novels) 66, 71
Doctor Who (TV show) 1, 11, 15, 213, 223; and audience 17; and Cybermen 199; establishing Torchwood institute 182; and fanfic 68, 74; fans 73; and fear of invasion 193; and Queen Victoria 192
Doctor Who Confidential 15, 66
Doctor Who Magazine 68
"Doomsday" 199
Doppelgänger 102, 104, 108, 111
Doty, Alexander 217
Draven, Eric 79
Dumbledore 55, 63
Dunn, Carrie 5, 6
Dyer, Richard 143, 144, 155, 158, 159

Eastenders 218
Edwards, Tim 160
Ellen 218
Ellis, John 49, 70
Emergency Protocol 4, 17, 54
"The Empty Child" 1, 86, 123, 168, 215, 219
"End of Days" 22, 25, 26, 45, 50, 51, 57, 58, 59, 84, 98, 124, 224
"The End of the World" 84
End Violence Against Women 210

Entertainment Weekly 181
ET: The Extraterrestrial 47
Eugene 25, 46, 47, 50
"Everything Changes" 13, 23, 32, 43, 44, 72, 91, 105, 107, 123, 128, 105, 154, 205, 206
Existential mulatto 197
Existentialism 22
"Exit Wounds" 50, 51, 62, 119, 125, 128, 130, 148, 172
Exoticism 116
Extraterrestrialism 20, 72
Extra-textuality 20

Face of Boe 64, 69, 84, 87, 88
Fag hag 136, 146
Fanfic 67, 70, 74
Fans 11, 69, 74; communities 67
Female agency 144
Female Gaze 143, 145
Female mating psychology 187
Female sexuality 165, 166, 175
Femininity 113
Field, Tiffany 44
The Fifth Element 156
Fight Club 160
Firefly 165, 167
The First Men in the Moon 213
Fiske, John 12, 69, 70, 143
"The Five Doctors" 123
Fletcher, Carys 92, 127
"Flowers of Evil" 138
Forster, E.M. 45
Foucault, Michel 184
"Fragments" 40, 57, 83, 118, 119, 129, 136, 172, 194, 222
Frankel, Valerie Estelle 3, 4
Frankenstein 36
Freud, Sigmund 30, 105, 108

Gaines, Jane 153
Galactus the Destroyer 84
Game Station 123
Gandalf 55, 56
Gardner, Julie 56, 91, 94, 169
Gatiss, Mark 66, 67, 73,
Gaultier, Jean Paul 156
Gauntlett, David 143, 204
Gay porn 168
Gendered identity and sexuality 153
Genres 13
Geraghty, Christine 137, 142
"Ghost Machine" 25, 49, 69, 84, 194
Gibson, Pamela Church 156, 160
Gilligan, Sarah 6
Ginn, Sherry 6

Gledhill, Christine 141
God 81, 82
Gollum 61
Gordon, Joan 37
Gorman, Burn 61
Gothic 102, 103, 111; villain 82
Gould, Joan 95, 96, 100
Gove, Ben 217
Graf Report 66
Gray 50, 60, 62, 63, 86, 125, 130, 148
The Great Devourer 99; *see also* Abaddon
"Greeks Bearing Gifts" 26, 33–34, 39, 47, 57, 94, 128, 187
Greenberg 168
"Gridlock" 84
Griffin, Susan 203

Hall, Stuart 138
Hallett, Lisa 124, 126, 191
Halloran, Beth 191, 195
Hamlyn, Anne 1612
Hands 49
Haraway, Donna 35, 189, 200
Harkness, Capt. Jack 13, 43, 53, 44, 49, 54, 57, 71, 104, 111; buried alive 87; as Byronic Hero 82; coat 161, 221; and death 40; in *Doctor Who* 55, 135; and Gwen 94; history 109, 122, 125, 130, 146, 147, 216, 220; homosexual encounters 137; introduction to 1, 53, 215; meeting Captain John Hart 159; origin of his name 60, 185; physical encounters on screen 217; and resurrection 26; sexuality 110, 184, 224; *see also* Omnisexuality
Harper, Owen 45, 129; bettering himself 128; and death 19, 20, 28, 40, 50–51, 52, 118, 129, 130; rage 58; and sexual encounters 44; as "urban warrior" 156; and Weevils 188
Harry 61
Hart, Capt. John 46, 61, 62, 72, 86, 123, 124, 146, 159, 160, 220
Hart, Kylo-Patrick 141
Hartigan, Mercy 199
Hartman, Yvonne 193, 199
Harwood's Haulage 126
Hawking, Stephen 18, 19
Haynes, Todd 139
Hegel, G.W.F. 113
Heimlich 31, 34
Hellraiser 14
Hercules 62
Heritage cinema 158
The Heroine's Journey 90
Hero's journey 53, 54, 56

Heteronormativity 218
Hippocratic Oath 129
The Hitchhiker's Guide to the Galaxy 54, 69, 121
HIV 140
Hogwarts 53
Hollander, Anne 157
Hollinger, Veronica 37
Holloway, Dr. Grace 214
Hollyoaks 218
Holman, Ray 156
Holmes, Diane 94, 129
Holmlund, Christine 153
Holquist, Michael 69
Homoeroticism 2
Homosexuality 2, 72, 218; and identity 136
"The Host" 166
Howards End 45
Hub 14, 17
Human identity 31
Humanity 44
Humphries, Mr. 217
Hurley, Kelly 104
Hurt, John 218
Hustle 155
Hutcheon 71

Ideology 22
Immortality 30, 56
Inman, John 217
Intellectual uncertainty 31
Interracial couples 201
Intimate Contacts 141
Invasion 48
"The Invasion" 192, 200
Isolation 43, 45, 46
Ivanova, Susan 167

Jenkins, Henry 69, 70
Jentsch, Ernst 30, 31
Jesus 26
Jim Henson Productions 165
John, Elton 139
Jonah 46
Jones, Ianto 36, 44, 57, 60; and costume 157
Jones, Martha 12, 16, 17, 18, 20, 27, 48, 60, 71, 73, 115, 117, 172, 222
Jones, Samantha 69

Kaftan 199
Kara 102
Keller 172
King, Stephen 103
King Arthur 63

Kirk, Capt. James T. 53, 58, 71, 166
"Kiss Kiss, Bang Bang" 50, 60–61, 86, 100, 124, 146, 159, 174, 205, 220–221
Kosh 55
Kristevan theory 118
kydd, Elspeth 6

The L-Word 218
Last of the Gaderene 67
Life and death 52
Liminal 102
The Lion King 69
Lisa 36, 39, 72, 114, 194, 199
Lister, Dave 121
Lord Chamberlains Act 136
Love, Sydney 137
Lovecraft, H.P. 216
Luke 63
Lyle, Samantha 221

MacDonald, Marianne 186
Mad Men 154
Maggie 46, 52
Magic cloak 55
Male sexuality 175
The Man from U.N.C.L.E. 67
Manfred 81, 85
Martha *see* Jones, Martha
The Martian Chronicles 213
Marvel Comic Books 84, 122
Mary 33, 34, 38, 47, 48, 72, 128, 187, 194
Masculine dress 153
The Master 59
Masters, James 53, 124, 160
The Matrix 91, 160
Mayfly 116
McCoy, Dr. 58
McHale, Brian 213
McKee, Dan 69
McLelland, Mark 71
"Meat" 27, 33, 37, 45, 47, 126, 181, 185
Merlin 55, 59
Metrosexuality 224
Middle-earth 53
Millett, Kate 204
The Milton Berle Show 217
Moffat, Stephen 73
The Monk 103
Moreton 224
Morgan, Ed 49
Mori, Naoko 60
Mortality 22
Moses 59
Mulatta heroine 197
Mulvey, Laura 143

Murdock, Maureen 90, 96
My Fair Lady 57
Myles, Eve 56, 100

The Naked Civil Servant 218
Narboni, Jean 22
Nation, Terry 73
Neale, Steve 159
Needham, Gary 220
Neighbors, R. C. 2
"New Earth" 64, 84
"The Next Doctor" 199
Non-consensual penetration 204, 208, 211, 212
Non-sexual penetration 208

Obi-Wan 55, 63
Odysseus 62
Old Testament 58
Omnisexuality 1, 86, 103, 109, 110, 170
Opening narration *see* Voiceover
Orgasmic energy 48
Orientalism 118
Orpheus 62
The Other 31, 36, 39, 106, 113, 114, 115, 117, 118, 119, 195, 196, 199; racial Other 200
"Out of Time" 23, 49, 72, 129, 170, 172, 173, 183, 188

Pajaczkowsaka, Claire 161
Pan-sexual 221; *see also* Omnisexuality
Paradise Lost 88
Parker, Andrew 221
Parker, Henry 46
Parker, Peter 54
"The Parting of the Ways" 83, 86, 123, 215
Peeren, Esther 219
Pharm 116
The Phenomenology of Spirit 113
Pinkola Estés, Clarissa 62, 98
Police Woman 138
Possessed 49
Post-9/11 world 184
Potter, Harry 54, 58, 59, 63
POV (point of view) 17, 18, 19
Powers, Tom 5
The Predator 216, 223
Pretty Woman 57
Prime Directive 188
Proferes, Nicholas 19
Prometheus 88
Psychic paper 54
Pterodactyl 33
Pugh, Sheenagh 70

Pullen, Christopher 5
The Punisher 124
Punter, David 106
Purvis, Tony 217, 218

Q 79, 82
Queen Victoria 182, 192
Queer as Folk 71, 135, 149, 182, 214, 218, 224

Rabanne, Paco 156
Rabiger, Michael 12, 17
"Random Shoes" 25, 46, 50
Rape 48, 203, 204, 210
Rassilon 123
Ratings 16, 19
Rawcliffe, Daniel J. 4
Realism 16
Red Dwarf 121
Relationships 169
Representation of sexuality 214; *see also* Sexuality
"Reset" 12, 16, 19, 24, 47, 48, 49, 51, 115, 118, 129, 171, 222
Resurrection Gauntlet 13, 23, 39, 40, 45, 50, 97, 123, 129
Resurrection Glove *see* Resurrection Gauntlet
Return of the Jedi 61
Rhys 45, 49, 126
Rice Burroughs, Edgar 213
Rift 11, 16, 43, 58
Riker, William T. 166
Ripley, Ellen 102, 104, 107
"The Rise of the Cybermen" 69
Romance 142
Romantic Period 80, 88
Romantopia 171
Rosenberg, Dale 186
Roundheads 67
Royle, Nicholas 110
Russo, Vito 139

Said, Edward 118
Salmon, Catherine 171, 186, 187
San, Dr. Abigail 211
The Sarah Jane Adventures 66, 69, 223
Sartre, Jean-Paul 113
Sato, Toshiko 34, 39, 44, 46, 48, 51, 57, 72, 118, 127, 128
Scott, Ridley 102
Screwdriver 54
The Second Coming 182
Segal, Lynne 203, 204, 221
Severed hand 49, 59, 69, 85
Sex and the City 154, 218

Sexual activity 34, 117, 216; acts 17; boundaries 216; contact 44; fluidity 204; identity 135; orientation 110; relationships 72; storylines 70; tension 136
Sexuality 71, 72, 74, 176
Shadows 63
Shakespeare, William 33
Shape-changers 94
Shape-shifter 38, 95, 117
Sheridan, Capt. John 55, 63
The Shining 103
Showgirls 140
Sinfield, Alan 139
Singularity 18
Singularity Scalpel 18, 116
Six Feet Under 218
Skywalker, Luke 54, 61
Slade, Brian 140
Slash fiction 67, 68, 70, 71, 72, 186, 187
"Sleeper" 35, 122, 185, 191, 195, 206, 209, 221, 223,
Slitheen 55
"Small Worlds" 26, 40, 85, 105, 106, 110, 172, 194
Solo, Han 54
"Something Borrowed" 27, 38, 48, 95, 117, 118, 169, 223
"The Sound of Drums" 193
Sparrow, Jack 54
Spinning Straw into Gold 95
Spock 58, 71
Spooks 155
Stanley, Liz 113
Star Trek 13, 67, 68, 71, 82, 166, 188
Star Trek: The Next Generation 79, 166
Star Wars 63, 125, 216
Starsky & Hutch 67
Stein, Atara 82
Steinman, Erich 139
"The Stolen Earth/Journey's End" 73, 87
Stone, Sharon 141
Storyteller 12
Suspension of disbelief 15
Swearing 2, 16, 17
Sweet as You Are 141
Sycorax 193
Symons, Don 171, 186

Taboo language *see* Swearing
Tales from the City 218
Tanazaki, Dr. 114, 198
The TARDIS 55, 56, 59, 83, 100
Tasker, Yvonne 159
Television Quarterly 138
Tennant, David 160
The Tenth Doctor 68

The Terminator 216, 223
Terminator 2: Judgment Day 80
The Texas Chainsaw Massacre 216
Theory of relativity 12, 18
Thornhamm, Sue 217, 218
Thorslev, Peter L., Jr. 79, 80, 81, 82, 85, 86, 87
Time Agency 54, 83, 60, 86, 123, 147, 158
Time Lords 64, 85
The Time Machine 213
Time Travel 214
"To the Last Man" 27, 46, 72, 172, 185, 204
Toberman 199
"Tomb of the Cybermen" 199
Tommy 46
"Tooth and Claw" 69, 182, 192
Torchwood Declassified 15, 108
Torchwood Magazine 142, 156
Touch 43, 50, 52
Tractor beam 214
Tragic mulattas 191, 196, 198, 200
Transgressive 48
Truman, Will 218
Tucker, John 123
Tucker, Ken 181
28 Days Later 216
2001: A Space Odyssey 156
Tyler, Rose 1, 53, 54, 55, 56, 68, 71, 84, 86, 123, 169

Uncanny 30, 35, 40, 41, 102, 108
"An Unearthly Child" 125
"Utopia" 86

Vader, Darth 61, 63
Van Zooner, Liesbet 143
Vaughn, Tobias 200
Velvet Goldmine 139
Violence 16
Vogler, Christopher 55, 58, 61, 94
Voiceover 11, 20
Voldemort 61

Wagner 70
The War of the Worlds 192, 213
War on terror 216
Weevils 14, 32, 33, 40, 41, 50, 57, 91, 188; first view 106
Wells, H. G. 192, 213
Whedon, Joss 103, 167
White, Jonathan David 135, 140
The Wicked Lady 158
Wika, Courtney Huse 3
Wilde, Oscar 139

Will & Grace 136, 137, 138, 218
Williams, Raymond 182
Winters, Paul 6
Wise, Sue 113
Witch-King 62
Wolfe, Susan J. 3
Wolverine 122
"World War Three" 193
The Writer's Journey 55

The X Files 182
X-Men 122
Xena: Warrior Princess 218
Xenophobia 193

Zeus 80, 88

www.ingramcontent.com/pod-product-compliance
Ingram Content Group UK Ltd.
Pitfield, Milton Keynes, MK11 3LW, UK
UKHW041939140426
5217IPUK00014B/557